The Mind of Thomas Jefferson

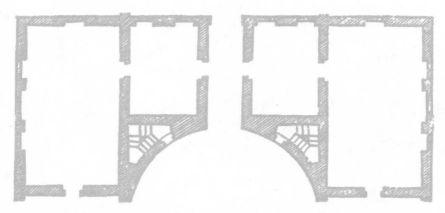

THE MIND *of* THOMAS JEFFERSON

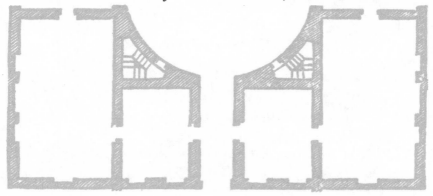

Peter S. Onuf

University of Virginia Press
Charlottesville and London

University of Virginia Press

© 2007 by the Rector and Visitors of the University of Virginia

All rights reserved

Printed in the United States of America on acid-free paper

First published 2007

1 3 5 7 9 8 6 4 2

LIBRARY OF CONGRESS CATALOGING-IN-PUBLICATION DATA

Onuf, Peter S.

The mind of Thomas Jefferson / Peter S. Onuf.

p. cm.

Includes bibliographical references and index.

ISBN-13: 978-0-8139-2578-3 (cloth : alk. paper)

ISBN-13: 978-0-8139-2611-7 (pbk. : alk. paper)

1. Jefferson, Thomas, 1743–1826—Political and social views. 2. Jefferson, Thomas,
1743–1826—Philosophy. 3. Jefferson, Thomas, 1743–1826—Influence. I. Title.

E332.2.O59 2007

973.4'6092—dc22

2006014637

for Annette Gordon-Reed
and Jan Ellen Lewis

Contents

CONTENTS

Acknowledgments

Thomas Jefferson has been a fascinating and rewarding subject for me for many years. He has also introduced me to new friends in the community of Jeffersonians, helped me renew and sustain old friendships, and brought excellent students to Charlottesville to study Jefferson and his times with me. Among my former students, Andy Burstein and Joanne Freeman in particular have helped me understand the Sage of Monticello. Their influence will be apparent in many of the essays collected here. I have also learned much from visiting scholars, including Csaba Levai from Hungary and Ari Helo from Finland, the latter a coauthor of one of the essays in the present collection.

Under the direction of Doug Wilson, Jim Horn, and Andrew O'Shaughnessy, the Robert H. Smith International Center of Jefferson Studies at Monticello has been a magnet for Jeffersonians; Kenwood and, since its construction, the Jefferson Library have been the site for many stimulating seminars and conferences. The Early American Seminar at the ICJS is an ongoing source of intellectual excitement.

My good friend Tom Dowd, formerly of the University of Virginia's School of Continuing and Professional Studies, enabled me to get to know an extraordinarily diverse and accomplished group of "students" who attended his summer Symposia on the Lawn over the past decade. I prepared the essay "Jefferson's Religion" for Tom's most recent symposium: it is dedicated to him.

Dick Holway at the University of Virginia Press has been a great editor and friend for many years. Without his support, this book would never have been published.

I also wish to acknowledge the continuing and enriching friendship of the Amigos, including el Jefe, David Konig, Alan Taylor, Paul Gilje, and Don Higginbotham. This book is dedicated to two of the Amigos, Annette Gordon-Reed and Jan Ellen Lewis. Annette and my sometime coauthor Jan understand Jefferson better than anyone I know. They are also wonderful friends.

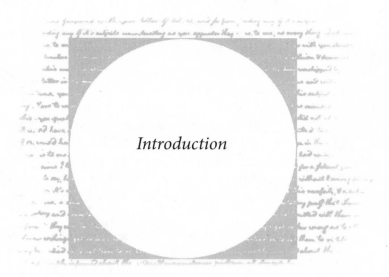

Introduction

Notwithstanding the assaults of generations of iconoclastic critics, Thomas Jefferson remains an American icon. A touchstone for partisans of all persuasions, the author of the Declaration of Independence has risen above partisanship as America's "inventor," the great apostle of democracy and national self-determination. His eloquent formulations of "self-evident . . . truths" constitute the American creed: "all men are created equal"; "they are endowed by their Creator with inherent and unalienable Rights," including "Life, Liberty, and the pursuit of Happiness"; and the governments men institute to secure these rights derive "their just powers from the consent of the governed."[1]

Historians may insist, and Jefferson would have agreed, that these principles were hardly original; they may acknowledge that he was a gifted writer but emphasize the crucial editorial role of fellow congressmen who purged the document of most (but not all) of its embarrassing rhetorical excesses; or they may be appalled by the bald hypocrisy of a Virginia slave owner holding forth on the rights of man. But Jefferson's language and the man himself seem impervious to historians' qualifications and caveats. Because modern Americans know what Jefferson really meant, they know their man. They think they know Jefferson because Jefferson—in visionary moments—seems to know them. Jefferson's Declaration announced a new epoch in world history, transforming a provincial tax revolt into the opening salvo of a great struggle to liberate humanity from the tyrannies of the past; his first inaugural address, of March 4, 1801, reaffirmed the universal republican principles of 1776 while envisioning a glorious, specifically American, future in this "chosen country, with room enough for our descendants to the thousandth and thousandth generation."[2]

The essays in this collection are not designed to debunk, diminish, or demolish either the Jefferson image or the mythic narrative of our history that make Jefferson and his fellow founders loom so large in the national imagination. Instead, I hope to raise fresh questions about what was on Jefferson's mind as he looked forward, so hopefully and yet so fearfully, to an uncertain future.

Jefferson's language continues to resonate, but its radical edge has been lost. In an eighteenth-century world where all men were self-evidently created unequal, the principle of equality threatened to turn the world upside down, subverting social and political order, even family governance. But what does "equality" mean now, when most right-thinking Americans take it for granted, assuming it to be compatible with—and even to make legitimate—the glaring inequalities in contemporary society that we also take for granted? And what about that "chosen country," now that there is no longer "room enough" for further waves of settlement and improvement? In what sense are Americans still Jefferson's "chosen people," the virtuous, independent yeoman farmers who surged westward to conquer a continent, now that family farmers have virtually disappeared? Are Americans chosen to act as proxies and exemplars for the human race, or chosen instead to be uniquely free and unequally prosperous?

My point is not that complacent and conservative Americans have betrayed Jefferson's radical legacy, but, rather, to underscore what should be obvious: we live in a radically different world than Jefferson's, yet one that must remain inextricably linked to ours—simultaneously foreign, yet uncannily familiar—as long as the nation itself survives. The historian's challenge is to sustain the tension between past and present, to restore our subjects to their own uncertain world while reconnecting it to ours by fresh translations from the increasingly foreign language of a distant time and place. The national idea is timeless and transcendent, an ongoing collaboration across the generations. The historian's role is to protect us against facile appropriations of the past to serve present purposes, to challenge the assumption that the founders' "original intentions"—whether they are supposed to be "liberal" or "conservative"—can be fully known and should be authoritative guides to future action. The myth of nationhood that Jefferson and his fellow nation makers articulated and enacted encourages such abuses by collapsing the past into the present. In response, historians must struggle to keep past and present apart, not to destroy, but rather to reinvigorate our cross-generational conversation.

My hope is to spark some conversations with and about Thomas Jefferson, to engage in the rich and complex legacy he has left us in his voluminous correspondence as well as in the great public papers that have played and will play such a crucial role in defining the meanings and purposes of American nationhood.

Who Was Thomas Jefferson?

If Americans know Jefferson, they don't know much about his private life. Jefferson could be indiscreet, but he kept his own secrets, destroying his correspondence with his wife, Martha, and revealing nothing about his long-term relationship with his slave Sally Hemings. Jefferson's autobiography (drafted in 1821) is a sketch of his public career, virtually bereft of illuminating details about his private life.[3] It was, instead, yet another effort to secure his legacy as a Revolutionary founder and to guarantee his own everlasting fame.

Most modern Jefferson biographers have agreed with Merrill D. Peterson that Jefferson was "impenetrable."[4] But this impenetrability is as much a function of their unwillingness to probe as of their subject's unwillingness to be probed. Jefferson's defenders make their ignorance into a virtue, invoking an upright and stainless "character" that makes the improprieties attributed to him seem like "moral impossibilities."[5] To be fair, Jefferson constructed a formidable self-defensive barrier, leaving us all in the position of a baffled Maria Cosway, recipient of the famous dialogue between Jefferson's "Head" and his "Heart."[6]

Jefferson's dialogue is one of the strangest, most mystifying "love letters" in the language, seeming to reveal everything while in fact revealing nothing. Heart gets the best lines, yet its sentimental "pulsations" are contained by the dialogue's frame, an artifice that serves Head's purposes. The paradoxical effect of Jefferson's artful performance is distancing—Heart is too self-absorbed, too busy explaining itself to Head, to speak directly to another heart—leaving Cosway to wonder if she had any role at all to play in Jefferson's inner drama.

Scholars have mined the rich veins of the Head-and-Heart dialogue for illuminating insights into Jefferson's political and social thought. American hearts had triumphed in the American Revolution, whatever part Jefferson's heart may have played in his private affairs: "If our country, when pressed with wrongs at the point of the bayonet, had been governed by it's heads instead of it's hearts, where should we have been now? Hanging on a gallows as high as Haman's. You," Heart tells Head, "began to calculate and to compare wealth and numbers: we threw up a few pulsations of our warmest blood: we supplied enthusiasm against wealth and numbers: we put our existence to the hazard when the hazard seemed against us, and we saved our country."[7]

Throughout his career, Jefferson expressed his fundamental political beliefs with eloquence and clarity even as he sought to suppress, disguise, or conceal private interests and impulses. The Head-and-Heart dialogue epitomizes the contrast between Jefferson's "self-evident" principles and the protective shield he constructed around his inner life. The boundary between his transparent public and opaque private worlds has enabled subsequent generations of Americans to take Jefferson at his word, to make his words their own, and so conflate "Jefferson" and "America." Of course, the apotheosis of Jefferson has generated its dialectical opposite, a persistent, powerful impulse to demolish his exalted image and pull the great man off his pedestal. Perversely, however, iconoclasts reinforce, even as they seek to reverse, the synecdoche: the "real" flesh and blood Jefferson was a liar and a hypocrite, all talk and no action, a man of no character. The apostle of democracy and equal rights, they say, was a slave owner who held his own children in bondage; thin-skinned and duplicitous, he was a partisan ideologue who pretended to be above the political fray; profligate and self-indulgent, he cultivated an aristocratic lifestyle while plunging ever further into debt. This anti-image has always shadowed Jefferson's more benign public image, reflecting in darker shades the icon's familiar outlines. Image and anti-image alike pay fealty to Jeffersonian principles, and so follow Jefferson's own script even while reaching radically different conclusions about the man himself.

There are encouraging signs that Jefferson scholarship is finally breaking free from this vicious circle of celebration and condemnation. As the historiographical essays in this book suggest, we know more now—and can speculate more intelligently—about the private Jefferson than ever before. Probing Jefferson's life is not an end in itself, nor is the point to come to some sort of definitive judgment on whether he is worthy enough to retain his place in the founders' pantheon. Instead, I argue, the great value of historicizing Jefferson—of putting him in his proper place and time—is that it enables us to bridge the gap between private and public, practice and profession, that Jefferson himself took such pains to cultivate, and thus to take the measure both of his thought and of our own.

The Jefferson image itself was never fixed but always a work in progress.[8] As Jefferson and his followers constructed a public persona for the reluctant party leader, he simultaneously fashioned an alternative, private, "self," at home in the idealized domesticity of Monticello. In yet another flirtatious letter to a married woman, Alexander Hamilton's sister-in-law Angelica Schuyler Church, Jefferson anticipated returning to Virginia at the end of his term as Washington's secretary of state: "I am then to be liberated from the hated occupations of politics, and to sink into the bosom of my family, my farm, and my books. I have my house to build, my fields to farm, and to watch for the happiness of those who labor for mine." When both of his surviving daughters were married and had gathered their families around him, "I shall imagine myself as blessed as the most blessed of patriarchs."[9] As Jan Lewis persuasively argues, Jefferson's conceptions of home and world, of the "blessings of domestic society" and the "torments" of politics, were reciprocal constructions, evoked at a distance, one from the other, in the sentimental effusions of his familiar correspondence.[10]

Andrew Burstein's illuminating work on the inner Jefferson focuses on his letter writing, the nexus between "private" and "public" worlds that defined each other and could not be kept apart.[11] In a sentimental age that scorned artifice and prized authenticity, the familiar letter was the ideal medium for self-expression. But, of course, the selves inscribed in the most heartfelt language were utterly banal and conventional; as they strained toward the "natural," literary scholar Jay Fliegelman shows, Jefferson and his fellow sentimentalists reached new heights (or depths) of artifice.[12] Burstein shows how the sensitive and suggestible Jefferson so eagerly followed in novelist Laurence Sterne's footsteps in his own "sentimental journey" through France, a kind of homecoming for this displaced provincial in the great "republic of letters."[13]

Of course, the artifice of sentimentalism is increasingly conspicuous to us, as is the futility of the quest for "natural language." Yet it is precisely the historical and cultural specificity of Jefferson's literary performances that gives us access to the hidden depths and dark recesses of his life. Or, we might better say, the very assumption of a deep and "impenetrable" inner life—an assumption that comes all too naturally to us in our own solipsistic, therapeutic age—is fundamentally misleading, for Jefferson's "self" is hidden in plain sight. The materials he deployed in his self-construction project drew from the common stock—the conventional and unconventional ideas, the literary forms and experiments of his age—that he collected in his library and personal archive and recycled in his own writing. We reflexively turn to psychology in our quest for the inner springs of character, for psychology now provides the conventional methodology and language for self-examination and self-explanation. But our psychologized view of our world is no less time bound than the moral philosophy of Jefferson's sentimental age. Historically sensitive literary analysis is thus a much more promising route into Jefferson's depths (or surfaces) than psychohistory.

Late in life, in a famous self-effacing moment, Jefferson disclaimed any "originality of principle or sentiment" in authoring the Declaration of Independence. It was not "copied from any particular and previous writing," he told Henry Lee, but "was intended to be an expression of the American mind, and to give to that expression the proper tone and spirit called for by the occasion. All its authority rests then on the harmonizing sentiments of the day, whether expressed in conversation, in letters, printed essays, or in the elementary books of public right."[14] Jefferson always said this about his political principles—after all, if they were not "self-evident," he was a fraud—but surely would have insisted on the "originality" and uniqueness of his private self. But I would reverse this self-serving formulation. Notwithstanding the intellectual debts that he acknowledged and that subsequent scholars have so carefully calculated, Jefferson's social and political theory—his adumbration of the "American mind"—was much more original and consequential than he could comfortably acknowledge; by contrast, and not surprisingly, the "inner Jefferson" predictably voiced "the harmonizing sentiments of the day." His only originality was in his idealized definition of domesticity as a distinct, isolated, and self-contained sphere of private life—and this was a definition, Jan Lewis tells us, that derived from his understanding and experience of a life devoted to public service.

Recent scholars have subjected the Jefferson archive to new and revealing questions. But we also need to know more about what Jefferson did not say, to interrogate the silences in and around his life that have contributed so much to his status as an icon who seems to rise above the sordid realities of his own slaveholding world. Over the last generation, historians have focused intensively on Jefferson's implication in slavery and on the implications of slavery for Jefferson. Only recently, however, in the wake of DNA evidence establishing the strong likelihood of his long-term sexual relationship with his slave Sally Hemings, have they begun to put private and public Jeffersons back together again, bringing the planter-statesman back down to earth and resituating him in his mountaintop home, in the midst of his white and black families. Jefferson was a beloved father and grandfather of his white family, but a more distant and problematic figure for Sally Hemings's children—offspring he owned but did not own. The complexities of life at Monticello—the peaceful, apparently harmonious, coexistence of related black and white families—must have shaped Jefferson's attitudes toward race and slavery.[15]

The distinction between "public" and "private" that Jefferson cultivated has encouraged commentators to distinguish between what he said (and might have believed) and what he did (and perhaps could not do) about slavery, bridging the yawning gap between precept and practice with judgments about his character. But I suspect that Jefferson was not gripped by guilt over slavery or torn by its contradictions. If he had been, he could not have found refuge at Monticello from the "torments" of political life, for he would have been constantly, inescapably tormented by his personal failure to take any effective action against this most barbarous and unjust institution. The "real" Jefferson was an enlightened slaveholder, evidently satisfied with the self he so arduously fashioned, not a guilt-ridden schizophrenic. Furthermore, as Ari Helo and I argue in the last chapter in this volume, Jefferson was a moralist acting (or not acting) in accord with his own enlightened, teleological understanding of history's moral imperatives. He did not stand at the bar of conscience or moral judgment and find himself wanting, as modern moralists would like to imagine. To the contrary, his enlightened moral sense, the "pure" principles that guided both his private life and his political career, constituted the solid and enduring foundation of his character, as he understood it.[16] Our moral sense leads us to take Jefferson apart, with the hope of isolating and preserving something in his life—or at least some inspiring words, however intended—that we can live by. But Jefferson's moral sense worked in the opposite way, not simply to reconcile or suppress what we like to see as fundamental, irreconcilable personal conflicts but rather to underwrite an abiding self-assurance that verged on self-righteousness. Jefferson the moralist lived comfortably with himself. He also lived comfortably at Monticello, where family members and slaves (including enslaved family members) struggled constantly to fulfill Jefferson's idealized conception of domesticity.

Jefferson and America

The essays collected here approach the private Jefferson—and proceed from him—in oblique ways. Although none directly discusses his life at Monticello, my premise in all of them is that Jefferson's life and thought are inextricably linked. Jefferson was no more a bundle of contradictions and conflicting impulses than we sophisticated, self-conscious moderns know ourselves to be: he made sense to himself and he can make more sense to us now if we engage him on his own terms and in his own cultural and moral contexts. I also believe that a fresh, historically informed engagement with Jefferson's thoughts will both complicate and make more vital the political principles that he articulated so eloquently and that continue to exercise such a powerful influence in our national self-understanding.

Jefferson's conception of the world historical significance of the American Revolution and his vision of the new nation's boundless promise remain inspiring, and it is hard for modern Americans to resist the complacent conclusion that the United States today represents the fulfillment of his prophecy, that his future is our past. But Jefferson's racially exclusive vision of American nationhood also raises profound and troubling questions. The "chosen people" of his inaugural address looked westward to a virgin continent, a vast, unpeopled domain awaiting progressive cultivation and civilization: he imaginatively obliterated Indian country in a single bold rhetorical gesture. In contemplating the future of a continent (and hemisphere) freed from the incubus of slavery, Jefferson imagined a similarly expansive whitening process. "It is impossible not to look forward to distant times when our rapid multiplication will expand itself beyond those limits," he wrote Governor James Monroe of Virginia in 1801, and "cover the whole northern, if not the southern continent, with a people speaking the same language, governed in similar forms, & by similar laws; nor can we contemplate with satisfaction either blot or mixture on that surface."[17] When African Americans were finally emancipated, Jefferson insisted, they had to be expatriated, leaving no "blot" on the American landscape.[18]

Jefferson's responsibility for an expanding "empire of slavery" is a controversial question in contemporary scholarship.[19] He certainly wanted African Americans to disappear, and the fulfillment of that hope was on

the face of it incompatible with the expansion and perpetuation of the peculiar institution; nor is there any reason to doubt that Jefferson loathed
slavery and that his racist speculations about black inferiority in *Notes on
the State of Virginia* were secondary and subordinate to his commitment
to emancipation.[20] Yet it is unquestionably true that Jefferson believed that
African Americans had to remain in slavery, however unjust the institution,
until a comprehensive emancipation scheme could be implemented; piecemeal, gradual emancipation could not work, and the growing population
of free blacks resulting from the 1782 liberalization of manumission law in
Virginia constituted a grave threat to racial hierarchy, social order, and the
success of the republican experiment in Virginia.

Of course, there is no reason on good Jeffersonian grounds why we cannot extricate race and nation, even if this was inconceivable to Jefferson
himself, convinced as he was of the eternal enmity of the captive black nation and fearful of the genocidal bloodbath that emancipation without expatriation would unleash. Jefferson's thinking about the immigration of
Europeans to America became progressively more liberal and his conception of the nation more inclusive in the post-Revolutionary period; and notwithstanding his animus to "merciless savages," he could also imagine racial
amalgamation of civilizing whites and civilized Indians on the expanding
western frontier. Jefferson's nation may have been "white," but whiteness
itself was a protean construct that could accommodate different emigrants
from European nations (or "races"), civilized Indians, and even mulattos
after three "crossings" with whites.[21] Jefferson wanted to keep whites and
blacks apart—miscegenation was an unnatural abomination—but he was
not nearly as obsessed with race purity as with the purity of republican principles.

Jefferson's nation was a great family of families, coming together across
the generations as republican civilization spread westward. This was not
the exclusive genealogy that romantic nationalists would later invent for
European peoples, but, rather, one that could absorb new streams of free-
dom-loving immigrants from all over the world. Jefferson's conception of a
dynamic and expansive American people, fulfilling its destiny through history, provided the essential foundation for his republican superstructure.
The progress of political enlightenment, the enjoyment of natural rights,
and the fulfillment of human potential were all predicated on the heartfelt principles that bound the nation in affectionate union. Jefferson's modern admirers often overlook his teleological framework, instead abstract-

ing universal and transcendent rights from the specific historical and cultural circumstances within which alone they could flourish. Natural rights, Jefferson insisted, could only be recognized and perfected within particular communities as they crossed the threshold of republican self-government and national self-determination. Outside the context of national history, man's natural rights remained merely potential and practically inoperative. For all the peoples of the world to gain the great boon of nationhood, millions of lives would be sacrificed and "rivers of blood" would flow.[22] In the case of the enslaved African nation, he hoped, a comprehensive scheme of emancipation and expatriation initiated and sustained by the "generous energy of our own minds" might yet spare the new nation a replay of "the bloody process of St Domingo." Whether such a scheme was adopted or not, "the hour of emancipation is advancing, in the march of time. It will come."[23]

The modern tendency to talk about rights in universal, ahistorical terms leads us to misunderstand Jefferson's language precisely when he seems to be speaking to us most directly. Lifting rights out of history, we universalize them; universalizing rights, we individualize them, thus authorizing claims against any and all oppressive regimes. Jefferson, by contrast, historicized rights, locating them in specific civic contexts within which—and only within which—the most enlightened and "civilized" peoples could enjoy them. In other words, we overlook the nation (or, perhaps, we confuse the nation with the world), imagining ourselves beyond history and the further bloody struggles Jefferson anticipated. Thinking beyond history, we read Lockean and Jeffersonian social contract theory in reverse, moving backward from the formation of political society to the sovereign individual and the natural rights he supposedly exercised in the state of nature, before history. For Jefferson, by contrast, the contract theorists explained mankind's progress through history, from the barbarism of its natural state to society and civilization, thus previewing the Enlightenment's more elaborate "conjectural history."[24]

The libertarian assumption of a never-ending struggle between the individual, with his "natural" (property) rights, and society, exercising its voracious (property-consuming) power through the state, was alien to Jefferson. Jefferson instead saw the progressive development of society as the necessary precondition for the emergence of the modern individual in full enjoyment of his rights; by eliminating the despotic rule of privileged classes, a republican government would secure national unity and facilitate individual "pursuits of happiness" that in turn would promote the community's prosperity and well-being. Invoking Jefferson's authority, modern advocates of property rights look backward for justification: history authenticates their claims or entitlements just as genealogy once established the privileges of birth. But Jefferson looked to the future, insisting in a famous letter to James Madison in 1789, "that *the earth belongs in usufruct to the living.*" That meant that "the portion occupied by an individual ceases to be his when himself ceases to be, and reverts to the society."[25] For Jefferson, living individuals constituted a "generation," indebted to its predecessors for the liberty and property it now enjoyed and responsible for the well-being and progressive improvement of succeeding generations. In Joyce Appleby's eloquent formulation, "the future was the screen upon which Jefferson projected his faith in the unfolding of the human potential under conditions of freedom."[26]

Jefferson was never complacent about what he and his countrymen had achieved, in 1776 or in 1783—when the Peace of Paris was negotiated—or even in the "Revolution of 1800," when right-thinking Republicans finally captured the federal government. Even when the republican experiment seemed secure and counterrevolutionary forces at home and abroad were at bay, Jefferson believed that the new nation only stood at the threshold of progressive improvement. Many great obstacles still had to be overcome, and none was more conspicuous or perplexing than dealing with slavery, a fundamentally unjust and antirepublican institution that threatened to demoralize and destroy the republic. If slavery worked for Jefferson, and if he could live with it very comfortably at Monticello, he knew that the survival of the institution would work against the republic's glorious future prospects, dividing the nation and thus perhaps even threatening to reverse the outcome of the Revolution itself, as he came to fear during the great controversy over the extension of slavery to the new state of Missouri in 1819–21.[27]

Jefferson's moral horizon extended far into the future (too far, many critics have charged), and he did not think moral perfection had been achieved in the new nation or that it could be easily or fully attained in the future. But history demonstrated that progress *had* been achieved. The American Revolution, the touchstone of Jefferson's faith, had inaugurated a remarkable new chapter in human history, raising his expectations—and therefore his anxieties—about the new nation's prospects. In 1799, as Republican hopes began to revive after the Federalist "reign of witches," Jefferson struck characteristically optimistic and anxious notes in a letter to William Green Munford, a young scholar at the College of William and Mary. "The generation which is going off the stage has deserved well of mankind for the struggles it has made, & for having arrested that course of despotism which had overwhelmed the world for thousands & thousands of years." The American Revolutionaries had achieved great things. It was now up to Munford's generation to carry on the good work, conscious of its enormous responsibilities: "If there seems to be danger that the ground they have gained will be lost again, that danger comes from the generation your cotemporary." But Jefferson reaffirmed his faith; he could not believe that the younger generation would fail. That Munford and his peers, with "the enthusiasm which characterises youth should lift its parricide hands against freedom & science, would be such a monstrous phaenomenon as I cannot place among possible things in this age & this country."[28]

The essays that follow are organized into four groups. Those in the first section discuss recent efforts to illuminate Jefferson's mental world and to assess his significance in American political culture. Jan Lewis and I offer some thoughts on how our thinking about Jefferson today reflects developments in contemporary American culture. But we are also interested in the "nation" problem, for no amount of scholarly distance or detachment can reduce Jefferson to a mere historical figure. Indeed, we suggest, Jefferson lives today and will live as long as there is an American nation and Americans seek to know who they are as a people and what their role is in world history. The concluding essay in this section exhorts diplomatic historians to take a leading role in Jefferson scholarship by focusing on how the author of the Declaration of Independence understood the challenges of international relations and sustaining and perfecting the federal union that shaped the new nation's history.

Scholars have given disproportionate attention to Jefferson's republican faith without situating it in its historical and geopolitical context. Jefferson's worldview was, to risk circularity, determined by his view of the world. The West loomed particularly large in his geopolitical imagination, as I show in the essays in part 2, for it was here that the United States would meet its greatest challenges, both from hostile foreign empires and Indian nations and, more ominously, from the fickle loyalties of frontier people. The West is where the glorious narrative of American progress would be inscribed; but it might also be the site of the experiment's great failure, as centrifugal forces tore the union apart and paved the way for counterrevolution. Jefferson's faith in the future of the West and in Westerners' loyalties stood in conspicuous counterpoint to his chronic suspicions about the loyalties of anti-expansionist Federalists in the North.

Jefferson could not take the virtuous good citizenship of his fellow Americans for granted, even those untainted by Federalist heresies. The essays in part 3 focus on Jefferson's efforts to promote the moral progress of the new American republic. His first great challenge was to dismantle the established church in Virginia. The Bill for Establishing Religious Freedom— drafted in 1779 and, thanks to Madison's leadership in the legislature, finally enacted in 1786—was one of Jefferson's proudest achievements. But disestablishment left a vacuum that the new republic would have to fill. Because popular enlightenment was the necessary moral foundation for a successful republican experiment, Jefferson unsuccessfully campaigned for a broad-based public education system: his only successes, the establishment of the University of Virginia and the new military academy at West Point, served republican ruling elites, not the generality of citizens. Yet Jefferson did not despair. Perhaps, after all, popular religion might provide the most solid foundation for popular virtue. Freely competing in the new religious marketplace that separation of church and state created, religious teachers would offer a more rational, republicanized version of Christianity. Jefferson's hopes for popular Christianity—and his willingness to call himself a "Christian"—reflected his personal quest for a religious faith that would sustain his republican commitments.

In the final group of essays, I explore the implications of Jefferson's republican faith for the small world he inhabited so masterfully at Monticello. This is where I approach most closely to the private Jefferson and am most indebted to recent scholarship. Jefferson's idea of the nation constitutes the conceptual bridge between the larger world of politics and prudence and the "pure principles" that were so crucial to his self-understanding. Jefferson was a moralist, and his moral sense comes most clearly into view where disenchanted, moralizing moderns least expect to find it: in the master of Monticello's lifelong engagement with the problem of slavery. Here again we approach, if we do not penetrate, the inner Jefferson, for slavery represented not only a great moral challenge to the republic but a personal challenge to the father and master of unrecognized, mixed-race children. The great theorist of generational sovereignty and responsibility was acutely sensitive about the need to educate the rising generation: the right kind of education was absolutely essential to the republic's progressive enlightenment and continuing moral progress. But the institution of slavery was a school for despots, not republicans. And surely, he recognized, his ownership of his own children was an utter perversion and negation of this great and fundamental republican moral imperative.

Ari Helo and I reconstruct Jefferson's moral horizon in order to make clear how different his world is from ours. Of course, speculations about how Jefferson coped with the problem of slavery inevitably tell us as much about ourselves as they do about our subject. But that is my purpose in this volume: to make Thomas Jefferson more vital to us by restoring him more fully and more perfectly to his own time and place.

Notes

1. Declaration of Independence as Adopted by Congress, July 4, 1776, in Julian P. Boyd et al., eds., *The Papers of Thomas Jefferson,* 32 vols. to date (Princeton, NJ, 1950–), 1:429. On Jefferson (hereafter TJ) as "inventor," see Garry Wills, *Inventing America: Jefferson's Declaration of Independence* (New York, 1978). Pauline Maier's *American Scripture: Making the Declaration of Independence* (New York, 1997) offers the most comprehensive and deflationary account of TJ's authorship. The relevant literature is discussed more fully in the essays in part 1 in this volume.

2. TJ, First Inaugural Address, March 4, 1801, in Merrill D. Peterson, ed., *Thomas Jefferson Writings* (New York, 1984), 494.

3. "Autobiography," Jan. 6–July 29, 1821, in Peterson, ed., *Jefferson Writings,* 3–101.

4. Merrill D. Peterson, *Thomas Jefferson and the New Nation: A Biography* (New York, 1970), viii.

5. Ellen Randolph Coolidge to Joseph Coolidge, Oct. 24, 1858, reprinted in Annette Gordon-Reed, *Thomas Jefferson and Sally Hemings: An American Controversy* (Charlottesville, VA, 1997), 259.

6. For the famous dialogue between Head and Heart, see TJ to Maria Cosway, Oct. 12, 1786, in Peterson, ed., *Jefferson Writings,* 866–77.

7. Boyd et al., eds., *Jefferson Papers,* 10:451; Wills, *Inventing America,* 276–83; Richard K. Matthews, *The Radical Politics of Thomas Jefferson* (Lawrence, KS, 1984), 58–61; Jean M. Yarbrough, *American Virtues: Thomas Jefferson on the Character of a Free People* (Lawrence, KS, 1998), 34–35, 167–68.

8. Merrill D. Peterson's classic study *The Jefferson Image in the American Mind*

is complemented by Robert M. S. McDonald, "Jefferson and America: Episodes in Image Formation" (Ph.D. diss., University of North Carolina, 1998), an excellent account of TJ's image in his own lifetime.

9. TJ to Angelica Schuyler Church, Nov. 27, 1793, in Peterson, ed., *Jefferson Writings*, 1013.

10. Jan Lewis, "'The Blessings of Domestic Society': Thomas Jefferson's Family and the Transformation of American Politics," in Peter S. Onuf, ed., *Jeffersonian Legacies* (Charlottesville, VA, 1993), 109–46.

11. Andrew Burstein, *The Inner Jefferson: Portrait of a Grieving Optimist* (Charlottesville, VA, 1995); and Burstein, *Jefferson's Secrets: Death and Desire at Monticello* (New York, 2005).

12. Jay Fliegelman, *Declaring Independence: Jefferson, Natural Language, and the Culture of Performance* (Stanford, CA, 1993).

13. Burstein, *Inner Jefferson*, 42–67. Garry Wills initiated the "sentimental turn" in Jefferson scholarship in *Inventing America*, which includes an insightful discussion of Sterne's influence, 273–76. See also Burstein, *Letters from the Head and Heart: Writings of Thomas Jefferson* (Chapel Hill, NC, 2002); and, on the "republic of letters," Douglas L. Wilson, *Jefferson's Books* (Charlottesville, VA, 1996).

14. TJ to Henry Lee, May 8, 1825, in Peterson, ed., *Jefferson Writings*, 1501.

15. My understanding of the private Jefferson is indebted to the pioneering scholarship of Annette Gordon-Reed, in *Thomas Jefferson and Sally Hemings* and subsequent work, and to the various other authors collected in Jan Ellen Lewis and Peter S. Onuf, eds., *Sally Hemings and Thomas Jefferson: History, Memory, and Civic Culture* (Charlottesville, VA, 1999), including most notably Jan Lewis, in her essay "The White Jeffersons," 127–60.

16. TJ to Samuel Smith, Aug. 22, 1798, in Peterson, ed., *Jefferson Writings*, 1053. The most sympathetic and comprehensive account of Jefferson's moral philosophy is Yarbrough's *American Virtues*. See also Ari Helo, "Thomas Jefferson's Republicanism and the Problem of Slavery" (Ph.D. diss., Tampere University, Finland, 1999).

17. TJ to James Monroe, Nov. 24, 1801, in Peterson, ed., *Jefferson Writings*, 1097.

18. For a full development of this theme, see my *Jefferson's Empire: The Language of American Nationhood* (Charlottesville, VA, 2000).

19. The most forceful recent indictment is Roger G. Kennedy, *Mr. Jefferson's Lost Cause: Land, Farmers, Slavery, and the Louisiana Purchase* (New York, 2003).

20. The most authoritative edition now in print is William Peden, ed., *Notes on the State of Virginia* (Chapel Hill, 1954). This theme is eloquently developed by Jack N. Rakove, "Our Jefferson," in Lewis and Onuf, eds., *Hemings and Jefferson*, 210–35, esp. 221–24.

21. TJ to Francis C. Gray, March 4, 1815, in Lewis and Onuf, eds., *Hemings and Jefferson,* 262–63. For further discussion, see Joshua Rothman, *Notorious in the Neighborhood: Sex and Families across the Color Line in Virginia, 1787–1861* (Chapel Hill, NC, 2003).

22. This was a favorite trope of TJ's. For examples, see TJ to Benjamin Austin, Jan. 9, 1816, in Andrew A. Lipscomb and Albert Ellery Bergh, eds., *The Writings of Thomas Jefferson,* 20 vols. (Washington, DC, 1903–4), 14:387–93, quotation on 389; TJ to John Adams, Sept. 4, 1823, in Lester Cappon, ed., *The Adams-Jefferson Letters: The Complete Correspondence Between Thomas Jefferson and Abigail and John Adams,* 2 vols. (Chapel Hill, NC, 1959), 2:596.

23. TJ to Edward Coles, Aug. 25, 1814, in Peterson, ed., *Jefferson Writings,* 1345.

24. See the discussion in Nicholas Onuf and Peter Onuf, *Nations, Markets, and War: Modern History and the American Civil War* (Charlottesville, VA, 2006), chap. 1.

25. TJ to James Madison, Sept. 6, 1789, in Boyd et al., eds., *Jefferson Papers,* 15:392, emphasis in original.

26. Joyce Appleby, "Jefferson and His Complex Legacy," in Onuf, ed., *Jeffersonian Legacies,* 1–16, quotation on 14.

27. Onuf, *Jefferson's Empire,* chap. 4.

28. TJ to William Green Munford, June 18, 1799, in Peterson, ed., *Jefferson Writings,* 1066.

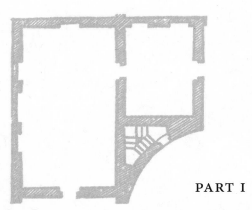

PART I

*Jefferson and the
Historians*

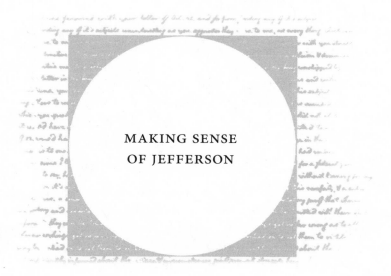

MAKING SENSE
OF JEFFERSON

In 1960 Merrill Peterson concluded in his book *The Jefferson Image in the American Mind* that Thomas Jefferson had finally, belatedly, ascended to a crucial "place in the symbolical architecture of this nation." It was now possible for scholars to take the measure of the man. "The scholarly wish to possess Jefferson for himself might never be realized," Peterson wrote, "but a Jefferson about whom politicians cease to contend, whose ideas suffer drastic erosion from all sides, and whose own history proves to be a rewarding field of study in itself—this figure invites the true scholar and begs the true historical discovery." In the academy, observed Peterson, the multiple Jeffersons of the party polemicists were already giving way to a new image of the culture hero—"the civilized man," with his multiplicity of interests and achievements.[1]

Peterson looked forward to the elaboration of a scholarly, nonpartisan Jefferson image. Historians no longer saw American history as a great, ongoing struggle between Jeffersonian democrats and Hamiltonian aristocrats, the "people" and the "interests." Indeed, as Peterson showed, this genealogy of the parties had always been somewhat suspect, and the confusion became complete when Democratic New Dealers invoked Jefferson's "progressive spirit" to justify their neo-Hamiltonian programs of state intervention: "After the Roosevelt Revolution, serious men stopped yearning for the agrarian utopia, politicians (and most historians too) laid aside the Jefferson-Hamilton dialogue, and almost no one any longer maintained the fiction that American government was run, or ought to be run, on the Jeffersonian model." The "disintegration of the Jeffersonian philosophy of government heralded the ultimate canonization of Jefferson."[2]

Peterson's *Jefferson Image* is superb cultural history but poor prophecy. This is not to say that historians have neglected Jefferson. When Peterson wrote, Dumas Malone was moving into high gear with his definitive six-volume biography, *Jefferson and His Time* (1948–81).[3] The greatest monument to Jefferson scholarship, the comprehensive edition of *The Papers of Thomas Jefferson*, continues its stately progress, more than a half century after it was launched.[4] Meanwhile, writing about Jefferson for both scholarly and general audiences has expanded exponentially.[5] Yet Jefferson's image is as controversial now as it ever has been.

Peterson underestimated the capacity of scholars to divide into hostile "parties," regardless of the state of party conflict in the larger political culture. The old history of the parties not only distorted Jefferson's image but also deflected more fundamental questions about the new nation's character. Identifying with either Jefferson or Alexander Hamilton reinforced the faith of historians and politicians alike in the vitality and future prospects of the American political system. But the proliferating "new" histories of the 1960s and 1970s opened up profound and troubling questions about the course of American history as advocates of fresh approaches and methodologies sought to reconstruct the field as a whole—in ways involving and affecting the image of Jefferson.

For students of Revolutionary and early national America, Jefferson remains a fascinating and contested figure. It is not simply a question of his ubiquity, or the massiveness of his archives, or the historiographical tendency to revise the revisionists. The compulsion to characterize Jefferson reflects the convergence of important trends in the discipline and in the larger culture. The discrepancy between his idealistic professions and his membership in Virginia's slaveholding planter elite presents an interpretative challenge—and provokes scholars to moral judgments.

Controversy over the Jefferson image became particularly intense in the 1990s. In *The Long Affair,* the Irish writer Conor Cruise O'Brien explicitly challenges Jefferson's "place" in the nation's "symbolical architecture," portraying his subject as a philosophical terrorist and slaveholding racist.[6] While most critics denounced O'Brien for his interpretative excesses, well-received studies by respected scholars also questioned Jefferson's standing in the pantheon. Joseph J. Ellis's prizewinning *American Sphinx,* the best single-volume biography now available, focuses on the psychological strategies that enabled Jefferson to sustain a dangerously adolescent idealism that at least squinted toward terrorism.[7] Echoing another of O'Brien's arguments, Pauline Maier's *American Scripture* downplays Jefferson's role as "author" of the Declaration of Independence: in countless communities across the continent, ordinary Americans drafted their own declarations, anticipating and shaping the document Jefferson wrote and that the Continental Congress edited into its familiar, "scriptural" form. These writers all ask whether Jefferson really deserves his exalted position among the Revolutionary founders, an even more urgent question in the wake of DNA tests suggesting the strong possibility that he conducted a long-standing sexual relationship with his slave Sally Hemings.[8]

For most commentators today, Jefferson's fitness as a national icon has been cast as a question of character. Though this certainly reflects our current predispositions, it is fair to suggest that Jefferson brought the character question on himself, for character was his own constant concern. He devoted his political life to exposing the secret machinations of "monocrats" and "aristocrats" while establishing a new republican regime based on "natural"—authentic and responsive—representation. Though he was an advocate of transparency, his modes of self-presentation left his private life opaque and elusive. The impulse to unmask Jefferson, to make sense out of his complex career, is a mark of his continuing significance in our public culture.[9]

The Character Issue

The Revolutionary period was a crucial transitional moment for Western moral theory and practice. This was the time when a universal human nature became recognized—or constructed—and when natural philosophers naturalized racial (and gender) differences. "Equality" and "nature," the key premises of Jeffersonian thought, were contemporaneous constructs. The appropriation and elaboration of these ideas helped Jefferson and his Revolutionary colleagues solve compelling problems as they established a new republic on the periphery of the "civilized" world, but doing so inevitably raised new issues.[10]

The dissonance of planter privilege with enlightened theory constitutes an illuminating text for this broad political and ideological transformation.

The ways in which Jefferson resolved, or perhaps more accurately simply lived with, these conflicting demands constitute his "character." That character, for all its fascination, many present-day scholars find discomfiting, if not repellent. Jefferson's inner life, insofar as it can be recovered, manifests little evidence of distress, so thoroughly did he rationalize and repress his wants and griefs. Peterson writes that Jefferson was "an impenetrable man," a conclusion echoed in the title of Joseph Ellis's *Sphinx*.[11] A generation ago, when Fawn Brodie offered an "intimate history" of Jefferson, making what turns out to be a plausible case for the relationship with Hemings, she was roundly castigated for unsubstantiated and implausible speculations.[12] But more recent writers, however they weighed in on the Hemings question, have operated under the assumption that the real Jefferson *can* be known. The most successful of these works, Andrew Burstein's *The Inner Jefferson*, a sensitive study of Jefferson as a literary sentimentalist, and Annette Gordon-Reed's *Thomas Jefferson and Sally Hemings,* an eloquent and exhaustive reconsideration of the evidence and arguments concerning the relationship, show that this will be no easy task, for these two Jeffersons don't seem to have too much in common.[13] But the effort to put Jefferson back together again, to make sense of his character, has already yielded impressive results. Denial of the possibility of Jefferson's relationship—and of the centrality of slaveholding in all aspects of his life—has been the major obstacle to understanding. This obstacle has now been removed.

We know Jefferson better, but where does that leave us? Jefferson's characteristically judgmental frame of mind, along with the dualistic, not to say Manichaean, view of the world it reveals, tempts historians to judge him in turn, sometimes harshly, on moral grounds. Critics underscore the discrepancy between the Declaration's appeal to natural rights and Jefferson's failure to do anything about slavery, at Monticello or anywhere else. However successful historians may be in explaining this apparent contradiction, Jefferson will continue to be a controversial figure as long as race remains the great and unresolved American dilemma.[14] There is a powerful moral animus in present-day writing on the subject—an animus that sometimes strains scholarly standards of dispassionate investigation. But it would be a mistake to reject this literature as presentist, as it is a mistake to dismiss forays into Jefferson's private life as prurient and unseemly.[15] There is a powerful integrative impulse in both enterprises. It is precisely because historians want to make sense of Jefferson, because they want to grasp exactly what it was that the Revolutionary founders intended and accomplished, that they are contesting this terrain so passionately.

The slavery problem, for Revolutionaries generally and Jefferson in particular, has especially complicated our understanding of the Revolutionary transformation and brought moral questions to the fore. Why did Jefferson never take steps to dissociate himself—or, more to the point, his slaves—from the horns of his dilemma? Surely, nobody knew better than Jefferson, Revolutionary reformer, that exceptional, unnatural historical conditions are subject to change. Thus we confront the difficult image of the democratic founder who professed a profound hostility to slavery but could never extricate himself from an institution that guaranteed the welfare and well-being of his "country," Virginia.

Republicanism and Liberalism

Jefferson has always inspired controversy, among friends as well as foes. In his own lifetime, even Jeffersonians could invoke the master's authority for dizzyingly various ends. At his death, Peterson reports, his eulogists were hard-pressed to make sense out of him: "he remained an enigma, a figure of contradiction, a man of many faces."[16] For us, Jefferson's contradictions should be an opening to understanding. Consciousness of our own ambivalent situation—at the far side of the modernity Jefferson helped invent—should enable us to construct a more dynamic and compelling Jefferson image from the contradictory influences and impulses of a long life.

Exponents of the republican synthesis set the stage for a more complex and satisfying view of Jefferson by resituating him in the Revolutionary narrative. The immediate effect of rediscovering the Real Whig tradition was to displace the liberal John Locke and his American disciple Jefferson from their preeminent place in the American founding.[17] But while the republican revisionists challenged the conventional depiction of Jefferson as the forward-looking inventor of American nationality, they assigned him a conspicuous role as a history-minded defender of colonial rights and privileges.[18] Lance Banning's *The Jeffersonian Persuasion,* published in 1978, and Drew R. McCoy's *The Elusive Republic,* which appeared two years later, pointed Jefferson backward, emphasizing the anachronistic premises of his political thought and—more explicitly in McCoy's work—his confused and agonizing encounter with modernity.[19] In doing so, both writers betrayed an

ambivalence about Jefferson's influence on the new American political order and about the salience of Jeffersonianism—with its legacy of Real Whig
paranoia about abuses of governmental power—for the constructive tasks
of state making in the new republic.

The revisionists' mixed feelings about Jeffersonianism is a function of
their understanding of America's imminent transition toward a recognizably modern, liberal capitalist regime. For them, Jefferson was important,
for better or worse, because he was oblivious to the shape of things to come.
Critics have challenged the revisionists' displacement of the liberal tradition
and their portrayal of Jefferson as a man at odds with his times.[20] Exponents
of liberalism recast the Revolution in progressive, forward-looking terms,
with Jefferson taking the lead role. Joyce Appleby's *Capitalism and a New
Social Order,* which came out in 1984, seeks to remove Jefferson and his followers from the republican synthesis. Her Jeffersonians are not the fearful
oppositionists that Banning and McCoy depicted, but, rather, champions of
a progressive "reconceptualization of human nature," Lockeans in politics
and Smithians in economics. Embracing capitalism, the great solvent of the
traditional order, they reject the authority of history. "This rejection of the
past," Appleby concludes, "constitutes the most important element in the
ideology of the victorious Jeffersonian Republicans."[21]

The echoes of the party struggles of the 1790s thus still reverberate in
the academy. The quarrel now, as then, centers on the fundamental character of the new American regime. But it does not follow that we are doomed
to perpetual reenactment of our primal political drama. In fact, exponents
and critics of the republican synthesis have reached a working, if somewhat
begrudging, consensus on once controversial questions. The liberal and republican Jeffersons may look in opposite directions, but they share a sense
of the world historical significance of the American Revolution.[22] Similarly,
both Jeffersons offer a radical critique of the corruption of the old regime,
inspired in the one case by an enlightened, liberal vision of the future and
in the other by an idealized, republican vision of the past. Finally, the questions of character, virtue, and the relation between self-interest and the public good were equally central to republicanism and emergent liberalism—if
these isms can be meaningfully distinguished at this period—and were particularly compelling at a time of political upheaval.[23]

The debate over republicanism thus has given us a better understanding
of the range and relevance of political discourse in Revolutionary America.
Since the advent of the republican synthesis, we have moved not in circles

but in a closing spiral, liberal critics building on the revisionists' achievements and revisionists recasting republicanism in ways that accommodate and explain the radical initiatives and innovations that constituted Revolutionary change. Revolutionary talk—a medley of appeals to hopes and fears, patriotic sacrifice and class interest, cosmopolitan aspirations and localist prejudices—was essential to the processes of mobilizing resistance, sustaining popular commitments, and constructing and legitimating new governments.[24] As a writer, Jefferson was fluent in all these idioms. His words bridged the great divide between an enlightened, elitist republic of letters and a new world of popular political speech in a democratizing republican society.

The implications of these historiographical developments for Jefferson's image are strikingly apparent in Gordon Wood's *The Radicalism of the American Revolution*, published in 1992.[25] Wood sees republicanism as a terminal phase of the "monarchical" old regime that prepared the way for a thoroughgoing democratization of American society. Genteel, enlightened republicans like Jefferson—poised on the cusp of modernity and facing both ways—were central figures in the Revolutionary transformation. Wood's Jefferson does not play the same central role in the history of American democracy as Appleby's Jefferson. For Wood, democratization is a great social and cultural transformation, precipitated by a Revolutionary republican elite whose assaults on the old regime jeopardized their own class position. *Radicalism* tells the story of democratic progress—the story first told by Jefferson, and then about him—in an appropriately ironic fashion, replete with unintended consequences. Jefferson and his fellow Revolutionaries were transitional figures, ambivalent about the radical changes they unleashed. From this perspective, Jefferson's ambivalence and inconsistency seem less the hallmarks of a flawed or superficial character than evidence of his central position in the new nation's drama, subject to the conflicting tendencies that made the Revolution radical.[26]

As the quintessential republican, Jefferson both embodied and envisioned fundamental changes in American society. It was his responsiveness to the historical moment, not his originality, that brought him to the fore. The conflicts and tensions Wood delineates are readily apparent throughout Jefferson's writings.

Herbert Sloan's explication of the September 6, 1789, letter to James Madison is a good example of what we can learn from a close reading of a Jefferson text. Jefferson here developed the "principle that *the earth be-*

longs in usufruct to the living," that "by the law of nature, one generation is to another as one independant nation to another." No generation, he told Madison, was entitled to impose a burden of debt on its successors or to "make a perpetual constitution, or even a perpetual law." Jefferson's conversations with revolutionary reformers in France, his ongoing and deeply troubling experience with indebtedness, the centrality of the debt problem in the Real Whig oppositionist thought he espoused, and his passionate commitment to generational self-determination all contributed to this extraordinary formulation of a radical democratic constitutionalism. Sloan's point is that the historical contingencies were crucially important, and that for Jefferson the political was personal and the personal political. "In our effort to understand his letter to Madison," Sloan writes, we should not attempt to "isolate" the "private Jefferson [from] the Jefferson of high politics."[27]

Next to the Declaration of Independence, the Jefferson text that has most fascinated scholars is his *Notes on the State of Virginia.*[28] What is most remarkable about the literature on this omnium gatherum, never-completed bag of a book is the extraordinary range of formal interpretative schemes— legal, natural scientific, pedagogic, and others—that have been offered by critical readers.[29] That all these readings make some sense is indicative of the richness of the *Notes*; they also suggest that Jefferson did not have the same control over his multiple voices that he usually displayed in his correspondence. In this extraordinary effort to conjure up in words his society and his place in it, the personal and the political are powerfully, and sometimes painfully, juxtaposed. Nothing, for example, could have been more painful and troubling than the radically incompatible characterizations of Virginia agriculturalists as virtuous and independent yeoman farmers (Query 19, "Manufactures") and as despotic slave owners (Query 18, "Manners"). That Jefferson was profoundly troubled by an institution that violated the premises of his political philosophy and jeopardized the future of the commonwealth is apparent in his invocation of a "just" God, whose "justice cannot sleep for ever."[30]

An undercurrent of malaise pervades the *Notes* and is by no means confined to the discussions of race and slavery. Jefferson's inventories and descriptions are offered in a hopeful, progressive spirit that anticipates a glorious future for Virginia and for America. Yet despair shadows this hope—despair that is not simply an expression of his chronic anxieties about popular slothfulness and ignorance but is more deeply grounded in a devastating judgment on himself and his slave-owning countrymen.[31] The "numbing" process Lucia Stanton describes in Jefferson's life with his own slaves, the scientific racism of the natural philosopher so conspicuously displayed in the *Notes,* and—in later life—righteous indignation at the crypto-Federalist centralizers who would "enslave" Virginia under the pretense of liberating her slaves are ways Jefferson would find to suspend or deflect that judgment. However much he suppressed his knowledge of his slaves' humanity or denied his own despotic impulses in a regime of benevolent rationality, the problem would never go away. It was a problem that writing the *Notes*—the great effort to represent his country to Europeans, to his fellow countrymen, above all to himself—had brought to the fore. This was the tragic counterpoint, the lengthening shadow of Jefferson's great project to smash the despotism of the old regime and spread universal enlightenment through words—the liberating words that articulated natural rights principles, the words by which free men signified and constituted the affectionate, durable bonds of republican government.

Jefferson's story cannot be reduced to lifelong advocacy of a single principle. Looking both ways—toward an idealized Saxon past and toward a progressively enlightened future—Jefferson invites wildly contradictory characterizations of his political thought.[32] What gave his project coherence, Jay Fliegelman convincingly argues in *Declaring Independence,* published in 1993, was a coincidental revolution in rhetoric and sensibility. Fliegelman's Jefferson is "a witness to, and conflicted participant in, a new affective understanding of the operations of language, one that reconceives all expression as a form of self-expression, as an opportunity as well as an imperative to externalize the self, to become self-evident."[33] Our lack of sympathy with Jefferson bespeaks our failure to appreciate the psychological tensions this imperative entailed: his poor performances in public speaking revealed a sensitive self-consciousness to the contradictory claims of self-construction and self-presentation in a democratizing political world. Jefferson's life at Monticello, as well as his performances on the great stage of public life, suggests ongoing inner conflicts—and ironic, if not tragic, outcomes—in full measure.

Self and Society

Jefferson's "self-evident" ideas about equality and natural society reflected the strenuous efforts of an ambitious young man to overcome arbitrary and artificial obstacles to his personal progress. Through reading, writing, and reflection, the bookish provincial sought to construct an intellectually consistent character and a satisfying image of himself in the world.[34] His almost monastic regimen enabled him to transcend his rustic isolation in Albemarle County: through his intellectual attainments, the natural philosopher gained access to the centers of enlightenment and power. Jefferson savored polite company and learned conversation, but these were the fruits of lifelong labors in the privacy of his study. A rigorous process of self-construction constituted the premise of the sociability he so cherished.

Jefferson's juvenile encounters with classical philosophy provided the models and texts that shaped his development. The classics did not merely offer philosophical consolations or a refuge from the real world. The Epicureans provided practical guidance in restraining unruly passions under a personal regime of balance and moderation. Jefferson's agenda in reading the classics was to make sense of his circumstances and to secure a philosophical ground for his forward-looking personal and political projects. The philosophers' injunctions to self-control, the life of reason, and the passionate friendship of enlightened souls all constituted a script for self-making and world making.[35]

However much Jefferson mined classical sources for building materials, nothing could be more modern than his self-construction project. He was no retrograde pastoralist; nor when he celebrated "those who labour in the earth [as] the chosen people of God" was he invoking the disinterested virtue of classical citizenship: he was talking about his rights-conscious neighbors.[36] The citizen's participation in affairs of state was not an end itself for Jefferson but a means of curbing state power. Jefferson did not have much good to say about cities, but this was because these were the prime sites for old regime corruption, not because he rejected urbanity or the progress of commercial civilization.[37] Yet it would be a mistake to conclude that Jefferson's modern uses of classical sources made him, or any of his fellow citizens in the Enlightenment's republic of letters, a fully modern man. Where Jefferson was most self-consciously modern—his apotheosis of reason, his naturalistic epistemology, his crusade for universal enlightenment and liberation—is where he now seems most characteristically a man of his time, not ours.[38]

Paul K. Conkin argues that Jefferson's intellectual quest was grounded in Judeo-Christian cosmology and inspired by hopes for the progressive enlightenment of his countrymen. His laborious compilations of Bible extracts that were free from the mystifications of priestcraft represented his lifelong effort to reconcile this cosmology with his fundamental ethical values and philosophical commitments.[39] Thus he came to view "Jesus as the foremost moral reformer in human history," Eugene Sheridan writes, and this "demythologized," primitive Christianity was—or should have been— the bedrock of republican virtue.[40] Jefferson sought to harmonize the gospels with classical philosophy and ethics in order to promote enlightenment and republican government. Ideally his labors would set an example for others, but their primary function was to construct and reinforce his sense of himself; his sense of self was predicated on preserving his privacy and remaining "a sect by myself."[41] Jefferson had no interest in publicizing his religious views or in aligning himself with anybody else's sect: throughout his life he was hostile to organized religion. The tension between his efforts to achieve harmony in society and politics—the philosophical ground and expression of Jefferson's conception of natural sociability—and the imperatives of privacy and personal autonomy was characteristic. The sentimentalist who espoused authenticity and transparency was always reluctant to expose his most serious thoughts.

Analysis of Jefferson's reading habits gets us closer to his fundamental values and assumptions. A fire that destroyed the family home Shadwell and most of the young Jefferson's personal papers left little evidence about his early life. This lacuna helps explain why his personality seems so elusive, for biographers generally shape their subjects' character from the homely details of their early years. But we do know quite a bit about the presumably formative reading experiences of the bookish young Jefferson, painstakingly reconstructed in Douglas L. Wilson's edition of *Jefferson's Literary Commonplace Book*. Jefferson's extracts from his reading of the 1760s and early 1770s began with classical authors and English poets he read before 1763, continued from 1762 to 1766 with his law studies and "most of the Greek entries," and concluded with his immersion in "poetry, classical and contemporary," during the period from 1768 to 1772 or 1773, when he set up his legal practice. Thereafter, as the imperial crisis deepened, poetry gave way to history and politics. Wilson suggests that the *Literary Commonplace Book* was "a deeply personal notebook with direct connections to the emotional events and preoccupations of [Jefferson's] formative years."[42]

In the pages of his commonplace book, the young philosopher first confronted disappointment in love and the death of a beloved friend; here he first rehearsed the great contest between Head and Heart.[43] Jefferson's commonplacing, Kenneth A. Lockridge argues, reveals his deepest conflicts.

Lockridge reads the cluster of misogynistic extracts as Jefferson's "tirades" against his mother's domination and against female power generally; they express pervasive anxieties—and "patriarchal rage"—characteristic of a provincial gentry in the making. Rhys Isaac culls the same materials for the "stories" out of which Jefferson fashioned an idealized conception of domesticity that resolved or suppressed his adolescent conflicts.[44]

The adult Jefferson had little time for poetry or for exploring the darker recesses of his psyche. But, as Burstein shows in *The Inner Jefferson,* the enlightened autodidact continued to fashion himself—and his world— through a regimen of reading and writing.[45] Jefferson's legal practice constituted the crucial link between adolescent reading and adult writing.[46] Reading opened up the great world for Jefferson; writing enabled him to take a leading role in its Revolutionary transformation. Yet he always longed to return to Monticello, where the never-ending process of building up and tearing down engaged his deepest interest—and drained his financial resources. Jefferson's sense of himself was most fully expressed in the construction of his mountaintop home and of the family life it contained. Isaac suggests that Jefferson sought to create "a place both of intimate domesticity and of more comprehensive sociability . . . of contemplative retreat and of continuing resort." The tension between Jefferson's private and his public world was prefigured in these intentions.[47] In later life that tension was most fully articulated in his reaction to the rancorous partisanship that came to characterize national politics in the 1790s. As Jefferson moved forward on the public stage, Jan Lewis argues, he was constantly drawn back to the consolations of Monticello and the love of his daughters and their families. The adult Jefferson's domestic idyll, his storied home, mobilized youthful fantasies to salve the wounds of public life.[48] But as countless friends, allies, and admirers visited Monticello, daughter Martha complained that Jefferson's sociability compromised the private enjoyment of his family life. The tension was basic to Jefferson's self-conception and to his ongoing negotiations with the world that defined him.[49] Jack McLaughlin's history of Monticello's construction offers glimpses into Jefferson's private life and character. Other lives were also involved in this project, as McLaughlin's discussion of the workforce reveals.[50] Isaac suggests that Jefferson's vision of domestic bliss depended not only on exploiting the unremitting labor of his slaves but also on suppressing the African-Virginian songs and stories he had heard as a child.[51] Lucia Stanton in her important work on the slave community at Monticello explores the relationships between Jefferson and his slaves.

Stanton reconstructs the circles of the African American community at Monticello, moving outward from the light-skinned Hemingses, who were said to have been relatives of Jefferson's wife and dominated the most skilled and trusted positions, to the industrial workers Jefferson directly supervised and to the great majority of agricultural laborers supervised by overseers. What is remarkable about these circles is Jefferson's instrumental approach to them, the general absence of affect and human feeling that his very occasional expressions of sentiment only cast into relief. Most concerned with sustaining orderly conditions and maximizing productivity, Jefferson did not sentimentalize slave ownership. The contrast with his ideas about domesticity and sociability within the circles of his white family and friends could not be starker.[52]

Jefferson's life at Monticello was predicated on the fundamental distinction between white domesticity and black slavery. His voluminous correspondence provided the crucial link between home and wider world and a more expansive social setting for his "self-fashioning."[53] Letter writing was also—and above all else—the medium of extending and sustaining his widening circle of friends, the practical expression of the sociability that grounded his political philosophy and shaped his political practice.[54] As he told his future foe Noah Webster Jr. in 1790, "No republic is more real than that of letters."[55]

The Jefferson archive provides extraordinarily rich testimony to his affectionate feelings for his vast network of friends. Jefferson addresses his correspondent as an "equal"; his concessions to the correspondent's predilections—or gender—presume a common ground to be illuminated and developed in future correspondence.[56] In other words, the letter—a tender or reaffirmation of friendship between equals—is both means and end for Jefferson, the practical embodiment of the republican idea. But the connection between letter writing, self-expression, and the fractious political life of the new American republic was troublesome for Jefferson. As Wilson observes, the imperatives of partisan politics led Jefferson to secrecy and concealment: "He could conscript others to pseudonymous pamphleteering and newspaper writing," and "he could even speak past his correspondents to an interested posterity . . . but he seems to have found it next to impossible to direct his writing squarely at the public."[57] However "real" it might be to Jefferson, the "republic" that he constituted through his correspondence had to be preserved inviolate—as he guarded the privacy of his home—from the conflicts of political life. At the same time, Jefferson's correspondence—like his home—constituted the center of a busily social and deeply political world. It was a paradox, like so many in Jefferson's life, that could be reconciled only by denial—in this case, denial that Jefferson and his allies pursued their own interested ends through partisan political action.

The relationship between Jefferson's two "republics" was less a problem for Jefferson the visionary reformer than for Jefferson the statesman-politician. As Harold Hellenbrand argues in his book on Jefferson and education, Jefferson could fashion acceptable roles for himself as the proponent of republican enlightenment that did not violate his fundamental principles. By thinking of the republic "in familial terms," and not the terms of self-promotion and partisan interests, he could sustain an apolitical conception of republican leadership. Hellenbrand asserts that Jefferson "thought of his policies as instruments of moral improvement that were understandable as such by reason. He functioned as the father/teacher in the republic; in his rhetoric, he played the role of the nation's mentor."[58]

The mentor role figures prominently in Jefferson's correspondence. It helped resolve one of the most troubling and dangerous questions of his personal and political life: how to establish an affectionate relationship between the generations that did not compromise the equality and moral autonomy of necessarily dependent sons. The authority of the mentor is temporary and contingent; it is based on the sentimental, familial premise that the good father sublimates self-interest on behalf of the child. If monarchy and aristocracy are simply the most extreme, legally institutionalized forms of generational tyranny, the fundamental republican imperative of equality demands the ultimate elimination of public debts, periodic constitutional revision, and self-denying father-mentors who equip their sons for an enlightened future. This self-denial is a form of self-construction: Jefferson expected republican fathers (who would not be "aristocrats") to take the essential role in the parade of generations (the progress of civilization) as exemplars and teachers who would wield parental love and filial gratitude to make their own sons into self-controlled, self-constructing republican fathers. There is more bourgeois father than "Patriot King" (who, after all, never abdicates) in this conception of republican leadership.[59]

Letter writing defined the parameters of Jefferson's world. He assumed different voices in performing different roles as a correspondent, but all expressed his fundamental belief in progress: his young charges would achieve a self-disciplined happiness; his countrymen would see their own true interests more clearly; and enlightenment would expand across the world. Historians who look for disclosures of an authentic self behind these many voices and roles will be frustrated. Jefferson's self is in his writing, and his fundamental commitments to equality, consent, and civility inform all his varied self-representations.

Statecraft

Jefferson's writings exercise a continuing fascination because they reflect and represent fundamental, unresolved problems in his political thought and practice as well as his private life. Our sense of these problems is not simply a function of anachronistic moralizing. Jeffersonian contradictions were abundantly apparent to contemporaries who were excluded or resisted inclusion in the widening circle of republican friends who seized the reins of power in the electoral "Revolution of 1800." These contradictions would also become apparent to Jefferson's legatees, if not to Jefferson himself, as the nation blundered into a second, nearly disastrous, war with Britain.

The discrepancies between Jefferson's idealized vision of the republic and his performances in office have been the subject of a large critical literature. Following the lead of critics in Jefferson's own time, Leonard Levy has emphasized the disjunction between his libertarian precepts and his resort to governmental coercion to muzzle—or at least chill—Federalist editors and, much more dangerously, to enforce his disastrous embargo on foreign trade in 1807 and 1808.[60] John Larson argues persuasively that the strict constructionist constitutionalism that served the Republicans so well in opposition crippled their efforts to promote the internal improvements they knew were essential to securing a fragile union.[61] Even Appleby, Jefferson's most eloquent proponent today, worries that the "fusion of democracy and capitalism" over which Jefferson originally presided has "raised formidable barriers to the public oversight of economic affairs" and to the continuing vitality and viability of the "democratic forms" that were liberating in his time.[62]

The ascendancy of a strict constructionist constitutionalism born of a fear of power subverted positive government for public purposes, but Jeffersonians could overcome their constitutional scruples when the purposes seemed sufficiently compelling. The Louisiana Purchase is the prime case in point, violating the fundamental principles that were, as Henry Adams writes, "the breath of his political life."[63] There were always exceptions and limits to the principles that Jeffersonians articulated in such absolute, unlimited terms. What would come to be called the new nation's "manifest destiny" to spread across the continent thus trumped any lingering concerns about the rights of Native Americans or, for that matter, of neighboring European colonies under the law of nations.[64]

The most pernicious aspect of Jeffersonian foreign policy, Robert W. Tucker and David C. Hendrickson argue in *Empire of Liberty,* was the conflation of a vaulting idealism with a willingness to employ any means, however devious, to promote American interests. Self-righteous "moralism . . . not only constituted the central aspect of [Jefferson's] diplomatic outlook but is also identifiable as the primary corrupting factor within it." "Unable to adjust to the existing world," Jeffersonians set the pattern for the characteristically American oscillation between "withdrawal from that world" and "the attempt to reform it by imposing one's will on it."[65] Paradoxically, this self-deluding "idealism" justified a disregard for the rights of others, even—as in the case of the black rebels of Santo Domingo—when they invoked the Jeffersonian rhetoric of self-determination.

The theme that runs through all such attacks on Jefferson's record is that inflated, idealistic rhetoric was at odds with realistic assessments of policy alternatives, authorized massive disregard for the rights of others at home and abroad, and precluded the development of the kind of civic life that could alone secure the promise of republican self-government to future generations. The critics' juxtaposition of Jefferson's words and deeds points to some of the central interpretative issues. Whatever else he was, Jefferson was no hypocrite in the conventional sense; as an exponent of "natural speech" and "self-evident" truths, he did not deploy glittering phrases with a cynical, instrumental disregard for what he took to be their meanings.[66] The disjunction of speech and act, so apparent to us, does not necessarily reveal a flawed character. It is nonetheless true that the self Jefferson fashioned and the ways he constructed and conceived his private world and public career have had momentous, often unintended, and sometimes tragic implications and consequences.

Jefferson's antipathy to political life—"a dreary scene where envy, hatred, malice, revenge and all the worse passions of men are marshalled, to make one another as miserable as possible"—is well known. If Jefferson was the father of the first modern political party, it was not a paternity he happily acknowledged.[67] When, at his first inaugural, he said, "We are all republicans, we are all federalists," he was seeking to overcome and banish party divisions. Parties were anathema to Jefferson because they set up artificial and corrupt barriers among representatives of the people who should be acting together for the common good. Ominously, party divisions tended to replicate and exacerbate sectional animosities. Jefferson therefore invoked a transcendent commitment to "federal and republican principles, our attachment to union and representative government."[68]

Good republicans fostered peace and harmony, not the violent animosities that partisans promoted and exploited. Partisanship, the antithesis and negation of friendship, jeopardized the affectionate bonds that sustained republican government. But Jeffersonian ideas of friendship and sociability, though hostile to party, also contributed to Jefferson's great successes in party leadership. As James Sterling Young shows in *The Washington Community,* a social history of the process of governance in the new national capital, Jefferson had a genius for drawing congressmen into his charmed circle and for achieving his political goals through indirection and gentle persuasion. "Friendship"—the close personal ties of congressional agents who took charge of key legislation, the receptive predisposition of his dinner guests—was instrumental, the functional equivalent of a more complex, and inevitably hierarchical, party organization.[69]

The "irony" of Jefferson's antipartisan politics, Michael Lienesch suggests, was that it intensified partisanship by opening up the political process and identifying popular sovereignty with "organized public opinion." This new sort of partisanship was supposed to merge governors and governed, representatives and represented, thus achieving the kind of transparency and authenticity that "natural language" would bring to public discourse.[70] Thus, when Republican oppositionists called for a return to the "principles of the revolution of 1776," they were seeking to show things as they really were, to unmask the villains, and to enable good republicans to recognize one another. Their own motives were self-evidently above reproach, for they sought only to restore the affectionate bonds of union on which the survival of the republic depended.[71]

For modern skeptics, such claims can only seem disingenuous and cynical—as they did in Jefferson's time to his Federalist opponents. But Jeffersonians were simply projecting into the realm of popular politics the precepts of the enlightened republic of letters. They believed that a true representation of the people's will was a powerful revolutionary force that would ultimately banish the mystifications and misrepresentations that sustained monarchical rule. The republican millennium was postponed during the

1790s, it was true, as artful aristocrats exploited popular credulity and used the new federal government to pander to selfish interests. Such setbacks did not deter the Jeffersonians but drove them to redouble their efforts to expose the malign motives of insidious opponents who merely pretended to be republicans. The conviction that Federalist machinations jeopardized the survival of the republic was powerfully confirmed by blatant assaults on civil liberties in the Alien and Sedition acts. Intoxicated with their own power, or so it seemed to strict republicans, Federalists stripped off their own disguises—and stood condemned.

Revisionist historians have illuminated the hopes and fears that animated Jefferson and his followers. Jeffersonian visions of the progress of political civilization were counterposed to chronic anxieties for the future of republican government. Imaginary networks of conspirators against liberty constituted the model—perhaps more accurately, the antitype—for the Revolutionary band of brothers who had fought for independence and now, as the "particular friends" of Jefferson and Madison, sought to redeem republican government from its secret enemies. The darker, fearful side of this Jeffersonian persuasion has been delineated by Lance Banning. More recently, Gordon Wood and Jay Fliegelman have emphasized the progressive and optimistic dimensions of Revolutionary thought and sensibility. Implicit in the unmasking of political enemies was the promise of a world without masks, a politics of authenticity and feeling in which interests and motives would be transparent and a true, unmediated representation would be possible.[72] The goal was unattainable, even when the monocrats were routed: politicians would simply learn to wear more democratic masks as they appealed to an expanding electorate.

The American founders are celebrated for their gritty realism, for their immunity to the utopian aspirations that corrupted and destroyed the French Revolution. Their revolutionary optimism was predicated not on the exercise but on the restraint of power. The contrast between the American Revolution of 1776—or Jefferson's "Revolution of 1800"—and the bloody debacle in France is certainly striking. If Jefferson occasionally gave vent to sanguinary sentiments, he showed no inclination to exterminate his enemies when he gained power: "Let them stand undisturbed as monuments of the safety with which error of opinion may be tolerated where reason is left free to combat it."[73]

The glib explanation for the peaceful transfer of power is that this was yet another instance—albeit a happy one—of the characteristically Jeffersonian

[36]

discrepancy between talk and action. But Jefferson remained constitution-ally averse to the abuse of power, an aversion that his years in opposition reinforced. The point of his "Revolution" was to banish forever the possibil-ity that the power of the central government would jeopardize the rights of states or citizens. Such consolidation of authority was incompatible with liberty, and liberty was the basis of union. Recognizing the primacy of these affectionate ties and committed to the fundamental principles of equality and consent, the triumphant Republicans would exercise power only to se-cure the broader sphere of natural society and free exchange against the depredations of the privileged and corrupt.

Conclusion

Grounded in the cosmopolitan aspirations of a young provincial who sought citizenship in the great republic of letters, Jefferson's vision of repub-lican government was both an extrapolation of conventional Enlightenment ideas about civility and sociability and a projection of his own ever-expand-ing circle of friends. Political life could be seen as a conversation among friends, recognizing diverse perspectives and interests while they sought a common ground and a common good. Similarly, a harmonious union of free states in America was predicated on the mutual interest and natural sociability of liberty-loving republicans, not on the energetic government favored by Federalists—or even on the party organization that Republicans had to develop in order to counter Federalist corruption.[74] In its most ex-travagant formulation, the fulfillment of Jefferson's project would see the nations of the world substitute peaceful, mutually beneficial exchange for violent conflict.[75]

But the republic in Jefferson's mind was never the same thing as the real republic he was instrumental in creating, and the discrepancy has become increasingly apparent. Simply to sketch the bold outlines of Jefferson's hopes for himself and his world is to invite mockery and derision. Peace on earth is no more in prospect now than it was in the dangerous days when Jefferson and Madison stumbled into war. The federal union has survived, but it bears little resemblance to Jefferson's union. And the collapse of the union during the Civil War and the subsequent transformation of the federal system are traceable to Jefferson's commitment to upholding the rights of slave states, a commitment that reflected his personal failure to take any effective steps against the institution of slavery. So, too, impasse and incapacity in politics today can be blamed on the diffusion of authority, the suspicion of power, and the disjunction between the private pursuit of happiness and the intensely public life of the commonwealth that Jeffersonianism authorized.

Yet these indictments of Jefferson and his legacy follow a Jeffersonian script. Our own skepticism about words and deeds hearkens back to Republican efforts to unmask the nefarious Federalist foe. But historians are now more inclined to direct this Jeffersonian skepticism at the Jeffersonians themselves. What could be more outrageously spurious than to claim, as Jeffersonians did, to speak for the people or to invoke the authority of natural language, affectionate feelings, and self-evident principles? Manipulators of public opinion, they traded in empty words; self-effacement disguised vaulting (or sordid) ambitions. If Jefferson could not acknowledge his true motives or moral lapses, most conspicuously as a slave owner, that simply makes him more of a monster of self-deception.

The present-day discomfort with Jefferson is a challenge to historical interpretation and self-reflection. Nothing is more Jeffersonian about our approach to him than to raise questions about his character as well as his statecraft. As Fliegelman suggests, the search for a natural republican language—and politics—was bound to fail: sentimentalism gave way to cynicism as the politics of authenticity subverted itself.[76] The "real" Jefferson will continue to elude and resist judgment. A greater measure of self-consciousness about our indebtedness to Jefferson, even in criticizing him, will not resolve the controversy he continues to inspire. But it should enable us to see him more clearly in his own context.

Jefferson's great political project, his struggle against despotic rule, expressed and confirmed his fundamental commitment to the self-evident principles of his political credo. In a revolutionary world of tenuous and shifting loyalties, secret enemies and doubtful friends, this commitment defined a common ground, the only solid foundation for a durable union of liberty-loving republicans. Historians will argue about the sources of republican principles and about their unifying or divisive effects in the dynamic context of revolutionary political change. But we should never assume that American independence, the union of American states, or the democratization of American political and social life were preordained. No one was more conscious of the fragility of the American experiment than Jefferson. As Gordon Wood writes, the "democratic revolution he had contributed so much to bring about" left him mystified and uncomprehending. The discrepancy between his vision of the new nation's glorious future and the actual course of its development was—or should have been—increasingly evident in his declining years. A perennial optimist, Jefferson could sustain his "sublime faith in the people" only by averting his gaze from the vulgarity and busy-ness of the rising generation.[77]

Jefferson's optimism, his belief in the liberating power of words, his faith in man's natural sociability and capacity for self-government inspire as much incredulity as assent. If his ideas now circulate as the debased coin of our democratic culture, they were real for Jefferson and revolutionary for his times. As Joyce Appleby contends, "Jefferson boldly levitated himself out of his social milieu and trained his great learning on the real problem of liberty at the end of the eighteenth century: how to make good on the Enlightenment promise that men, born with a capacity for benign self-direction, could work out their own destinies and bring into existence a world that reflected the fulfillment of desire rather than a compromise with despair."[78] The promise has not been fulfilled, even for the empowered and hopeful beneficiaries of the new dispensation. But that is America's story as much as it was Jefferson's. As long as that story is worth telling, Jefferson will continue to occupy a crucial place in our nation's history and "symbolical architecture."

Notes

This essay was originally published as "The Scholars' Jefferson," *William & Mary Quarterly* (hereafter *WMQ*) 50 (1993): 671–99; and in revised form as "Making Sense of Jefferson," the introduction to my *Thomas Jefferson: An Anthology* (St. James, N.Y., 1999). Minor changes, including updated citations, have been made in this version.

1. Merrill D. Peterson, *The Jefferson Image in the American Mind* (New York, 1960), 447, 453–54, 395–420.

2. Ibid., 375–76.

3. Dumas Malone, *Jefferson and His Time*, 6 vols. (Boston, 1948–81). See Merrill D. Peterson, "Dumas Malone: An Appreciation," *WMQ* 45 (1988): 237–52.

4. Julian P. Boyd et al., eds., *The Papers of Thomas Jefferson*, 32 vols. to date (Princeton, NJ, 1950–), has regained momentum under editors Barbara Oberg (editor of the continuing First Series) and J. Jefferson Looney (editor of the new Retirement Series). The most recently published volume in the First Series takes Thomas Jefferson (hereafter TJ) to the eve of his inauguration in 1801; the first two volumes of the Retirement Series (2005–2006) extend into 1810.

5. See Frank Shuffelton's "Bibliographic Essay," in Merrill D. Peterson, ed., *Thomas Jefferson: A Reference Biography* (New York, 1986), 453–79. The most complete bibliographies are Shuffelton, *Thomas Jefferson, Annotated Bibliography of Writings about Him, 1826–1980* (New York, 1983); and Shuffelton, *Thomas Jefferson, 1989–1990: An Annotated Bibliography* (New York, 1990). The Shuffelton bibliographies are now online; see http://etext.lib.virginia.edu/jefferson/bibliog/.

6. Conor Cruise O'Brien, *The Long Affair: Thomas Jefferson and the French Revolution* (Chicago, 1996).

7. Joseph J. Ellis, *American Sphinx: The Character of Thomas Jefferson* (New York, 1997), 127–28.

8. Eugene Foster et al., "Jefferson Fathered Slave's Last Child," *Nature* 396 (Nov. 5, 1998): 27–28. The title of this piece is misleading, as Foster emphasized in a subsequent communication: it is at least theoretically possible that someone else with Jefferson's DNA could account for the match between Jefferson's descendants and the descendants of Eston Hemings, one of Sally's children (Foster et al., "The Thomas Jefferson Paternity Case," *Nature* 397 [Jan. 7, 1999]).

9. For further discussion, see Peter S. Onuf and Jan Ellen Lewis, "American Synecdoche: Thomas Jefferson as Image, Icon, Character, and Self," in this volume.

10. David Brion Davis, *The Problem of Slavery in Western Culture* (Ithaca, NY, 1966); idem, *The Problem of Slavery in the Age of Revolution, 1770–1823* (Ithaca, NY, 1975), 169–84; Winthrop Jordan, *White over Black: American Attitudes toward the Negro, 1550–1812* (Chapel Hill, NC, 1968), 429–81. See also Jack P. Greene, "All Men Are Created Equal: Some Reflections on the Character of the American Revolution," in his *Imperatives, Behaviors, and Identities: Essays in Early American Cultural History* (Charlottesville, VA, 1992), 236–67; Charles A. Miller, *Jefferson and Nature: An Interpretation* (Baltimore, 1988); Thomas L. Haskell, "Capitalism and the Origins of the Humanitarian Sensibility, Part I," *American Historical Review* 90 (1985): 339–61.

11. For Peterson's "mortifying confession" that Jefferson "remains for me, finally, an impenetrable man," see his *Thomas Jefferson and the New Nation: A Biography* (New York, 1970), viii.

12. Fawn Brodie, *Thomas Jefferson: An Intimate History* (New York, 1974). The most extensive refutation of Brodie's charges is Virginius Dabney, *The Jefferson Scandals: A Rebuttal* (New York, 1981). For a fascinating account of this controversy and further citations, see Scot A. French and Edward L. Ayers, "The Strange Career of Thomas Jefferson: Race and Slavery in American Memory, 1943–1993," in Peter S. Onuf, ed., *Jeffersonian Legacies* (Charlottesville, VA, 1993), 418–56.

13. Andrew Burstein, *The Inner Jefferson: Portrait of a Grieving Optimist*

(Charlottesville, VA, 1995); Annette Gordon-Reed, *Thomas Jefferson and Sally Hemings: An American Controversy* (Charlottesville, VA, 1997).

14. The vast literature on Jefferson and slavery includes Robert McColley, *Slavery and Jeffersonian Virginia* (Urbana, IL, 1964; 2d ed., 1973); William Cohen, "Thomas Jefferson and the Problem of Slavery," *Journal of American History* 55 (1969): 503–26; John Chester Miller, *The Wolf by the Ears: Thomas Jefferson and Slavery* (New York, 1977); Paul Finkelman, "Jefferson and Slavery: 'Treason against the Hopes of the World,'" in Onuf, ed., *Jeffersonian Legacies*, 181–221; Paul Finkelman, *Slavery and the Founders: Race and Liberty in the Age of Jefferson* (Armonk, NY, 1996); Alexander O. Boulton, "The American Paradox: Jeffersonian Equality and Racial Science," *American Quarterly* 47 (1995); and Onuf, "'To Declare Them a Free and Independant People': Race, Slavery, and National Identity in Jefferson's Thought," *Journal of the Early Republic* 18 (1998): 1–46, republished in revised form in my *Jefferson's Empire: The Language of American Nationhood* (Charlottesville, VA, 2000), chap. 5.

15. On "presentism," see Douglas L. Wilson, "Thomas Jefferson and the Character Issue," *Atlantic Monthly* 270 (Nov. 1992): 62.

16. Peterson, *The Jefferson Image in the American Mind*, 13. For a sampling of attitudes toward TJ among his contemporaries, see Jack McLaughlin, ed., *To His Excellency Thomas Jefferson: Letters to a President* (New York, 1991).

17. The key text is Bernard Bailyn, *The Ideological Origins of the American Revolution* (Cambridge, MA, 1967). For progress reports on the historiography, see Robert E. Shalhope, "Toward a Republican Synthesis: The Emergence of an Understanding of Republicanism in American Historiography," *WMQ* 29 (1972): 49–80; idem, "Republicanism in Early American Historiography," *WMQ* 39 (1982): 334–56; Joyce Appleby, ed., "Republicanism in the History and Historiography of the United States," Special Issue, *American Quarterly* 37 (Fall 1985). For a provocative if perhaps premature postmortem, see Daniel T. Rodgers, "Republicanism: The Career of a Concept," *Journal of American History* 79 (1992): 11–38.

18. See particularly the seminal contributions of H. Trevor Colbourn: "Thomas Jefferson's Use of the Past," *WMQ* 15 (1958): 56–70; and *The Lamp of Experience: Whig History and the Intellectual Origins of the American Revolution* (Chapel Hill, NC, 1965), 158–84.

19. Lance Banning, *The Jeffersonian Persuasion: Evolution of a Party Ideology* (Ithaca, NY, 1978); Drew R. McCoy, *The Elusive Republic: Political Economy in Jeffersonian America* (Chapel Hill, NC, 1980). Forrest McDonald, who argues most forcefully for Alexander Hamilton's modernizing political economy, is an enthusiastic exponent of the republicanized version of Jefferson; see his *The Presidency of Thomas Jefferson* (Lawrence, KS, 1976); and *Alexander Hamilton: A Biography* (New York, 1979).

20. See particularly Michael P. Zuckert, *Natural Rights and the New Republicanism* (Princeton, NJ, 1994); and idem, *The Natural Rights Republic: Studies in the Foundation of the American Political Tradition* (Notre Dame, IN, 1996).

21. Joyce Appleby, *Capitalism and a New Social Order: The Republican Vision of the 1790s* (New York, 1984), 81, 83, 79. Appleby's essays—including "The 'Agrarian Myth' in the Early Republic" (1982) and "What Is Still American in the Political Philosophy of Thomas Jefferson" (1982)—are collected in her *Liberalism and Republicanism in the Historical Imagination* (Cambridge, MA, 1992). For a sympathetic account of Jeffersonian political economy, see John R. Nelson Jr., *Liberty and Property: Political Economy and Policymaking in the New Nation, 1789–1812* (Baltimore, 1987).

22. On the importance of historical consciousness in the civic humanist tradition, see particularly J. G. A. Pocock, *The Machiavellian Moment: Florentine Political Thought and the Atlantic Republican Tradition* (Princeton, NJ, 1975). Jay Fliegelman suggests that participants in the scholarly debate over the historical consciousness of putatively republican or liberal Revolutionary Americans "may be seen as schematizing a number of the late eighteenth-century dialectics" that he explores in his *Declaring Independence: Jefferson, Natural Language, and the Culture of Performance* (Stanford, CA, 1993), 186–87.

23. For discussion of these diverse sources, see Richard Vetterli and Gary Bryner, *In Search of the Republic: Public Virtue and the Roots of American Government* (Totowa, NJ, 1987); and the essay by Jean Yarbrough, "The Constitution and Character: The Missing Critical Principle?" in Herman Belz et al., eds., *To Form a More Perfect Union: The Critical Ideas of the Constitution* (Charlottesville, VA, 1992), 217–49. On Jefferson and character, see Jean M. Yarbrough, *American Virtues: Thomas Jefferson on the Character of a Free People* (Lawrence, KS, 1998).

24. Peter S. Onuf, "Reflections on the Founding: Constitutional Historiography in Bicentennial Perspective," *WMQ* 46 (1989): 341–75. For the ideological diversity of the founding era, see James T. Kloppenberg, "The Virtues of Liberalism: Christianity, Republicanism, and Ethics in Early American Political Discourse," *Journal of American History* 74 (1987): 9–33; and Isaac Kramnick, "The 'Great National Discussion': The Discourse of Politics in 1787," *WMQ* 45 (1988): 3–22.

25. Gordon S. Wood, *The Radicalism of the American Revolution* (New York, 1992). Wood's account of republicanism here departs significantly from his earlier emphasis on its "classical" premises in *The Creation of the American Republic, 1776–1787* (Chapel Hill, NC, 1969), esp. 46–90. On the break between classical and modern republicanism, see Paul Rahe, *Republics Ancient and Modern: Classical Republicanism and the American Revolution* (Chapel Hill, NC, 1992), 573–616.

26. On Jefferson's disillusionment with democratic society, see Wood's essay, "The Trials and Tribulations of Thomas Jefferson," in Onuf, ed., *Jeffersonian Legacies,* 395–417.

27. TJ to James Madison, Sept. 6, 1789, in Boyd et al., eds., *Jefferson Papers,* 15:392–98, emphasis in original; Herbert Sloan, "*'The Earth Belongs in Usufruct to the Living,'*" in Onuf, ed., *Jeffersonian Legacies,* 281–315, quotations on 282. For a fuller discussion of the debt problem, see Herbert Sloan, *Principle and Interest: Thomas Jefferson and the Problem of Debt* (New York, 1995).

28. The most authoritative edition now in print is William Peden, ed., *Notes on the State of Virginia* (Chapel Hill, NC, 1954).

29. A sample of some of the more interesting essays includes Lee Quinby, "Thomas Jefferson: The Virtue of Aesthetics and the Aesthetics of Virtue," *American Historical Review* 87 (1982): 337–56; Mitchell Breitwieser, "Jefferson's Prospect," *Prospects* 10 (1985): 315–52; Robert A. Ferguson, "'Mysterious Obligation': Jefferson's Notes on the State of Virginia," *American Literature* 52 (1980): 381–406; Harold Hellenbrand, "Roads to Happiness: Rhetorical and Philosophical Design in Jefferson's Notes on the State of Virginia," *Early American Literature* 20 (1985): 3–23; Pamela Regis, "Jefferson and the Department of Man," in her *Describing Early America: Bartram, Jefferson, Crèvecoeur, and the Rhetoric of Natural History* (DeKalb, IL, 1992), chap. 3; and James W. Ceaser, *Reconstructing America: The Symbol of America in Modern Thought* (New Haven, CT, 1997), 43–65.

30. TJ, Query 18 ("Manners"), in Peden, ed., *Notes,* 163.

31. Jack P. Greene, in "The Intellectual Reconstruction of Virginia in the Age of Jefferson" (in Onuf, ed., *Jeffersonian Legacies,* 225–53) emphasizes the reformist thrust of TJ's *Notes* and his contributions to "a positive sense of collective self for Virginia and Virginians" (250).

32. For treatments of TJ's political thought that demonstrate the range of interpretative possibilities, see David N. Mayer, *The Constitutional Thought of Thomas Jefferson* (Charlottesville, VA, 1994); and Richard K. Matthews, *The Radical Politics of Thomas Jefferson: A Revisionist View* (Lawrence, KS, 1984). Throughout a long, turbulent career, Mayer's Jefferson remains a Real Whig constitutionalist; Matthews's TJ, a democratic radical. In *The Political Philosophy of Thomas Jefferson* (Baltimore, 1991), Garrett Ward Sheldon discusses Jeffersonian "liberalism" in the context of the imperial crisis and his "republicanism" in the setting of Revolutionary reform in Virginia.

33. Fliegelman, *Declaring Independence,* 2. TJ's problems with public speaking are suggestively elaborated in successive sections on Patrick Henry, great orator of the Revolution, and in "Social Leveling and Stage Fright," 94–140.

34. For a good introduction to Jeffersonian thought, see Daniel J. Boorstin, *The Lost World of Thomas Jefferson*, with a new preface (1948; Chicago, 1981). On TJ's reading, see Douglas L. Wilson, "Jefferson's Library," and Meyer Reinhold, "The Classical World," both in Peterson, ed., *Thomas Jefferson: A Reference Biography*, 157–79, 135–56; also, Charles B. Sanford, *Thomas Jefferson and His Library: A Study of His Literary Interests and of the Religious Attitudes Revealed by Relevant Titles in His Library* (Hamden, CT, 1977); Douglas L. Wilson, "Jefferson and the Republic of Letters," in Onuf, ed., *Jeffersonian Legacies*, 50–76; and Burstein, *Inner Jefferson*, 42–67.

35. On TJ and the philosophers, see Karl Lehmann, *Thomas Jefferson, American Humanist* (New York, 1947); Carl J. Richard, "A Dialogue with the Ancients: Thomas Jefferson and Classical Philosophy and History," *Journal of the Early Republic* 9 (1989): 431–55; and Carl J. Richard, *The Founders and the Classics: Greece, Rome, and the American Enlightenment* (Cambridge, MA, 1994).

36. Douglas L. Wilson, "The American *Agricola*: Jefferson's Agrarianism and the Classical Tradition," *South Atlantic Quarterly* 80 (1981): 339–54; Paul Rahe, "Thomas Jefferson's Machiavellian Political Science," *Review of Politics* 57 (1995): 449–81. Wilson's piece is an important corrective to Leo Marx's influential account of Jeffersonian pastoralism in *The Machine in the Garden: Technology and the Pastoral Ideal* (New York, 1964). The Jefferson quotation is in TJ, Query 19 ("Manufactures"), in Peden, ed., *Notes*, 164–65.

37. Onuf, *Jefferson's Empire*, chap. 2; Thomas Bender, *Toward an Urban Vision: Ideas and Institutions in Nineteenth Century America* (Lexington, KY, 1975), 3–51.

38. C. A. Miller, *Jefferson and Nature*. See also Joyce Appleby, *Without Resolution: The Jeffersonian Tensions in American Nationalism*, Harmsworth Inaugural Lecture (Oxford, 1992). The "Jeffersonian tension," she writes, results from the "confounding of facts and ideals. America's natural-rights philosophy did not just express aspirations; it purported to explain reality" (17).

39. Paul K. Conkin, "Religious Pilgrimage of Jefferson," in Onuf, ed., *Jeffersonian Legacies*, 19–49. See the excellent collection of documents in Dickinson W. Adams, ed., *Jefferson's Extracts from the Gospels: "The Philosophy of Jesus" and "The Life and Morals of Jesus"* (Princeton, NJ, 1983). The fullest treatment is Charles B. Sanford, *The Religious Life of Thomas Jefferson* (Charlottesville, VA, 1984).

40. Eugene Sheridan, "Introduction," in D. W. Adams, ed., *Jefferson's Extracts from the Gospels*, 3–42, quotation on 42.

41. TJ to Ezra Stiles Ely, June 25, 1819, in Adams, ed., *Jefferson's Extracts from the Gospels*, 42. For discussion of how TJ edited "The Life and Morals of Jesus" to promote his "ideals of social harmony and democracy" (30), see Susan Bryan,

"Reauthorizing the Text: Jefferson's Scissor Edit of the Gospels," *Early American Literature* 22 (1987): 19–42. On the progress of evangelical religion in this period that emphasizes surprising affinities with Jeffersonianism, see Nathan O. Hatch, *The Democratization of American Christianity* (New Haven, CT, 1989).

42. Douglas L. Wilson, "Introduction," in Douglas L. Wilson, ed., *Jefferson's Literary Commonplace Book* (Princeton, NJ, 1989), 3–20, quotations on 8, 15–16. See also idem, "Thomas Jefferson's Early Notebooks," *WMQ* 42 (1985): 433–52.

43. For the famous dialogue between Head and Heart, see TJ to Maria Cosway, Oct. 12, 1786, in Boyd et al., eds., *Jefferson Papers,* 10:443–55.

44. Kenneth A. Lockridge, *On the Sources of Patriarchal Rage: The Commonplace Books of William Byrd and Thomas Jefferson and the Gendering of Power in the Eighteenth Century* (New York, 1992); Rhys Isaac, "The First Monticello," in Onuf, ed., *Jeffersonian Legacies,* 77–108.

45. Burstein, *Inner Jefferson.*

46. Dewey, *Thomas Jefferson, Lawyer* (Charlottesville, VA, 1986). On TJ's reading as a student, see ibid., 9–17. Although he never appeared in court after August 1774, the honing of "his forensic and writing skills" and the "assurance" he gained as a lawyer set the stage for his public career. The revisal of the laws was the centerpiece of his reform program for republican Virginia (see Peterson, *Jefferson and the New Nation,* 97–165; and Harold Hellenbrand, *The Unfinished Revolution: Education and Politics in the Thought of Thomas Jefferson* [Newark, DE, 1990]).

47. Isaac, "The First Monticello," in Onuf, ed., *Jeffersonian Legacies,* 90.

48. Jan Lewis, "'The Blessings of Domestic Society': Thomas Jefferson's Family and the Transformation of American Politics," in Onuf, ed., *Jeffersonian Legacies,* 109–46. On the importance of "home" to Virginians in this period, see Jan Lewis, *The Pursuit of Happiness: Family and Values in Jefferson's Virginia* (New York, 1983); "The strands of evangelical religion, republican belief, and domestic thought combine; in the era after the American Revolution, the pursuit of happiness took men and women home" (210).

49. His answer to the privacy problem was to retreat periodically from Monticello to the other home he built for himself sixty miles away at Poplar Forest.

50. TJ's slaves "poured their energies into an edifice that epitomized the taste and refinement of the class that enslaved them and of the man whose ringing phrases had declared freedom for all mankind" (see Jack McLaughlin, *Jefferson and Monticello: The Biography of a Builder* [New York, 1988], 94–145, quotation on 145). See also the suggestive comments in Breitweiser, "Jefferson's Prospect": "Jefferson's instrumental innovations at Monticello are aimed at projecting a *sprezzatura* that denies the labor that permits Monticello to be: it is a magic place" (317).

51. Isaac, "The First Monticello," in Onuf, ed., *Jeffersonian Legacies*, 100–101.

52. Lucia Stanton, "'Those Who Labor for My Happiness': Thomas Jefferson and His Slaves," in Onuf, ed., *Jeffersonian Legacies*, 147–80; and idem, *Free Some Day: The African-American Families of Monticello* (Charlottesville, VA, 2000). Stanton makes good use of James Adam Bear and Lucia C. Stanton, eds., *Jefferson's Memorandum Books: Accounts, with Legal Records and Miscellany, 1767–1826*, 2 vols. (Princeton, NJ, 1997).

53. See Burstein, *Inner Jefferson*; Wilson, "Jefferson and the Republic of Letters," in Onuf, ed., *Jeffersonian Legacies*, 50–76; and Robert Dawidoff, "Man of Letters," in Peterson, ed., *Thomas Jefferson: A Reference Biography*, 181–98. For a study of self-fashioning that emphasizes the importance of language, see Stephen Greenblatt, *Renaissance Self-Fashioning: From More to Shakespeare* (Chicago, 1980).

54. For a good example of how Jefferson sought to build political alliances through correspondence, see his letter to Elbridge Gerry, Jan. 26, 1799, in Merrill D. Peterson, ed., *Thomas Jefferson Writings* (New York, 1984), 1055–62. Garry Wills may have overrated Francis Hutcheson's influence, and underrated John Locke's, in explicating the Declaration, but he is certainly right to emphasize the social aspect of "happiness" in his *Inventing America: Jefferson's Declaration of Independence* (New York, 1978), 149–64, 248–65. On the importance of "feelings" and "sympathetic identification" as fundamental social bonds, see Fliegelman, *Declaring Independence*, 35–65.

55. TJ to Noah Webster Jr., Dec. 4, 1790, in Boyd et al., eds., *Jefferson Papers*, 18:132.

56. According to Frank Shuffelton, the "republic of letters" could only claim "to universality . . . if it allowed for the participation of both genders, although ideally it would allow for the expression in one person of that postconventional morality able to shift with ease from the viewpoint of one to the other" ("In Different Voices: Gender in the American Republic of Letters," *Early American Literature* 25 [1990]: 301). See also Burstein, *Inner Jefferson*, chap. 4.

57. Wilson, "Jefferson and the Republic of Letters," in Onuf, ed., *Jeffersonian Legacies*, 73.

58. Hellenbrand, *Unfinished Revolution*, 121. For further discussion of Jefferson's educational thought, see Lorraine Smith Pangle and Thomas L. Pangle, *Learning of Liberty: The Educational Ideas of the American Founders* (Lawrence, KS, 1993), chaps. 6, 13; and Joseph F. Kett, "Education," in Peterson, ed., *Thomas Jefferson: A Reference Biography*, 233–51.

59. On the influence of Henry St. John Bolingbroke's ideas about the Patriot Kingship of the first presidents, including Jefferson, see Ralph Ketcham, *Presidents above Parties: The First American Presidency, 1789–1829* (Chapel Hill, NC, 1984).

The logical incompatibility of these conceptions of paternal authority is more apparent in retrospect than in the experience of Revolutionary Americans. For analyses of the generational problem in this period, see Fliegelman, *Prodigals and Pilgrims: The American Revolution against Patriarchal Authority* (New York, 1982), esp. 40–51, on pedagogues; and Melvin Yazawa, *From Colonies to Commonweath: Familial Ideology and the Beginnings of the American Republic* (Baltimore, 1985), esp. 131–32, on Jefferson's educational ideas.

60. Leonard Levy, *Jefferson and Civil Liberties: The Darker Side* (Cambridge, MA, 1963). See also Burton Spivak, *Jefferson's English Crisis: Commerce, Embargo, and the Republican Revolution* (Charlottesville, VA, 1979).

61. John Larson, "Jefferson's Union and the Problem of Internal Improvements," in Onuf, ed., *Jeffersonian Legacies,* 340–69. See also Joseph H. Harrison Jr., "Sic Et Non: Thomas Jefferson and Internal Improvement," *Journal of the Early Republic* 7 (1987): 335–49.

62. Joyce Appleby, "Jefferson and His Complex Legacy," in Onuf, ed., *Jeffersonian Legacies,* 1–16, quotation on 15.

63. Henry Adams, *History of the United States of America during the First Administration of Thomas Jefferson,* 2 vols. (New York, 1889), bk. 2, 89.

64. Albert K. Weinberg, *Manifest Destiny: A Study of Nationalist Expansionism in American History* (Baltimore, 1935), 11–42; Alexander DeConde, *This Affair of Louisiana* (Baton Rouge, LA, 1976). For a nuanced account of Jeffersonian Indian policy, emphasizing the unintended consequences of good intentions, see Bernard W. Sheehan, *Seeds of Extinction: Jeffersonian Philanthropy and the American Indian* (Chapel Hill, NC, 1973); and Onuf, *Jefferson's Empire,* chap. 1.

65. Robert W. Tucker and David C. Hendrickson, *Empire of Liberty: The Statecraft of Thomas Jefferson* (New York, 1990), 179, 247. For another powerful indictment of Jeffersonian foreign policy, emphasizing the distorting effects of Jefferson's Anglophobia and a doctrinaire commitment to commercial sanctions, see Doron S. Ben-Atar, *The Origins of Jeffersonian Commercial Policy and Diplomacy* (London, 1992). A less critical and more balanced account of Jeffersonian foreign policy, focusing on the importance of securing the union, appears in James E. Lewis Jr., *The American Union and the Problem of Neighborhood: The United States and the Collapse of the Spanish Empire, 1783–1829* (Chapel Hill, NC, 1998). Also see idem, *The Louisiana Purchase: Jefferson's Noble Bargain?* (Chapel Hill, NC, 2003).

66. Fliegelman, *Declaring Independence.*

67. TJ to Martha Jefferson Randolph, Feb. 8, 1798, qtd. and discussed in Jan Lewis, "'The Blessings of Domestic Society,'" in Onuf, ed., *Jeffersonian Legacies,* 114. The best account of the political culture of the 1790s is Joanne B. Freeman, *Affairs*

of Honor: National Politics in the New Republic (New Haven, CT, 2001). See also Richard Hofstadter, *The Idea of a Party System* (Berkeley, CA, 1970), 122–28; and Robert M. S. McDonald, "Jefferson and America: Episodes in Image Formation" (Ph.D. diss., University of North Carolina, 1998).

68. TJ, First Inaugural Address, March 4, 1801, in Peterson, ed., *Jefferson Writings*, 493–94.

69. James Sterling Young, *The Washington Community, 1800–1828* (New York, 1966), 128–31, 163–81. See also Noble E. Cunningham Jr., *The Process of Government Under Jefferson* (Princeton, NJ, 1978); and McDonald, *Presidency of Thomas Jefferson.*

70. Michael Lienesch, "Thomas Jefferson and the American Democratic Experience: The Origins of the Partisan Press, Popular Political Parties, and Organized Public Opinion," in Onuf, ed., *Jeffersonian Legacies,* 316–39; and Fliegelman, *Declaring Independence.*

71. James Morton Smith, *Freedom's Fetters: The Alien and Sedition Laws and American Civil Liberties* (Ithaca, NY, 1956). On the crisis of the late 1790s, see also Stanley Elkins and Eric McKitrick, *The Age of Federalism* (New York, 1993); and James Roger Sharp, *American Politics in the Early Republic: The New Nation in Crisis* (New Haven, CT, 1993).

72. Banning, *Jeffersonian Persuasion.* See also Gordon S. Wood, "Conspiracy and the Paranoid Style: Causality and Deceit in the Eighteenth Century," *WMQ* 39 (1982): 401–41; idem, *Radicalism of the American Revolution;* idem, "Trials and Tribulations of Thomas Jefferson," in Onuf, ed., *Jeffersonian Legacies,* 395–417; and Fliegelman, *Declaring Independence.* I have borrowed the phrase "politics of authenticity" from Marshall Berman's study of Rousseau, *The Politics of Authenticity: Radical Individualism and the Emergence of Modern Society* (New York, 1970).

73. TJ, First Inaugural Address, March 4, 1801, in Peterson, ed., *Jefferson Writings*, 493.

74. Recent contributions to the history of federalism include Richard E. Ellis, *The Union at Risk: Jacksonian Democracy, States' Rights and the Nullification Crisis* (New York, 1987); and Peter B. Knupfer, *The Union as It Is: Constitutional Unionism and Sectional Compromise, 1787–1861* (Chapel Hill, NC, 1991).

75. For a balanced account of Jefferson's thinking about war and peace, see Reginald C. Stuart, *The Half-Way Pacifist: Thomas Jefferson's View of War* (Toronto, 1978). On Jefferson's hopes for peace through trade, see Merrill D. Peterson, "Jefferson and Commercial Policy, 1783–1793," *WMQ* 22 (1965): 584–610. On the history of federal theory and of the development of Jeffersonian and Madisonian ideas about union, see Peter Onuf and Nicholas Onuf, *Federal Union, Modern World:*

The Law of Nations in an Age of Revolutions, 1776–1814 (Madison, WI, 1993); J. E. Lewis, *American Union and the Problem of Neighborhood*; Onuf, *Jefferson's Empire*; and David C. Hendrickson, *Peace Pact: The Lost World of the American Founding* (Lawrence, KS, 2003).

76. Insofar as self-expression, the great imperative of the new politics of feeling, "is prescribed and determined by a set of rules and expectations, the natural self that is ostensibly revealed is, in fact, concealed by or collapsed into a theatricalized self-construction" (see Fliegelman, *Declaring Independence,* 164–72, on self-effacement; quotation on 2–3).

77. Wood, "Trials and Tribulations of Thomas Jefferson," in Onuf, ed., *Jeffersonian Legacies,* 412–13.

78. Appleby, "Jefferson and His Complex Legacy," in Onuf, ed., *Jeffersonian Legacies,* 4–5.

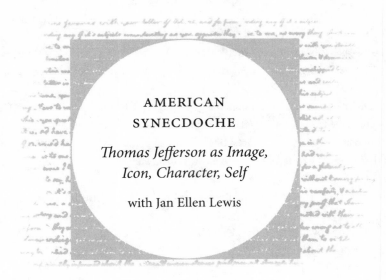

AMERICAN
SYNECDOCHE

*Thomas Jefferson as Image,
Icon, Character, Self*

with Jan Ellen Lewis

For generations of Americans, Thomas Jefferson's relation to their nation has been essential, bordering on identity. As the historian James
Parton put it in 1874, and Jefferson biographers have repeated ever since,
"If Jefferson was wrong, America is wrong. If America is right, Jefferson
was right."[1] More recently the filmmaker Ken Burns has said that "one approaches Thomas Jefferson with the sense that he is, in a biographical sense,
the Holy Grail of American History."[2] Pauline Maier has suggested that it
is not so much Jefferson as the Declaration of Independence that has been
sacralized, "remade into a sacred text, a statement of basic, enduring truths
often described with words borrowed from the vocabulary of religion."[3]
Whether the focus is on Jefferson himself or the document with which he is
most closely associated, and whether one worships him or calls him a false
god, the intellectual moves are similar: Jefferson is identified with the nation. Studying him becomes a way to discuss American nationhood—and a
substitute for studying the nation's history. Given our long history of equating Jefferson with the nation, is it possible still to historicize him, to situate
and understand him within the context of his times? Or, to put the question
another way, how can historians hold on to the historical Jefferson in the
face of powerful cultural pressures to make him a proxy for all that is right
or wrong with America?

Ken Burns's televised documentary *Thomas Jefferson: A Film by Ken*

Burns raises serious questions about the role of historians in shaping the public's understanding of history and the ways in which historians participate in and respond to the images of history that are now reaching mass audiences. The opportunity for professional historians to play a role in such productions is certainly seductive. Both of us gladly complied with the invitation by Florentine Films (Burns's production company) to speak on camera about Jefferson. Both of us—like a number of our colleagues—ended up on the cutting-room floor. The insult to our vanity notwithstanding, it is not clear that *Thomas Jefferson: A Film by Ken Burns* would have been a better production with us as talking heads. We know better than to equate historians with history. The real question is: Is Burns's *Thomas Jefferson* good history?

It is not necessarily a problem that Jefferson scholars would find little new in Burns's recycling of familiar materials. Burns's claim on our attention is not original research or interpretation, but his capacity to frame the familiar in a new way and to make it speak to our civic soul and aesthetic sensibility. With their ability to reach huge audiences, Burns and his fellow documentarians are becoming the custodians of our national historical consciousness. Hence it is troubling that the line separating Burns's "fact" and Oliver Stone's "fiction" is less distinct than one might suppose. In Thomas Jefferson, Burns dispenses, by and large, not only with professional historians but also with the fetish of authenticity that has, for instance, so conspicuously characterized the costume dramas of James Ivory and Ismail Merchant. The soundtrack uses the Shaker hymn "Simple Gifts" to convey folk simplicity, anachronistic photos of plantation slaves to suggest tobacco-planting field hands in Jefferson's Virginia, an 1833 painting of *Black Hawk and His Son, Whirling Thunder* to illustrate the Indian policies of Jefferson's presidency, and, without any sense of postmodernist playfulness or even modernist irony, a Jefferson impersonator and a children's book author to play the role of "historians."

Burns takes these liberties with the promise of giving us the real Jefferson. From the opening shots of a mist-enshrouded Monticello at dawn and the expert witnesses' remarks about Jefferson's contradictions and sphinx-like nature, Burns suggests that he is in pursuit of the truth. No fewer than eighteen shots zoom in on the eyes in a Jefferson portrait, as if Burns's camera could take us literally inside Jefferson's head, penetrating the inner man. Likewise, Jefferson's home, Monticello, becomes a visual proxy for the man himself and the objects in the home for the furnishings of his mind. The camera pans across rooms empty except for objects, a visual image reinforced by repeated shots of Jefferson's empty chair. Yet these are objects without function: like Jefferson's ideas in Ken Burns's documentary, they have no purpose and no relationship to other objects or ideas. The only relationship that matters is the one between Burns himself and his subject, for Burns's conceit is that his all-seeing camera can reveal the truth behind a portrait or inside a bookstand, as if meaning could be disclosed by the right camera angle. It is as if the objects of Jefferson's material world had the same meaning to him as they do to Burns's camera, as if Thomas Jefferson were, in fact, a film by Ken Burns, rather than a historical figure.

At the end of the film, Burns's talking heads are still speaking portentously about Jefferson's mysteries. But the filmmaker knows better. In the film's final shots, the camera recedes from a Jefferson portrait, pans across a portrait from the right, holds a close-up, pans across another portrait from the left, and finishes with another close-up. Burns no longer needs to take us behind Jefferson's eyes. Jefferson is now the same from whatever direction the camera looks. And to underscore his point, Burns concludes with a beautiful, fiery sunset: the mists surrounding Monticello and its owner have been dispelled!

Burns's image of Jefferson stands in contrast to the most recent scholarship on Jefferson, which is skeptical, and indeed often critical. By failing to engage these debates, Burns misses an opportunity to engage his audience as well. The only exceptions are the opening and closing sections with the cacophony of voices talking about Jefferson's complexities and the twenty minutes or so devoted to race, slavery, and the Sally Hemings issue. Here our gaze is deflected from transparent objects and images to the conflicting testimonies of talking heads—historians, "historians," and a Hemings descendant. But in Burns's film, all authorities are created equal, and they tend to cancel each other out in a way that inert images and objects are never allowed to do. The talking heads have moving, ultimately disposable, parts.

This is why Clay Jenkinson, a Jefferson impersonator who is identified on-screen as a "historian," is so important a presence in Burns's film.[4] By seeming to collapse the distinction between scholarly interpretation and Jefferson himself, Jenkinson allows Burns to appear to engage Jefferson directly, without the mediation of historians and their distracting agendas— while at the same time giving his film an academic gloss. As Burns has put it (in an interview posted to the film Web site), "We're not here to debate as much as we are to cohere." The hard work, then, is that of the filmmaker, who explains that "what I engage in is a very, very difficult process of distilling information." Although Burns repeatedly raises the issue of race in his films—coproducer Camilla Rockwell says, "Any film by Ken is going to have race as a central focus"[5]—he treats it as an incoherence, an insoluble problem in an otherwise explicable past. Hence the function of Burns's banal camera work, his anachronistic sounds and images: He presents the public with what it already knows—familiar images of slavery and Native Americans, authentic-sounding music, conventional cinematography—in the process enclosing and neutralizing what is dangerous and disturbing in a reassuring visual package. It is as if Burns believes his aesthetic can solve the problem of race in this country—a conceit perhaps not unlike Jefferson's. Indeed, the subtext of the entire documentary is about the collapsing of distinctions—between scholarship and Jefferson himself, between authentic and anachronistic images, between artist and subject, and, finally, by way of the Jeffersonian synecdoche, between the artist and the nation.

Unlike Burns, most contemporary Jefferson scholars have not dissolved themselves into their subject, but they do generally assume, either explicitly or implicitly, that Jefferson is in some sense a proxy for the nation. Present-day historians have been trained to discount Parton's equation of Jefferson with the nation, and great white men have been in ill repute for some time, as have the celebratory excesses of national history in the exceptionalist mode. But what is remarkable about recent studies of Jefferson by popular and academic historians is the extent to which they continue to embrace the premise of a "pantheon" of American gods even as they take potshots (or, in the more extreme cases, launch warheads) at the Sage of Monticello. In marked contrast to Burns's *Jefferson*, recent works by Conor Cruise O'Brien, Joseph J. Ellis, and Pauline Maier all offer critical perspectives on their subject. O'Brien magnifies the Sage's significance; Ellis and Maier invert the looking glass: a much diminished Jefferson comes into sharp, psychological focus in Ellis's *Sphinx*, while the Virginian threatens to disappear altogether in Maier's wide-angled account of the drafting and reception of the Declaration of Independence. Yet for all their differences, all of these books are variations—or interrogations—of Parton's theme. They ask us to consider the civic consequences of the Jeffersonian synechdoche.

Conor Cruise O'Brien's trashing of Jefferson in *The Long Affair* has been widely and appropriately assailed by reviewers, but the Irish writer deserves credit for laying his cards on the table. O'Brien has no doubt that there is a pantheon: a cast of larger-than-life founding heroes who provide successive generations of Americans with a framework for historical self-understanding. Does Jefferson belong in this select company? O'Brien insists that this question can be answered (negatively) on objective grounds, contemptuously dismissing the pathetic efforts of "liberal Jeffersonians" to refurbish their idol's image. Here's the short version of *The Long Affair*: while representing the new nation in Paris in the years immediately preceding the French Revolution (1785–89), Jefferson contracted the Revolutionary contagion; this ideological absolutism made him a (rhetorical) terrorist who would (in theory) drench the earth in blood in vain pursuit of the perfect and pure; the Haitian revolution had a chilling effect on his affair with France, but Jefferson's inveterate hostility to the black republic revealed the deeper, darker core of his racism. O'Brien thus concludes that there is no "usable" Jefferson who can serve our present needs: instead, we're stuck with the one we've got (or rather, that O'Brien has given us), a radical racist ideologue forever fixed in and condemned by "history." Historians, custodians of our civic culture, must therefore knock Jefferson off his pedestal. Jefferson is certainly "wrong," and if we fail to banish him from the national pantheon, America will certainly, tragically, go wrong as well. If Jefferson is America, America is . . . Timothy McVeigh.

O'Brien's pseudopositivism (his book strings together long quotations from original sources, with a few "talking head" secondary sources thrown in) clearly signals his alienation from fashionable humanities scholarship: no relativism, no constructivism, no "invented traditions," thank you, just the facts. Leaving aside the dubious historicity of *The Long Affair* and its breathtaking leaps into the interpretative unknown, what is most striking about O'Brien's stance is the enormous cultural power he claims for himself and other right-minded authority figures. The Jefferson image may be beyond rehabilitation, but historians can—if they only would—read him out of our civic culture, exorcising a dangerous ideologue who licenses contemporary extremists to represent themselves as patriotic Americans. In O'Brien's fanciful scenario, we historians would not only enjoy a monopoly over "history" but the even more crucial function of deciding what historical themes and which historical figures offer the most appropriate image of the civic culture we mean to celebrate and sustain today.

Joseph Ellis and Pauline Maier are also self-conscious participants in the ongoing conversation about American civic culture and historical self-understanding. Ellis's *American Sphinx* and Maier's *American Scripture* are both worthy contributions to historical scholarship. Neither writer wants to banish Jefferson from the pantheon (quite), though both suggest that his historical importance is vastly overrated. O'Brien gives short shrift to Jefferson's "authorship" of the Declaration: as it is "increasingly perceived as a collective document, Jefferson may be increasingly cast in the prosaic and subordinate role of a draughtsman."[6] Maier agrees: the story of the drafting "is not of a solo performance or even, to extend the metaphor, a performance of chamber music with a handful of players."[7] Ellis makes a similar point, showing how preoccupied Jefferson and his congressional colleagues were during these stressful months with other, more immediately compelling issues than justifying themselves to "a candid world" and emphasizing how much Jefferson would have preferred to be back home in Virginia, taking a leading role in what he considered to be the much more important work of drafting his state's first constitution.

O'Brien's solution to the supposed crisis in what he provocatively calls "American civil religion (official version)," is to invest the authorless text "with the aura of the sacred."[8] This is precisely what our historians would not do: their prescriptions are instead for more heavily populated pantheons, the proliferation, not the death, of authors. In Maier's capacious conception, Jefferson is granted his due as a gifted turner of phrases, but is surrounded—and brilliantly edited—by his congressional colleagues; more importantly, he is also surrounded by countless more-or-less ordinary Americans in localities up and down the seacoast who are busily churning out their own declarations. Maier's intention, signaled in the semi-ironic title of her book, is, contra O'Brien, to desacralize the American Scripture, and so make it a vital link—part inspiration, part provocation—between the Revolutionary generation and ours: "The vitality of the Declaration of Independence rests upon the readiness of the people and their leaders to discuss its implications and to make the crooked ways straight, not in the mummified paper curiosities lying in state at the [National] Archives."[9]

Maier is no less interested than O'Brien in the state of our civic soul. Like O'Brien, she thinks that the cult of divinely inspired authorship, reading the Declaration reverently as Constitutional Originalists read their sacred text, is ultimately demoralizing. But where O'Brien sets up shop as iconclastic reformer, preaching a new civic religion, Maier's civic impulses take a more indirect, sublimated, form. In her account of the drafting of the declaration(s) as a formative event in the history of American civil society, Maier speaks to currently fashionable concerns; but she also evokes an old-fashioned image of American consensus, a creedal nationalism that lays heavy emphasis on pragmatism, procedure, and principles that were so deeply imbedded as to be almost unconscious and instinctive. Her assault on American filiopietism and scripturalism is anything but a demolition job in the postmodern mode: Maier instead offers an expansive and attractive conception of the Revolutionary founding that is designed to revive and rehabilitate our civic self-consciousness, if not our civil religion.

Maier's pantheon, if we may call it that, is nothing less than the nation itself, the arena within which successive generations have struggled to define their civic identities, not a place where "false gods" are worshiped but rather where we must "define and realize right and justice in our time."[10] Ellis's ambitions are perhaps more modest than those of O'Brien and Maier: Americans won't revere an authorless text, nor in this cynical age are exhortations to good citizenship likely to grip the public imagination; yet, despite the best efforts of modern scholarship, ordinary folk (or, more accurately, those extraordinary folks who still buy books) still love their great men. Jefferson will not be downed, and even those who would blast him away— or contextualize him into insignificance—can only get a hearing from the so-called general public because they are writing about him.

As Ellis tackled Jefferson's life, he encountered an "American icon," an "electromagnetic" figure who "symbolized the most cherished and most contested values in modern American culture."[11] *American Sphinx* is a character study framed as an episodic biography. It burrows into Jefferson, discovering elaborate psychological mechanisms for protecting and projecting adolescent fantasies: the vision of a good society in the Declaration "came from deep inside Jefferson himself," eloquently expressing personal cravings for a world in which all behavior was voluntary and therefore all coercion unnecessary.[12] Ellis's Jefferson has the narcissism of youth; he's an adolescent who could not grow up. Such an approach would seem radically at odds with Maier's contextualism, but the net effect in both cases is deflationary: the history of ideas doesn't amount to much, and Jefferson's were, in any case, half-baked. Recognizing the dangerous and delusionary character of these adolescent impulses in Jefferson, Ellis suggests, modern Americans will be better able to recognize and restrain their own idealistic excesses. As a chastened Jefferson recedes from preeminence, other voices from the founding, more sober and circumspect—more adult—will be easier to discern. If our ears are properly attuned, we may even hear the voices of Maier's ordinary folk, declaring their own independence.

[56]

Ellis the realist would settle for a little more Adams and a little less Jefferson. The famous late-life correspondence between Jefferson and Adams, which Ellis has so eloquently rehearsed both in *Passionate Sage*,[13] his superb history of Adams's retirement years, and in *Sphinx*, offers an image of Ellis's pantheon. Jefferson never recanted his youthful idealism, remaining "a dedicated political warrior" to the (increasingly) bitter end of his life, but he treasured his "fourteen-year dialogue with Adams": it proved "impossible to dismiss his irascible old colleague." Jefferson and Adams "were the proverbial opposites that attracted"; "if the American Revolution had become a national hymn, they were its words and its music," their Revolution "an ongoing argument between idealistic and realistic impulses."[14]

Ellis's brief against Jefferson is not all that different from O'Brien's: their commentaries on the infamous "Adam and Eve" letter ("Were there but an Adam and Eve left in every country, and left free, it would be better than it is now") evoke similar horrors. For Ellis, Jefferson's complacent acceptance of mass slaughter points toward the "revolutionary realism . . . in the Lenin and Mao mold"[15]; O'Brien gives us Pol Pot and right-wing militias as contemporary avatars.[16] But while O'Brien concludes that Jefferson must be read out of the American pantheon, Ellis would neutralize Jefferson by bringing other, more sensible, icons back to life, to check and balance his pernicious influence: Ellis would not kill Jefferson off, he would institutionalize him. Civic life, it would seem, still requires heroes.

Membership in a pantheon suggests a larger-than-life, iconic quality. These are not quite ordinary mortal human beings we're dealing with here. The task of Jefferson biographers has traditionally been to give their subject a "life," although some have concluded, with Albert J. Nock, that Jefferson's private life is "inpenetrable."[17] In any case, the genre of biography tends to defeat its practitioners' humanizing purpose, even when warts and all are conspicuously on display: Why bother spend so much time and effort on a subject who does not represent something much bigger, in this case America? Even the warts tend to take on a portentous character when the humanizing gives way to demonizing in revisionist accounts. The great man remains great, after all, even if greatly culpable. So too high-minded efforts to knock Jefferson off his pedestal altogether focus our gaze on the pedestal itself—and remind us of the missing figure.

Treatments of Jefferson that make him a god, standing or fallen, or ask him to stand for the entire nation, necessarily distort his human qualities.

Only in fiction should personal character and emotional attributes be asked to bear the whole weight of the narrative. The most successful of the recent studies of Jefferson are those that have best uncoupled not Jefferson and his pedestal but the man and the nation. Jefferson's proper context is not the array of gods and demigods in the American pantheon, but, rather, the social and intellectual milieux that shaped him—and within which he acted.

Andrew Burstein's *The Inner Jefferson: Portraits of a Grieving Optimist* and Annette Gordon-Reed's *Thomas Jefferson and Sally Hemings: An American Controversy* each give us what might be called "possible" Jeffersons. Although they are both sympathetic to Jefferson (if in different ways), these two books differ dramatically in their approaches, their methods, and their styles, not to mention their conclusions. Burstein's is a profoundly sympathetic attempt to read the "inner Jefferson" by closely examining what he read and what he wrote to those nearest and dearest to him. Burstein situates Jefferson in what Henry May once labeled "the sentimental Enlightenment," and his book helps illuminate both Jefferson and that intellectual context.[18] Gordon-Reed's study is not so much of Jefferson himself as the historians' controversy about whether he engaged in a long relationship with his slave Sally Hemings and fathered her children. Gordon-Reed, a law professor, is most interested in the ways in which historians handle evidence. In the process of sifting through everything we know that has any bearing on the issue, and in insisting that we consider evidence from black sources as seriously as we take that from whites, she reminds us forcefully that Jefferson lived in a thickly populated plantation world inhabited by whites and blacks both. Despite their differences (Burstein lines up with the naysayers on the Hemings affair),[19] Burstein and Gordon-Reed both give us Jeffersons who live in rich, complex worlds—Burstein's, a mental and felt world of books and correspondents, reading and writing, and Gordon-Reed's, an embodied world of masters and slaves. In the end, these are very different worlds, one that of the head and heart, the other (implicitly) that of the body. And though we would like to know more about the coexistence of these domains, the Jeffersons who inhabit them are plausible, even compelling: both Jeffersons correspond to the available evidence; both are successfully situated in complex and comprehensible worlds.

The proliferation of possible Jeffersons does not constitute the failure of the biographical enterprise. We would suggest, rather, the opposite. The search for a single, definitive, "real" Jefferson is a fool's errand, setting us off on a hopeless search for the kind of "knowledge" that even (or especially?)

eludes sophisticated moderns in their encounters with each other—and themselves. If, in this age of full disclosure and true confessions, we are increasingly reluctant to rush to judgment on questions of character, how can we expect historians and biographers to explain to us an intensely private man who has been dead more than a century and a half? Perhaps the public's desire to know "the character" of a man such as Thomas Jefferson, and, even more, to know if it is good or bad, is a form of compensation for the dim recognition that we are doomed to cluelessness in our own world, like Plato's cave, a domain of shadows and hand-me-down light.[20]

Ironically, it is the thin-skinned Jefferson himself, with his obsessive concerns with privacy and his reputation (or "character" in his world and to posterity), who tantalizes us with the prospect of discovering the "real" Jefferson. On his deathbed, he complained to his grandson that the enemies who had slandered him and besmirched his character "had never known *him.* They had created an imaginary being clothed with odious attributes, to whom they had given his name."[21] Jefferson has seduced us with the promise of intimacy, the prospect of meeting the real Jefferson, the true "*him.*" Yet this notion that intimates might know—and only intimates could know—the real person is itself a time-bound notion, one coming into being precisely during Jefferson's lifetime.[22] Likewise, as Burstein notes, the concept of an "inner life," which we take for granted today, was the creation of Jefferson's time, and Jefferson himself was "part of the transition from neoclassical to romantic, from visible to inner life."[23] Jefferson's inner self, the true *him,* was not so much, then, a core, coherent self that could be "known" to contemporaries or to successive generations of scholars (or filmmakers), transparent to their empathetic, unmediated gaze. Instead, Jefferson's true *him* was the Jefferson he knew himself to be, his notion of himself, the person he hoped his intimates might come to know—and that his enemies (and hostile biographers) would never begin to comprehend. This self was necessarily hidden, for the very notion of an "inner life," the premise of Burstein's book, required that it be distinct from the public self, the "imaginary being" that others saw. Yet however hidden, and therefore "real," this private Jefferson might be, it was nonetheless as much a self-conscious construction as the artfully projected public image. Both were artifacts of their times.

Burstein's Jefferson, then, is one of several possible Jeffersons: the inner Jefferson, the Jefferson as Jefferson saw himself. Burstein takes us as close as we are likely to get to Jefferson's interior world, the fragile and vulnerable *him* that he was still brooding about on his deathbed. At the same time that

Burstein shows us this "inner Jefferson," he demonstrates how slippery such a concept was. It is not only that Jefferson embodied the transition between two very different notions of the self, but also that he defined himself in relation to others. "The essential Jefferson," Burstein writes, "was the private individual, an engaging and considerate friend. . . . Friendship was . . . essential to his own pursuit of happiness."[24] Jefferson was at once private and social; his privacy derived its meaning from its relation to his social world, the one in which a private man was a friend to other private persons. "John Donne's dictum 'No man is an island' applies particularly well to the age of Jefferson . . . and to Jefferson's own ideal of developing friendship and good feelings among men."[25] Consequently, this Jefferson can only be understood in relation to his friends and his family, the chosen community in which he found himself and which he believed vital to his existence. This was a community, as Burstein shows, of fellow letter writers and sentimentalists, people who valued the distinctive mixture of expressiveness and restraint that characterized the waning days of the Enlightenment in America in its transition to a Romantic sensibility.

Like Burstein, Gordon-Reed situates Jefferson in a community, a densely populated social world not of sentimentalists of the same elite social class but of black slaves and their owners and employers. As Gordon-Reed makes clear, too often previous students of Jefferson have tried to study him in isolation from this community. In responding to Ken Burns's question about the possibility of a relationship between Jefferson and Sally Hemings, children's book author Natalie Bober responded, "I think we must consider who Thomas Jefferson was," as if the question could be answered by reference to character rather than evidence.[26] Although this is not her immediate purpose, Gordon-Reed shows us a Monticello inhabited by blacks and whites, a world of lived experience alongside the world that Burstein shows us, a "dream world" of enlightened sentiment and bold ideas.

In the world of Thomas Jefferson that Gordon-Reed re-creates, certain things happened: Over a period of fifteen years, Jefferson's slave Sally Hemings bore six children, all or some of whom who had a strong resemblance to Jefferson. His family later acknowledged a family connection, claiming that one of Jefferson's nephews, either Peter or Samuel Carr, was the father. Although Jefferson was typically at home only a few months a year during this period, he was always at Monticello during the periods when Hemings would have conceived her children. The Carr brothers might have been there as well, as they lived in the vicinity, but there is no evidence of Hemings having conceived a child when Jefferson was *not* around. All of Hemings's four surviving children were freed at about the time they turned twenty-one, although generally in ways that would not have attracted the notice of the community. Beverley Hemings, for example, ran away from the plantation, and no effort seems ever to have been made to find him and bring him back. Such indifference to a runaway was unusual for Jefferson, and although he freed several slaves over his lifetime, freeing an entire family as they reached the age of twenty-one was exceptional. Sally Hemings herself was also freed, informally, after Jefferson's death.

Gordon-Reed attempts not so much to explain this remarkable confluence of events as to evaluate how historians and witnesses have explained them. Members of the Hemings family asserted that Jefferson had promised Sally Hemings freedom for herself and any children she might bear if she returned with him from France, where he was serving as his nation's ambassador. Members of the Jefferson family denied not only that Jefferson *was* the father of Hemings' children but that he *could* have been. As Jefferson's granddaughter Ellen Coolidge put it, "The thing will not bear telling. There are such things, after [all], as moral impossibilities."[27] By and large, subsequent historians have repeated these explanations and elaborated upon them more than they have weighed the evidence, and all too often, Gordon-Reed argues, white historians treated similar sorts of evidence from white and black sources differently.

One of Gordon-Reed's chief accomplishments is to problematize the usefulness of a term such as "character" for historical explanation. Is the concept of "moral impossibility" a meaningful term for historical analysis? Gordon-Reed notes, for example, that some historians have argued that Jefferson could not have been the father of Madison Hemings because Hemings was conceived when Jefferson's daughter Polly was home at Monticello dying. But, she argues, "Human beings have sex for many reasons other than depraved lust."[28] They have sex when they are happy, and they have sex when they are sad or depressed or frightened or need comfort. Gordon-Reed shows that the use of "character" as an explanatory mechanism necessarily flattens the human experience. It speaks to our emotional needs—Ellen Coolidge's defense of her grandfather rests more upon the plaint "How could he have done this to us?" than evidence—more than the complexity of human life. Like the pantheon paradigm, the use of character as an explanation requires us to evaluate human beings in terms of black and white, as it were, either on the pedestal or off.

Gordon-Reed gives us another possible Jefferson. Although she by no means asserts that Jefferson was the father of Hemings's children, she certainly demonstrates that this is the best explanation currently available for the evidence we confront. She does not attempt to infer Jefferson's state of mind if and when he had sex with Sally Hemings while his daughter was dying; she suggests only that if he did, he might have been frightened or he might have been depressed or he might simply have needed comfort. Her evaluation of the evidence requires us to imagine a different Jefferson—one very different from Burstein's. This Jefferson would have persuaded a young slave woman to return with her master to Virginia by promising her and her children freedom. He would subsequently have fathered at least six children by her, seen four of them survive to adulthood, and kept his promise to their mother. There is additional evidence of affection, or at least care, for this family, enough at least for us to begin to imagine even if we cannot reconstruct a mulatto family that lived next to Jefferson's white one at Monticello, one that inhabited a tenuous, liminal space in the plantation world, somewhere between slavery and an unenforceable promise of freedom. Of course, this possible Jefferson in this possible Monticello gives rise to its own critique. As Brenda Stevenson has suggested, it runs counter to historians' depictions of the ravages of slavery and may portray the institution in a light we find unacceptably romantic.[29] In the end, Gordon-Reed's revisionist effort may lead only to another American synecdoche, in which Jefferson and his plantation world stand for a multiracial America in which racial reconciliation is achieved by interracial sex.[30] The desire to make Jefferson stand for the nation may be too strong for historians to check.

For now, however, Burstein and Gordon-Reed offer alternatives to the powerful cultural imperative to make Thomas Jefferson represent America in order that we may judge the country right or wrong. Although both authors' Jeffersons are sympathetic, neither is a god—not because of imperfections but because they live in the world, surrounded by other people. These new, possible Jeffersons are complex men, living in complex worlds. They remain impenetrable, but perhaps no more so than any of the rest of us. These Jeffersons shift our attention to the worlds they inhabited, and they invite us to find him not in some inner, essential core but somewhere between those worlds, one of words and feeling and one of promises kept and promises broken.

Notes

This essay was originally published, with Jan Ellen Lewis, under this title in *American Historical Review* 103, no. 1 (February 1998): 125–36. A review essay, it focused on a then recently released film and several important books on Thomas Jefferson (hereafter TJ): Ken Burns, *Thomas Jefferson: A Film by Ken Burns* (Florentine Films, 1996); Andrew Burstein, *The Inner Jefferson: Portrait of a Grieving Optimist* (Charlottesville, 1995); Joseph J. Ellis, *American Sphinx: The Character of Thomas Jefferson* (New York, 1997); Annette Gordon-Reed, *Thomas Jefferson and Sally Hemings: An American Controversy* (Charlottesville, 1997); Pauline Maier, *American Scripture: Making the Declaration of Independence* (New York, 1997); and Conor Cruise O'Brien, *The Long Affair: Thomas Jefferson and the French Revolution, 1785–1800* (Chicago, 1996). Jan Lewis and I acknowledged our personal involvement with the Burns film and with two of the books discussed. I was the supervisor of Burstein's dissertation, subsequently published as *The Inner Jefferson*; and Jan and I both served as reviewers of Gordon-Reed's *Thomas Jefferson and Sally Hemings* for the University of Virginia Press.

1. See, for example, Merrill D. Peterson, *The Jefferson Image in the American Mind* (New York, 1960), 234; Ellis, *American Sphinx*, 3.

2. PBS Web site for *Thomas Jefferson: A Film by Ken Burns,* http://www.pbs.org/jefferson/.

3. Maier, *American Scripture*, xviii.

4. According to his Web site, http://www.clayjenkinson.com, Jenkinson has degrees in humanities and literature; he has taught at several colleges and universities and is now scholar in residence at Lewis and Clark College in Oregon.

5. PBS Web site for *Thomas Jefferson: A Film by Ken Burns,* http://www.pbs.org/jefferson/.

6. O'Brien, *Long Affair,* 321.

7. Maier, *American Scripture*, xviii.

8. O'Brien, *Long Affair,* 319.

9. Maier, *American Scripture*, 215.

10. Ibid.

11. Ellis, *American Sphinx*, x–xi.

12. Ibid., 59.

13. Joseph J. Ellis, *Passionate Sage: The Character and Legacy of John Adams* (New York, 1993).

14. Ellis, *American Sphinx,* 257, 250, 251.

15. Ibid., 127.

16. O'Brien, *Long Affair*, 150, 313–14.

17. Qtd. in Merrill D. Peterson, *Thomas Jefferson and the New Nation: A Biography* (New York, 1970), 29.

18. Henry F. May, *The Enlightenment in America* (New York, 1978). For a more recent, and very suggestive, account, see Jay Fliegelman, *Declaring Independence: Jefferson, Natural Language, and the Culture of Performance* (Stanford, CA, 1993).

19. Burstein, *Inner Jefferson*, 228–31. He subsequently changed his mind. See his brilliant discussion of the Hemings issue in *Jefferson's Secrets: Death and Desire at Monticello* (New York, 2005).

20. For further discussion of the "character issue," see "Making Sense of Jefferson," in this volume.

21. Sarah N. Randolph, *The Domestic Life of Thomas Jefferson* (Charlottesville, VA, 1947), 369, emphasis in original.

22. See Lucia McMahon, "'While Our Souls Together Blend': Narrating a Romantic Readership in the Early Republic," in Peter N. Stearns and Jan Lewis, eds., *An Emotional History of the United States* (New York, 1998).

23. Burstein, *Inner Jefferson*, 287.

24. Ibid., 149.

25. Ibid., 195.

26. Burns, *Thomas Jefferson*.

27. Ellen Randolph Coolidge to Joseph Coolidge, Oct. 24, 1858, in Gordon-Reed, *Thomas Jefferson and Sally Hemings*, 259.

28. Gordon-Reed, *Thomas Jefferson and Sally Hemings*, 196.

29. Brenda Stevenson, "Founding Father's Folly?" *Washington Post Book World*, June 15, 1997, 4.

30. Sean Wilentz, "Life, Liberty, and the Pursuit of Thomas Jefferson," *New Republic* 216, no. 10 (March 10, 1997): 32–42.

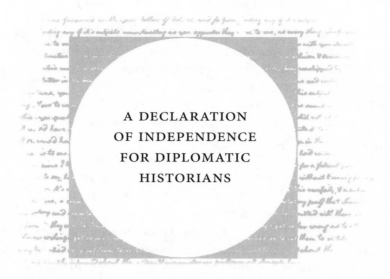

A DECLARATION
OF INDEPENDENCE
FOR DIPLOMATIC
HISTORIANS

As Thomas Jefferson insisted in 1825, the Declaration of Independence was "the fundamental act of union of these States."[1] According to the text of the Declaration, this union claimed "the separate and equal station to which the laws of nature and of nature's God entitle them." Now that the old "political bands" with Britain had been "dissolve[d]," the new nation was entitled by the law of nations to negotiate new "political" (that is, diplomatic) ties with other European powers. Independence was clearly a means toward higher ends: far from leaving the American states in their natural, anarchic condition with respect to one another, it drew them into a new, and unprecedented, "union," a union that could in turn forge further alliances—or unions—across the Atlantic. The conventional narrative of the American founding posits a clear distinction between the Declaration, marking the destruction of the old regime and the articulation of the "inherent and inalienable rights" (of individuals) on which the new American republics would be established, and the Constitution, creating a "more perfect union" (of states) that secured the new nation's independent standing in the larger world. But we should listen more carefully to Jefferson, who saw his Declaration as an "act of union"—and who later feared that the federal Constitution *jeopardized* union by concentrating too much power in the new national government. We should not rush through the first paragraph of the Declaration in order to get to the "self-evident" truths of the second.

For Jefferson the great, self-enacting claim of the Declaration is to be found in its opening sentence, where he asserts that the Americans constitute "one people." The Lockean logic in the next paragraph does nothing to explicate or substantiate, but instead deflects attention away from, that bold claim to nationhood. The natural rights talk of the second paragraph may have been pregnant with profound implications for later generations of democrats and libertarians, but it is Jefferson's *first* paragraph that changed the world.[2]

Jefferson and his Revolutionary colleagues first invoked the law of nature and nations in order to define satisfactory terms of union—*within* the British Empire. Only when rebuffed by a corrupt and tyrannical imperial administration did they declare independence and form a more limited American union. "Union" was not the belated outcome of the Revolution, but, rather, its central and defining problem from the very outset: American constitutionalism was shaped by the Revolutionaries' experience in successive world systems. Frustrated in their quest for imperial reform, American patriots became proponents of an independent federal union and a more liberal world order.

The original intentions of the American Revolutionaries have always been difficult to discern because of the vast discrepancies between their world—and their words—and ours. The biggest obstacle to contemporary understanding is *not* the anachronism of an agenda-driven "originalist" jurisprudence but rather the unexamined premises of our national history. The basic unit of analysis, the "nation," is taken for granted, and the intentions of the founders are therefore assumed to revolve around *its* magnificent prospects—and their forecast of our great achievements. But the Revolutionaries could not have had our idea of what a "nation" is, or of how it might be situated in the "world." Indeed, it is the indeterminacy of these terms (at least by our definitions) and their distinctive configuration that demand scholarly attention. Students of international thought and practice can and should make a major contribution to this continuing debate.

Diplomatic historians have played only a marginal role in the recent historiography of Revolutionary and early national America. One simple explanation for this is specialization: foreign policy specialists confine themselves to the history of diplomacy, narrowly defined. The "real" Revolution does not take place in their domain—nor, by most recent accounts, does it take place on the battlefield (where, in any case, military historians hold sway). But diplomatic historians have conceded too much.[3] The Revolution constituted an epochal moment in international history, a "new order for the ages." The Revolutionaries' agenda was shaped by political and economic developments in the Atlantic world and their goals were articulated in the cosmopolitan idiom of the Enlightenment.

Not only was the Revolution played out on a world stage but the definition of the world was its overarching issue. This definition has two crucial dimensions, both of fundamental concern to diplomatic historians. The more familiar has to do with relations among states: here, as I suggested above, it is important to emphasize affinities in contemporaneous understandings of "empire," "union," and "world." But the Revolution is as important for offering a new definition and model for the constituent part, the "nation," as it is for promoting change in the "international system" as a whole. Indeed, Jefferson's Declaration was supposed to constitute a more perfect world order for the colony-states, a transcendent and inclusive national identity for the American people, and a legitimate (recognizable) government to represent union and nation, states and people, in the larger world.

All of this might be self-evident to a historian who had *not* kept up with historiographical trends. The ideological turn in American Revolutionary scholarship, the so-called republican synthesis, has led to the general neglect of the political and constitutional issues that most concerned earlier generations of colonial and imperial historians. As long as the interpretive focus had been on the constitution and governance of the British Empire, the interimperial, diplomatic context was never far from view. After all, the Revolution would not have taken place without the elimination of the French presence in North America resulting from Britain's decisive victory in the Seven Years' War; subsequent British efforts to consolidate their geopolitical advantage—by pacifying a radically destabilized frontier, by rationalizing administration and raising taxes—provided the proximate causes for colonial rebellion. But this is all so familiar that it has faded into the dim historiographical background. Constitutional and diplomatic questions have been cast still deeper in the shadows as political historians focused on ideological appeals, group psychology, and the progress of popular mobilization. The exceptionalist tendencies of the ideological school have been powerfully reinforced by the community study approach of the "new" social historians with their bottom-up view of the world.

The narrowly provincial bias of the ideological approach led historians of the American Revolution to neglect problems of imperial organization and international politics. After all, as John Adams told Jefferson in 1815,

"The Revolution was in the Minds of the People, and this was effected, from 1760 to 1775, in the course of fifteen Years before a drop of blood was drawn at Lexington"—and before other nations were drawn into its vortex.[4] Drawing deeply (in characteristically provincial fashion) on the British Real Whig tradition and its American permutations, focusing obsessively on the putative "great transition" from republicanism to liberalism, the ideological historians could tell the subsequent history of constitution writing, political mobilization, and state building with only the most perfunctory reference to the international context. Given the prevailing view, so influentially articulated by Gordon Wood, that constitutional reform was at best only coincidentally concerned with problems of interstate relations, the international context inevitably would seem still more peripheral, and even less consequential.[5]

The republicanists' formulation of the role of ideas and ideology, powerfully strengthened by the (mis)appropriation of the work of anthropologist Clifford Geertz and historian of science Thomas Kuhn, has obscured the cosmopolitanism of the American Revolution.[6] On one hand, their conceptual genealogy took them back to British opposition and ultimately Florentine and classical sources; on the other, close analysis of the colonial American reception of this tradition underscored its distinctively British and provincial cast. Ironically, the Americans' derivativeness, their lack of originality, and their anachronism—manifest in their putatively "paranoid" inability to understand the world they lived in—set them apart as a distinctive, "exceptional," people.

The ideological historians defined the subject of contemporaneous debate in timeless terms that deflected attention away from the broader geopolitical context and issues that precipitated the imperial crisis, focusing instead on the supposedly fundamental questions—of citizenship and character, liberty and power, private and public interest—that continue to absorb political theorists. With the "real" subject of debate so narrowly defined, it was easy to discount and distinguish other, more cosmopolitan streams of thought. Obsessed as they were with defending themselves against a corrupt and grasping ministry, American patriots would have little interest in reading and thinking about the larger world.

The good news is that the republican paradigm has begun to collapse, at least in its original site, under the weight of accumulated anomalies.[7] Diplomatic historians have an important stake in this demolition and renewal project, for it was the republicanists'—and social historians'—definition of the Revolution that pushed them to the far margins of the field. One of the immediate benefits of this paradigm crisis will be that diplomatic historians will begin to recognize and build on their own historiographical tradition. As they do so, they will find themselves well situated to define the future course of Revolutionary and early national historiography.

The study of "republicanism" itself would have followed a more cosmopolitan path had the ideological historians paid more heed to Gerald Stourzh, whose brilliant studies of Franklin and Hamilton focused on the development of Revolutionary American ideas about empire, foreign policy, international law, and world order.[8] The rising tide of republican revisionism also led diplomatic historians to discount and dismiss Felix Gilbert's classic essay on the intellectual origins of American foreign policy.[9] Rather than building on promising beginnings in their own field, diplomatic historians increasingly positioned themselves as consumers of hand-me-down intellectual history. If the new nation's founders subscribed to—and were defined by—the tenets of Real Whig, "classical" republican ideology, the more cosmopolitan currents of thought delineated by Stourzh and Gilbert would barely lap against American shores.

The interpretive wheel has begun to turn, however, now that republicanism's historiographical charisma is so rapidly fading. The vacuum is already being filled. Important work by scholars such as John Phillip Reid and Jack P. Greene on the crisis of the British imperial constitution has begun to restore a more cosmopolitan perspective to Revolutionary historiography that diplomatic historians will find increasingly congenial.[10] Their traditional concerns—war and peace, foreign relations, and international politics—will become, by this redefinition, much more integral to the main historical narrative. Revolutionary diplomacy will not be treated as a secondary plotline (with most of the action offstage); nor will constitutional historians continue to give such scant notice to the founders' foreign policy concerns, so ably summarized in Frederick Marks's *Independence on Trial*.[11]

But I also see a great opportunity for foreign policy historians to take the lead in exploring new questions. "Presentism" may in this case be a conceptual advantage, for the present state of the world strongly suggests the historicity of the nation-state and of the international regime. As we come to terms with a complex contemporary world order in which classical definitions of sovereignty and state capabilities cease to make much sense, we should be better equipped to see what the world was like *before* the ascendancy of the "modern" international system.

The language of Jefferson's Declaration of Independence suggests that eighteenth-century Anglo-Americans did not make a clear distinction between *domestic*—or imperial—and *foreign* relations. This apparent confusion invites us to take a closer look at the world from the perspective of the Revolutionary generation—and *not* according to the way we have reflexively parceled out the historiographical terrain among specialists.[12] Patriot leaders understood their colonies to be "states," and they hoped to reform the imperial constitution through agreements that could be described as "treaties." Indeed, the argument against parliamentary sovereignty suggested that imperial connection could only be "federal," a relationship constituted by treaty. Jefferson recalled that John Adams and other congressional radicals insisted that the American colonies had always been "independent" with respect "to the people or parliament of England," "that so far our connection had been *federal* only & was now dissolved by the commencement of hostilities."[13]

For eighteenth-century Americans, "empire" was a protean concept, a bundle of emergent, potentially contradictory definitions.[14] As a complex, extended polity, the British Empire provided a template for American federalism, but it was also a kind of embryonic world order. One of the empire's leading weaknesses was the absence of authoritative definitions and common understandings that could have legitimized ministerial reform efforts. The shared language of British constitutionalism did not promote, but instead probably impeded, the articulation of an *imperial* constitutional order. Not surprisingly, leaders of the colonial resistance movement turned in frustration toward natural law—the law of nature and nations—in defense of their political rights and civil liberties. But American patriots did not see their efforts to codify a new constitutional order as a rejection of the imperial connection: quite the contrary, most of them continued to believe, until the bitter end, that the negotiation of strategic and commercial "treaties" would lay the foundation of a more perfect and enduring *Anglo-American* union.[15]

If the extended polity of the British Empire was an inchoate states system, the European balance of power was equally inchoate—and particularly so in the extra-European world. Indeed, at the time of the American Revolution, the law of nations was the law of European sovereigns: Europe *was* the "world." In declaring their independence, Americans boldly claimed membership in this "international" community—the "commonwealth" or "federal republic" of *European* sovereignties. They did not seek to isolate themselves from Europe, nor were they eager to participate—without powerful allies and on radically unequal terms—in the anarchic struggle of all against all that was supposed to be the natural state of nations. On the contrary, for Americans independence was the threshold of union, both among the American states and with prospective European trading partners.

Visionary republican Revolutionaries wanted to change the world: by extending the boundaries of the European system, by enhancing the system's capacity for progressive improvement through the practice of enlightened diplomacy, by perfecting a legal regime among their own state-republics that would eliminate the causes and pretexts of war.[16] Through painstaking and protracted negotiation of the Articles of Confederation (1777–81), the states gave constitutional form to the union enacted in Jefferson's Declaration. Not surprisingly, the terms "treaty" and "constitution" were used interchangeably: "The Treaty [of Confederation] is the Constitution, or mode of Government for the collective North-American Commonwealth."[17]

When "nationalists" later sought to reform or replace the Articles, they argued that federal ties alone were insufficient to sustain American independence. In his "Vices of the Political System," James Madison described the Articles as a "federal constitution," an alliance of "independent and Sovereign States" that could *not* preserve the union. Madison clearly intended to transform the union into a kind of state, founded on "the great vital principles of a Political Cons[ti]tution" and monopolizing all the essential powers exercised by a true sovereignty.[18] But the Federalists were at a loss for words to articulate their redefinition of the union. Whatever their original intentions, they insisted that the states would be preserved and strengthened under the new dispensation: it would not be a "consolidated" government. No matter how "perfect" the whole, union was still defined by its constituent parts, the states. And the new Constitution drafted at Philadelphia was, like the Articles, "federal" (from the Latin *foedus*, "of or pertaining to a covenant, compact, or treaty")—a term that would continue to be used to denote alliances between independent sovereignties.[19]

Historians and political theorists give Madison and his fellow nationalists too much credit for calling themselves "Federalists" and so preempting their opponents' proper ideological position and self-designation. Conceptual confusion arguably gave the Federalists the short-term advantage in the ratification debates, but it is also true that it would frustrate the designs of subsequent generations of centralizers and modernizers. American federalists—whatever they might be called—would continue to invoke the authority of Vattel and other law of nations writers; states' rights constitutionalists would invoke the Declaration of Independence and the Articles of Confederation as they sought to impose a strict construction on the federal Constitution. The supposedly decisive transformation of the union from a loose federation of sovereign states to a more highly integrated, centrally directed "compound" national republic thus was much less apparent to contemporaries than it is to modern commentators.

The interpretive problems here derive from the failure of scholars to take ideas seriously—or, perhaps more accurately, to take the right ideas seriously. Contemporaneous talk about federalism is explained away: as being merely instrumental and often obfuscatory (for those of an anti-intellectual, materialist bent) or as expressing more fundamental, underlying concerns (for the ideological school). What these scholars fail to understand is that the central problem in American political discourse from the imperial crisis through the Civil War was the definition of the federal union. This discourse periodically was refreshed by referring to its natural law (law of nations) sources and, increasingly, to the principles that supposedly had animated previous generations of patriots, in 1776, 1787, and 1798.[20]

The extent to which Madison, the "father of the Constitution," betrayed his nationalist faith and embraced Jeffersonian states' rights heresies in 1798 remains controversial.[21] My strong inclination is, with Lance Banning, to emphasize the Virginian's primary commitment to sustaining a "federal balance" that would preserve his state's corporate identity, rights, and interests while at the same time enabling the government of the union to function effectively on the world stage.[22] This balancing act was not inspired simply by prudential concerns for the multifarious, often conflicting interests that would have to be rationalized and reconciled in the "extended republic." During and after the ratification debates, Madison and other so-called nationalists, including James Wilson of Pennsylvania, demonstrated their continuing indebtedness to the cosmopolitan premises of internationalist thought: the Constitution formed a "more perfect union"; the law of nations would be enforceable without recourse to violent sanctions; the new system represented the culmination of a "peace plan" tradition that had engaged the most enlightened minds in Europe.[23] Predictions of "rising glory" invoked this new world, and the regime of piety, virtue, prosperity, and social happiness that it would inaugurate.

Few Revolutionaries shared Alexander Hamilton's vision of the United States as a great hemispheric power, modeled on Britain. For Jefferson, whose "federal and republican principles" triumphed in the election of 1800, the American union represented the antithesis of the Old World's detested balance of power.[24] Yet the United States *did* become something of a "power" in the conventional European sense, whatever the pretensions of Jefferson and his followers. Robert Tucker and David Hendrickson's merciless evisceration of Jeffersonian "statecraft" makes much of this ironic, if not tragic, discrepancy between profession and practice.[25] For these critics—and for most other historians of early American foreign policy—the advantages of closer ties with Britain are self-evident, and the challenge is to explain why Jeffersonians failed to recognize this. But this line of criticism assumes that the "United States" was a "nation" with identifiable national interests that could have been rationally pursued. To the contrary, partisan and sectional conflict in the early republic revealed the fragility of a union always seemingly poised on the brink of disintegration. As a result, "federal" relations with European powers could not be extricated from the federal bonds among Americans: not surprisingly, the characteristic response to an unpopular "foreign" policy—whether it was the Federalist tilt toward Britain in the 1790s or the anti-British tilt of Republican commercial diplomacy thereafter—was to threaten disunion.

The problem of national identity brings us back to the Declaration of Independence. The Declaration had enacted a weak union, a union without constitutional form or authoritative sanctions, because the bonds that tied the American patriots were so powerful. Joined in an act of parricide, risking death for their treason against the Crown, Jefferson and his fellow Revolutionaries "mutually pledge to each other our lives, our fortune, & our sacred honor." For Jefferson, the claim to nationhood set forth in the Declaration's opening paragraph depends, in theory, on the social contract principles of the subsequent paragraph. But it is Jefferson's sense of betrayal and rejection—*"the last stab of agonizing affection"*—by the British people—*"unfeeling brethren"*—that gives those general principles their particular force.[26] The patriots' exalted state of Revolutionary brotherhood reflected, even as it negated, a fantasy of transatlantic union, the myth of a transcendent British national identity. Anglophilia was thus transmuted into Anglophobia and one people became two. No federal alliance or constitution could make the "union" the American patriots now declared more perfect, for in the act of killing the king they had made themselves into a new nation.[27]

The paradox of the Declaration is that the strong assertion of national *identity* should entail such a weakly articulated national *government.* Jefferson and his followers do not deserve all the credit—or blame—for this paradoxical state of affairs. As Charles Royster has shown, patriotic Americans generally defined independence and nationhood in highly idiosyncratic and, from the perspective of the would-be central government, highly self-serving ways.[28] Indeed, to an extraordinary extent Americans measured their patriotism against the exactions and abuses of any distant, despotic governmental authority—and that distance, as resistance to federal excise taxes showed, did not have to be very great.[29]

Yet it would he a mistake to embrace the High Federalist perspective on Jeffersonian heresies, a perspective that diplomatic historians (sharing Hamilton's predilection for "energetic" and effective government) find all too congenial. Citizen-soldiers, inspired by popular patriotic fervor, might not provide effective firepower on the battlefield, and tax resisters could make life difficult for Hamilton's Treasury, the most visible hand of the early federal state. But Jeffersonian Republicans did show, through ideological appeals and party organization, how the "fiction" of popular sovereignty could be mobilized into effective political power. They successfully promoted and exploited nationalist sentiment in ways that Anglophiliac Federalists found dangerously unsettling and (literally) alienating.

Jefferson's inaugural address defined the limits of national community, thrusting beyond its pale "any among us who would wish to dissolve this Union or to change its republican form." Jefferson forecast a welcome respite from the party battles of the 1790s, a renewed commitment to the "federal and republican principles" of 1776, and a practical refutation of the Federalists' "theoretic and visionary fear that this Government, the world's best hope," lacked the "energy to preserve itself." "On the contrary," Jefferson exclaimed, in words that could only provoke incredulity and derision among Hamiltonian High Federalists, "I believe this . . . the strongest Government on earth."[30] "Strength" was predicated on a union of principle and sentiment, not in Jefferson's estimation on the national government's coercive resources or deep pockets. By defeating the Federalists at the polls, Republicans reenacted and revivified the patriotism of 1776, and so presented to the world an irresistible, impregnable force.

Jefferson's implicit identification of Republicanism and Americanism became increasingly explicit in later years. His most remarkable statement on this theme, one of particular interest to diplomatic historians, may be found in a letter he wrote to William Duane, editor of the *Aurora,* a leading Republican newspaper, in 1811. "During the *bellum omnium in omnia* of Europe," wrote Jefferson, the "union" of all our country's "friends" was absolutely essential in order "to resist its enemies within and without. If we schismatize on either men or measures, if we do not act in phalanx, as when we rescued it from the satellites of monarchism [in 1800], I will not say our *party*, the term is false and misleading, but our *nation* will be undone. For the republicans are the *nation*."[31] These proscriptive sentiments are somewhat embarrassing for modern Americans who are taught that party competition is a good thing: surely the "nation" is much more than any "party." But our perspective may be "false and misleading," for we are too inclined to take our national identity as a given and to assume that our contentious ancestors were all in fact "good" Americans who, alas, sometimes, in the heat of partisan controversy, failed to recognize each other's patriotism. British colonists were not born but became "American," and the becoming—the professions and practices that signified active consent—followed no preordained path.

The revival of scholarly interest in invented traditions, imaginary communities, and the formation of national identities offers a new perspective on the political and ideological work of Jefferson and his fellow republicans. For one thing, it suggests that Jeffersonian Anglophobia is not simply a perversely personal, deeply irrational quirk or anomaly, the result of one man's misreading of European diplomacy and politics. American national identity was constantly being renegotiated as successive administrations responded to real and imagined threats at home and abroad. The Federalists' achievement was to gain a measure of legitimacy and stability for the new federal government; Jefferson and the Republicans tapped a broader and deeper vein of patriotic sentiment by harking back to the moment of the new nation's birth in the midst of a revolution against British authority.[32] This primal act of national definition did not necessarily translate into anti-British policies for later generations, or even for Jefferson himself. But for the triumphant Jeffersonians of 1800, it did require eternal vigilance against forces at home and abroad that would exercise illegitimate and despotic power at the expense of liberty and union.[33]

The legacy of Jefferson's Declaration of Independence, and the revolutionary changes it represented and inspired, is profoundly ambivalent. On one hand, the Declaration constituted a weak federal alliance or "union" that constantly threatened to fly apart; the principles it articulated offered powerful arguments against subsequent efforts to give that union more energy or structure. At the same time, however, the Declaration boldly proclaimed the birth of a new people. In declaring themselves independent, the Americans launched a new epoch in the history of Western political civilization, offering glimpses of the awesome and unprecedented power of nationalist regimes to mobilize people and resources.

We might conclude that Jefferson's federal constitutionalism and his appeal to popular patriotic sentiment worked at cross purposes, in the former case to disperse energy and authority in a complex polity, in the latter to mobilize popular resources and initiatives in the larger project of nation building. Or we might suggest a dialectical, or complementary, relationship: for Jefferson to believe in a fully consensual federal union of equal, independent, and self-governing states, he *had* to believe in a fundamental homogeneity of sentiments, principles, and interests in the American people—that is, in their national identity. The diplomatic historian might suggest yet another reading of the Declaration and the story it tells of our national beginnings. For the American Revolution was first and foremost an episode in the history of the European states system: a provincial fragment of the British people made themselves into the new American nation *not* because they knew that this was their destiny but, rather, because they hoped to secure their rights within a more perfect British imperial order. Yet if the birth of the American nation was inadvertent, its implications would be far-reaching, both for the old European system of diplomacy and, more profoundly, for the new world of nation-states that emerged from its ruins.

Notes

This essay was originally published in *Diplomatic History* 22 (1998): 71–83.

1. Minutes of the Board of Visitors, University of Virginia, March 4, 1825, in Merrill D. Peterson, ed., *Thomas Jefferson Writings* (New York, 1984), 479. For the text of the Declaration, see ibid., 19–24.

2. For a brilliant discussion of this theme, see J. G. A. Pocock, "States, Republics, and Empires: The American Founding in Early Modern Perspective," in Pocock and Terence Ball, eds., *Conceptual Change and the Constitution* (Lawrence, KS, 1988), 57–61.

3. I strongly endorse Melvyn P. Leffler's call to arms: "If diplomatic historians listen closely [to colleagues in other fields] we should hear that we are being summoned to play a central role in the future writing of American history" (Leffler, "New

Approaches, Old Interpretations, and Prospective Reconfigurations," *Diplomatic History* 19 [1995]: 174). This central role should begin with the reinterpretation of the Revolution. For an assessment of the current state of the historiography, see William Earl Weeks, "New Directions in Early American Foreign Relations," *Diplomatic History* 17 (1993): 73–96.

4. Adams to Jefferson (hereafter TJ), Aug. 14, 1815, in Lester J. Cappon, ed., *The Adams-Jefferson Letters: The Complete Correspondence between Thomas Jefferson and Abigail and John Adams*, 2 vols. (Chapel Hill, NC, 1959), 2:455. Bernard Bailyn uses this quotation as the epigraph of his *Ideological Origins of the American Revolution* (Cambridge, MA, 1967), the most important and influential book in the republican canon.

5. Gordon S. Wood, *The Creation of the American Republic, 1776–1787* (Chapel Hill, NC, 1969). See my critical commentary in "State Politics and Ideological Transformation: Gordon S. Wood's Republican Revolution," *William & Mary Quarterly* (hereafter *WMQ*) 44 (1987): 312–16.

6. For an illuminating discussion of these appropriations, see Joyce Appleby, *Liberalism and Republicanism in the Historical Imagination* (Cambridge, MA, 1992), 328–30, passim.

7. The influence of the republican interpretation spread far beyond its original site, the study of political mobilization in the colonies' emergent public sphere. In a playful postmortem, Daniel T. Rodgers notes that republicanism has continued to flourish in outlying fields—in labor history, the history of American political culture in later periods, and legal history—even as rapidly declining interpretive yields have led students of revolutionary political thought to look elsewhere for inspiration (see Rodgers, "Republicanism: The Career of a Concept," *Journal of American History* 79 [1992]: 11–38).

8. Gerald Stourzh, *Benjamin Franklin and American Foreign Policy* (Chicago, 1954); idem, *Alexander Hamilton and the Idea of Republican Government* (Stanford, CA, 1970).

9. Felix Gilbert, *To the Farewell Address: Ideas of Early American Foreign Policy* (Princeton, NJ, 1961). James Hutson's assault on Gilbert played a key role in the "republican" turn away from Enlightenment cosmopolitanism: with John Adams as his skeptical proxy, and republicanism providing the intellectual ballast for a "realistic" assessment of the new nation's proper course in a dangerous world, Hutson could turn the Revolution's idealist impulses inward, away from the larger world (see Hutson, "The Intellectual Foundations of Early American Diplomacy," *Diplomatic History* 1 [Winter 1977]: 1–19; and idem, *John Adams and the Diplomacy of the American Revolution* [Lexington, KY, 1980]). The persuasiveness of Hutson's argument, David

Fitzsimons has recently shown, depends on how we understand "republicanism"; see Fitzsimons, "Thomas Paine's New World Order: Idealistic Internationalism in the Ideology of Early American Foreign Relations," *Diplomatic History* 19 (1995): 569–82, esp. 575–76, for astute commentary on Hutson's reliance on the "republican synthesis" in dismissing Gilbert's depiction of a "liberal internationalist" strain in early American thinking about foreign policy.

10. John Phillip Reid, *The Constitutional History of the American Revolution*, 4 vols. (Madison, WI, 1986–95). Reid argues, in conscious opposition to the ideological school, that the Americans' understanding of the customary British (imperial) constitution was plausible and orthodox, not the artifact of republican paranoia and anachronism. In other words, the Revolutionaries were engaged in a transatlantic debate over the constitution of an extended polity. Jack P. Greene offers a broader reading of this debate, with more direct links to issues of federal organization (and world order), in *Peripheries and Center: Constitutional Development in the Extended Polities of the British Empire and the United States, 1607–1788* (Athens, GA, 1986).

11. Frederick Marks, *Independence on Trial: Foreign Affairs and the Making of the Constitution* (Baton Rouge, LA, 1975). For a discussion of constitutional historiography that urges more attention to federalism and foreign policy issues, see Peter S. Onuf, "Reflections on the Founding: Constitutional Historiography in Bicentennial Perspective," *WMQ* 46 (1989): 341–75.

12. For a brilliant example of how diplomatic history written with a consciousness of the problematic distinction between "domestic" and "foreign" can challenge and revise conventional assumptions in early American political history, see James E. Lewis Jr., *The American Union and the Problem of Neighborhood: The United States and the Collapse of the Spanish Empire, 1783–1829* (Chapel Hill, NC, 1998).

13. TJ's notes on debates in Congress, June 7, 1776, *Autobiography*, Jan. 6, 1821, in Peterson, ed., *Jefferson Writings*, 15, emphasis added.

14. Reid, *Constitutional History of the Revolution*; Greene, *Peripheries and Center*. See also Richard Koebner, *Empire* (Cambridge, UK, 1961); Klaus E. Knorr, *British Colonial Theories, 1570–1850* (Toronto, 1944); and David Armitage, *The Ideological Origins of the British Empire* (Cambridge, UK, 2000).

15. On the turn to natural rights, and the quest for union within the empire, see the valuable discussion in Stephen A. Conrad, "Putting Rights Talk in Its Place: *The Summary View* Revisited," in Peter S. Onuf, ed., *Jeffersonian Legacies* (Charlottesville, VA, 1993), 254–80, esp. 260–61. Confusion about the role and authority of Congress as putative successor to the British Crown's prerogative powers suggests continuities in Revolutionary constitutionalism that the decision for independence has obscured; see Jerrilyn Greene Marston, *King and Congress: The Transfer of Political Legitimacy,*

1774–1776 (Princeton, NJ, 1987). On the importance of treaties in revolutionary thought, see Peter Onuf and Nicholas Onuf, *Federal Union, Modern World: The Law of Nations in an Age of Revolutions, 1776–1814* (Madison, WI, 1993), 108–13. The following two paragraphs reprise themes developed at greater length in our book.

16. The idea that the United States was a prototype for a "more perfect" world order was fashionable among world federalists such as James Brown Scott during the era of the League of Nations (see Scott, *The United States of America: A Study in International Organization* [Washington, DC, 1920]). For signs of renewed interest in this theme, see the interesting essays by Daniel H. Deudney in "The Philadelphian System: Sovereignty, Arms Control, and Balance of Power in the American States-Union, circa 1787–1861," *International Organization* 49 (1995): 191–228; and idem, "Binding Sovereigns: Authorities, Structures, and Geopolitics in Philadelphian Systems," in Thomas J. Biersteker and Cynthia Weber, eds., *State Sovereignty as Social Construct* (Cambridge, UK, 1996), 190–239.

17. *The Constitutions of the Several Independent States of America: The Declaration of Independence; The Articles of Confederation; The Treaties between His Most Christian Majesty and the United States of America* (Philadelphia; reprint, London, 1782), vii.

18. James Madison, "Vices of the Political System," April–June 1787, in J. C. A. Stagg et al., *The Papers of James Madison, Congressional Series,* 17 vols. (Chicago and Charlottesville, VA, 1962–91), 9:351–52.

19. *Oxford English Dictionary.* See Pocock, "States, Republics, and Empires," in Pocock and Ball, eds., *Conceptual Change and the Constitution,* 60–61.

20. See the suggestive work by Andrew Lenner: "A Tale of Two Constitutions: Nationalism in the Federalist Era," *American Journal of Legal History* 40 (1996): 72–105; "John Taylor and the Origins of American Federalism," *Journal of the Early Republic* 17 (1997): 399–423; and *The Federal Principle in American Politics* (Madison, WI, 2000).

21. See the spirited assault on Madison's inconsistent stands on federalism issues in Kevin R. Gutzman, "A Troublesome Legacy: James Madison and 'The Principles of '98,'" *Journal of the Early Republic* 15 (1995): 569–89.

22. Lance Banning, *The Sacred Fire of Liberty: James Madison and the Founding of the Federal Republic, 1780–1792* (Ithaca, NY, 1995).

23. Peter S. Onuf, *Origins of the Federal Republic: Jurisdictional Controversies in the United States, 1775–1787* (Philadelphia, 1983), 205; F. H. Hinsley, *Power and the Pursuit of Peace* (Cambridge, UK, 1963).

24. The quotation is from TJ's First Inaugural Address, March 4, 1801, in Peterson, ed., *Jefferson Writings,* 494. For further discussion of Jefferson and the

problem of union, see my *Jefferson's Empire: The Language of American Nationhood* (Charlottesville, VA, 2000), chap. 4.

25. TJ, the self-deluded idealist, wanted "both empire and liberty" and thought "he could have the one without sacrificing the other" (see Robert W. Tucker and David C. Hendrickson, *Empire of Liberty: The Statecraft of Thomas Jefferson* [New York, 1990], 20; see also Doron S. Ben-Atar, *The Origins of Jeffersonian Commercial Policy and Diplomacy* [New York, 1993]).

26. Emphasis in original. My understanding of TJ's sentimental politics is indebted to Jay Fliegelman, *Declaring Independence: Jefferson, Natural Language, and the Culture of Performance* (Stanford, CA, 1993).

27. Winthrop D. Jordan, "Familial Politics: Thomas Paine and the Killing of the King, 1776," *Journal of American History* 60 (1973–74): 294–308.

28. Charles Royster, *A Revolutionary People at War: The Continental Army and American Character, 1775–1783* (Chapel Hill, NC, 1979).

29. Thomas P. Slaughter, *The Whiskey Rebellion: Frontier Epilogue to the American Revolution* (New York, 1986).

30. TJ, First Inaugural Address, March 4, 1801, in Peterson, ed., *Jefferson Writings*, 493–94.

31. TJ to Col. William Duane, March 28, 1811, in Andrew A. Lipscomb and William Ellery Bergh, eds., *The Writings of Thomas Jefferson*, 20 vols. (Washington, 1903–4), 13:28–29, emphasis in original.

32. On the Federalists, see Stanley Elkins and Eric McKitrick, *The Age of Federalism: The Early American Republic, 1788–1800* (New York, 1993), esp. chap. 1 ("Legitimacy"), 31–74. A persistent source of terminological confusion is the identification of Federalists as nationalists. Hamiltonian centralizers may have been state builders, but they did not promote or develop "nationalist" sentiment in the modern (Jeffersonian) sense of the term.

33. This theme is elaborated in my essay "Federalism, Republicanism, and the Origins of American Sectionalism," in Edward L. Ayers et al., *All Over the Map: Rethinking American Regions* (Baltimore, 1996), 11–37, esp. 11–15. The best study of American nationalism is David Waldstreicher, *In the Midst of Perpetual Fetes: The Making of American Nationalism, 1776–1820* (Chapel Hill, NC, 1997).

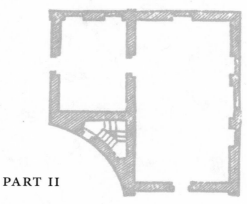

PART II

*Jefferson's
World*

THOMAS JEFFERSON,
FEDERALIST

W e are all republicans, we are all federalists," Thomas Jefferson told the American people in his first inaugural address. A "President above Parties" who believed factionalism jeopardized the safety and security of republican government, Jefferson was here setting forth the common principles shared by all patriotic Americans. Jefferson's election—the "Revolution of 1800"—would, he confidently predicted, put an end to the frenzied, hysterical, party struggles of the 1790s. Moderate Federalists who had voted for John Adams would soon see the errors of their ways. But "if there be any among us who would wish to dissolve this Union or to change its republican form, let them stand undisturbed as monuments of the safety with which error of opinion may be tolerated where reason is left free to combat it." In contrast to the Adams Federalists, who had sought to suppress their opponents with the Alien and Sedition Acts and had instead spurred Jeffersonian Republicans on toward their electoral revolution, Jefferson would allow his critics to discredit and disgrace themselves before the sovereign people.[1]

If, as Richard Hofstadter suggests, the peaceful "transit of power" from Federalists to Republicans marked an epoch in the history of party government, it does not follow that Jefferson saw a place for a "loyal opposition" in the new republican order.[2] Having vindicated the principles of 1776—and of 1798—the triumphant Republicans would themselves cease to be a "party." As Republican party activists had insisted for almost a decade, they were the true representatives of the sovereign people. When they assumed the reins of power, the American people at last began to govern themselves. In perverting and corrupting the power of the federal government, the Federalists had accentuated the distance between the people and their self-professed rulers and then sought to bridge the distance with the kind of coercive force that propped up the monarchies of the Old World. Alexander Hamilton and his minions were enemies of the "republican form," determined to transform the new American regime into a replica of the British Constitution they so much admired. But the success of their counterrevolutionary project depended on secret machinations, behind the scenes: the corruption of the people's representatives by bankers, speculators, and treasury operatives or expansive interpretations of the federal Constitution that enhanced executive power at the people's expense. The Republicans routed the specter of a counterrevolutionary monarchical revival not only by driving Adams and his supporters from office but more profoundly and lastingly by shining the bright light of an enraged public opinion on the murky recesses of Federalist administration.

Jefferson's extraordinary interpretation of his rise to power seems unwarranted by what had been, after all, a rather narrow victory at the polls that was only finally secured—on the eve of the inauguration—after thirty-six congressional ballots.[3] But Jefferson, with his already legendary distaste for the "torments" of political life, was not concerned with the wheeling and dealing that had broken the congressional stalemate. The people had already spoken: they had called Jefferson to the presidency, not his running mate Aaron Burr. And many voters who had supported Adams—because of the habitual submissiveness that sustained monarchical rule, or the all-too-plausible mystifications of "aristocrats" and "monocrats"—were good, educable republicans at heart. In bringing the good news to his fellow Americans, then, Jefferson was not a party leader with a policy agenda but, rather, a guardian of liberty, a patriotic mentor to his people. As the heavy hand of Federalist administration was lifted—with the end of excise taxes, the reduction of the national debt, the dismantling of the fiscal-military apparatus that threatened to plunge the new nation into a never-ending cycle of wars—the American people would reap the fruits of peace and prosperity. Jefferson would win the people's favor by doing nothing, or by undoing what the Federalists had done. Necessarily, increasingly conscious of their good fortune, Americans would repudiate the few remaining enemies of union and republican government, leaving them to stand as "monuments" to their own folly.

As Jefferson sought to define the meaning of his election, he looked back to 1776, to the first principles of a republican revolution that had toppled despotism in America. From this perspective, Jefferson could be confident that the "Revolution of 1800" would succeed: if the patriots of 1776 had overcome the greatest power on earth—despite the Crown's numerous American Tory supporters—then it should be easy enough to purge the Federalists, latter-day Tories who sought to reverse the Revolution's outcome. The persistent identification of the Federalists as "Anglomen," justified by Hamilton's financial program and a decided Federalist tilt toward Britain in the French revolutionary wars, served to exaggerate the Federalist menace as long as Jefferson and his Republican colleagues remained in opposition. But this identification served equally well to minimize the Federalist threat once Jefferson was elected. It was enough to recognize what the Federalists' true intentions really were, as sufficient numbers of voters finally did in 1800—for these enemies of the Revolution to be cast into the political wilderness, permanently.[4]

Jefferson's cast of mind, his sense of the world historical significance of his election, makes sense to us now in light of the historiographical reconstruction of Revolutionary American republican thought over the last generation.[5] The great lesson of the "republican synthesis" is that although Jefferson and his contemporaries were the founders of the American political tradition and the inventors of the first recognizably "modern" political parties—they thought, wrote, spoke, and acted in an entirely different world from ours. In fact, the political and constitutional continuities between their times and ours have been the greatest obstacles to understanding: because we still use them, we think we know what all the words mean. But Jefferson's obsessive fears of "power" and "corruption" and his notions of "liberty," "virtue," personal and political "independence," and "equality" were all embedded in a view of the world astonishingly unfamiliar to modern readers.

The literature on republicanism helps us understand why Jefferson saw the American Revolution as a crucial epoch in the great and ongoing struggle between the forces of despotism and darkness, on one hand, and of freedom and enlightenment, on the other. Yet this is only part of the story. In the following pages, I want to shift attention away from the first term in Jefferson's statement—"We are all republicans"—to the second—"we are all federalists." I will argue that "federal principles," the preservation of the framers' "more perfect union," was as important to Jefferson as vindicating republican government.

One reason why Jefferson's federalism is now obscure to us is that we have not had the benefit of a "federal synthesis" to balance or, perhaps more accurately, to extend and elaborate the "republican synthesis."[6] But there are further obstacles to understanding Jeffersonian federalism. Most daunting is the general belief that Jefferson and Madison only belatedly turned to states' rights: the Kentucky and Virginia Resolutions of 1798 were inspired by political desperation as Republican oppositionists sought to counter Federalist control of the national legislature and executive. The compact theory of union was grounded not in principle but rather in political expediency.

Jefferson's celebration of the union in his inaugural—a union he was prepared to destroy in 1798 through state "nullification" of federal authority—thus seems disingenuous, if not downright hypocritical. An unfriendly critic might conclude that Jefferson was projecting his own disunionist intentions on to his opponents, whose only "crime" was to attempt to buttress the authority of the federal government in a period of global political crisis—and the "Quasi-War" with France—when national security was in jeopardy. In calling himself a "federalist" supporter of the union, Jefferson must therefore be indulging in obfuscatory word play, perhaps in a sort of revenge against the nationalists of 1787 who called themselves "federalists." In other words, it was the spirit of anti-federalism, not the federalism of the framers, that Jefferson articulated and exploited in his inaugural address.

Jefferson has never lacked defenders, of course, but these defenders are clearly most comfortable in speaking to Jefferson's republicanism—his eloquent statements of natural rights and his lifelong advocacy of equality and government by consent—not to his federalism.[7] Merrill D. Peterson thus attributes Jefferson's recourse to federalism to a temporary fit of "hysteria" as he sought to vindicate freedom against the Federalists' "odious laws." But this was a potentially "dangerous" line of defense that ultimately fostered "delusions of state sovereignty fully as violent as the Federalist delusions he had combated." Invoking Jefferson's authority, states' rights advocates would lead the nation into in a bloody civil war.[8]

My point is that Jefferson's friends have been complicit in an interpretation of the inaugural and of his political career generally that systematically discounts and misrepresents his principled commitment to the American experiment in federal republican government. Federalism may not—for better or worse—rank very high in our own scheme of values, and we certainly continue to draw inspiration from Jeffersonian conceptions of the natural and universal rights of individuals. But when Jefferson called himself a "federalist," he meant what he was saying. It is worth noting that, in the next paragraph of the inaugural, when Jefferson returned to the Revolutionary legacy, he reversed the sequence of the first formulation: "Let us then, with courage and confidence pursue our own federal and republican principles, our attachment to our union and representative government."[9] Jefferson did not privilege "republicanism" over "federalism" (as we may), nor would he be willing to distinguish or dissociate these "principles."

Our challenge, then, is to try to understand exactly how these principles are related, how one depends on the other. The republican synthesis offers a good point of departure. Dissatisfied with the stripped-down Lockean liberalism that earlier generations of scholars and commentators found in the Declaration of Independence and other Revolutionary state papers, republican revisionists have sought to provide richer, alternative readings of early American political thought. These writers and their critics have challenged conventional understandings of fundamental principles of the American regime and illuminated obscure and neglected corners of the founders' conceptual universe. Yet only when republican revisionists and neoliberal critics overcome their common liberal presuppositions and move beyond the classically liberal obsession with the character, rights, virtue, public spiritedness, and happiness of individuals will they grasp the broader concerns of American Revolutionaries and constitution writers.[10] The Revolutionaries were not simply founding new republics; they hoped to construct a new order for the ages, a federal republican regime that would preserve peace (in the world, among the states), sustain republican government (in the states), and secure the liberty and natural rights of individual citizens.

Thomas Jefferson's political thought offers a good point of departure for a new history of Revolutionary federalism. It is the premise of this essay that neither the response to the Federalists in 1798 nor Jefferson's supposed reservations about the new federal Constitution a decade earlier constituted the crucial turn toward federalism in his career. I will argue instead that a fresh reading of the Declaration of Independence shows that Jefferson was always a federalist and that the federal principle was always preeminent in his thought. The text of the Declaration does not disclose a fully elaborated theory of federalism, and certainly not an institutional framework for a functioning federal system. But it does set forth, both in its ringing phrases and in the silences around them, what might be called the federal myth, the foundation principles for a new world order.

Jefferson's first sustained piece of political writing, *A Summary View of the Rights of British America* (1774), constituted a "plan for federal union" in a reformed British empire. "We are willing, on our part, to sacrifice every thing which reason can ask to the restoration of that tranquillity for which all must wish," wrote Jefferson. For their part, let the British "be ready to establish union and a generous plan." Jefferson was one of several writers who, as they denied parliamentary sovereignty over the American colonies, emphasized the king's role in sustaining imperial ties. "This is the important post," Jefferson reminded George III, "in which fortune has placed you, holding the balance of a great, if a well poised empire." In effect, Jefferson, John Adams, James Wilson, and other patriot writers argued for a new imperial constitution or treaty—the words were used interchangeably—that would guarantee the autonomy and fundamental rights of the empire's far-flung member states in return for a perpetual alliance, or union.[11]

It is easy to discount the federalism of the *Summary View*. The political situation in 1774—like that of 1798—put a premium on states' rights; Jefferson's opposition to central government—imperial or federal—was presented as a plan for constitutional union, with the threat of revolution or "nullification" barely concealed. Clearly, Jefferson was in both instances looking ahead, to one "revolution" or other, and had no real interest in sustaining the kind of "balance" he urged on George III. The very suggestion that George "held the balance" was tantamount to a declaration of independence, for it presupposed the autonomy of the various political communities to be balanced. After all, it had long been the premise, or conceit, of British diplomacy that Britain "held the balance" in the European system. It followed that the free and independent American states, like the sovereignties of Europe, would be linked to Britain through the mechanisms of the balance of power. Jefferson thus redefined the political and constitutional crisis that threatened the very survival of the British Empire in international terms. As a result, he exaggerated the role of royal prerogative (that included the conduct of foreign policy) in sustaining Anglo-American union. But to inflate George III's authority—and responsibility—was simply to prepare the way for the radically deflationary rhetoric, in Thomas Paine's *Common Sense* and in Jefferson's Declaration of Independence, that would mark the final push toward independence.[12]

This reading of the *Summary View* seems plausible enough. But the assumption that Jefferson and other patriot leaders sought a complete break with Great Britain in 1774—that when Jefferson called for "union" he really meant "disunion"—is unwarranted. Americans were by no means eager to make war against the mother country and only reluctantly and belatedly proclaimed their "separate and equal station" among the powers of the earth. When Americans sought to reform the imperial constitution, they were trying to construct an Anglo-American "peace plan," a new and higher level of political association that would eliminate sources of conflict and banish the use of coercive force among member states.[13]

When American radicals were at last persuaded that British corruption and obduracy precluded a constitutional resolution of the imperial crisis, they turned to the balance of power to secure their rights. The balance was a progressive mechanism, they believed, capable of sustaining an expanding regime of law and civility among independent states. Influential Enlightenment theorists thought of the balance-of-power system as a kind of "federal republic" or "commonwealth," an emergent political community constituted by treaties. The impossibility of a true federal union within the British Empire thus forced the Americans to seek "union" elsewhere, through alliances with other powers.[14]

Critics of the liberal, "individualist" reading of the Declaration are right to emphasize the republican, communitarian context for individual rights claims, but they fail to take their insight to the limits of Jefferson's thinking.[15] Independence was a means toward union, not an end in itself. Seen in this light, the continuity between Jefferson's thinking in 1774 and 1776, and beyond, becomes apparent. His commitment to republicanism proceeded from, and always was predicated on, his commitment to securing the corporate rights of Virginia and the other American states. But this does not mean that Jefferson was a "localist" rather than "cosmopolitan." Jefferson's developing conception of federalism transcended this polarity: in Jefferson's view, individual freedom depended on republican self-government that in turn depended on a "more perfect union" of free states in a progressively more civilized and peaceful world system. This is the underlying logic of the Declaration of Independence.

The affective ties of allegiance that bound American subjects to their British king constituted the biggest obstacle to independence. Recasting those ties in sentimental and familial terms, Jefferson's Declaration emphasized George III's betrayal of his trust. Just as James II had "abdicated" in the

Glorious Revolution of 1689, now George un-kinged himself. American independence was instigated by a usurping despot and a bad father. The juxtaposition of seventeenth-century constitutionalism and eighteenth-century sentimentalism proved to be a powerful, revolutionary force.[16]

Commentators turn to the second paragraph for a positive statement of the Revolutionaries' goals, epitomized by the stirring invocation of "life, liberty, & the pursuit of happiness." But the immediate object of the Declaration, "to dissolve the political bands which have connected . . . one people . . . with another," is set forth in its opening sentence. Jefferson is here referring to Americans collectively, but subsequent references are to the separate "colonies" or "states."[17]

A portion of Jefferson's draft, excised by Congress, provides the historical narrative that justifies the focus on provincial rights. The respective colonies were founded "at the expense of our own blood & treasure, unassisted by the wealth or the strength of Great Britain: that in constituting indeed our several forms of government, we had adopted one common king, thereby laying a foundation for perpetual league & amity with them: but that submission to their parliament was no part of our constitution." The idea that the colonists founded new communities and then "adopted one common king" was an American variation on the equally implausible myth of Anglo-Saxon constitutionalism, according to which the existence of the English nation preceded the institution of monarchy and therefore constituted a fundamental limit on monarchical authority. The novelty of the Jeffersonian myth of expatriation, more fully elaborated in the *Summary View*, was that it gave a spatial dimension and contemporary salience to a myth of origins: the "ancient constitution" survived—but was now threatened—in Anglo-America.[18]

Jefferson's colleagues may have rejected this passage because its historical claims were untenable, perhaps even laughable. But they did not reject Jefferson's conception of the empire as a federation of free states that they now, reluctantly, were forced to abandon. Jefferson's version of colonial history was a bold effort to identify the embattled assemblies with the corporate integrity of colony communities. The first six substantive charges against the king in the adopted Declaration all refer directly, and subsequent charges refer indirectly, to royal interference in the legislative process. The imminent threat is that the assemblies will cease to exercise any effective legislative power, if they continue to meet at all. In other words, the implicit claim that the assemblies—or their ad hoc, Revolutionary successors—"represent" the colonies, and that Congress can in turn speak for the colonies, is made in the face of the virtual immobilization of representative government in Anglo-America.[19]

It is this identification of representatives with their colony communities and of Congress with the American "people" that constitutes the most crucial rhetorical move in the Declaration. With the expatriation argument suppressed, the argument is made—probably more effectively—by ellipsis and indirection. Jefferson assumes that everyone will agree that the colonies are "states," that they possess inviolable corporate rights that the "people" must vindicate. But, of course, this is precisely what advocates of parliamentary supremacy did not accept. In other words, Jefferson silently stipulates that the empire must be seen as a federal union, not a unitary polity; the universalistic pretensions of a king-in-parliament are thus fractured and subverted by the particular claims of colony communities. Here was an ironic, localistic counterpoint to the universalistic claims, the "self-evident" truths, of Jefferson's second paragraph. For it was in response to the royal assaults on their corporate rights and privileges catalogued in the Declaration that the colonists invoked their "inalienable rights" as free men and took up arms. The challenge was to frame specific local grievances and customary claims in all-embracing, universal terms. This was Jefferson's great achievement in the Declaration, and it depended on his assumption that colonies had constitutions, that they were "states" that could claim rights.

As "sovereignty" was transferred from king to people, it traveled a circuitous route. Deposing the king created a vacuum of legitimate authority that representatives of the people quickly filled. The most significant consequence of this upheaval, and the great unrecognized achievement of the Declaration, was the invention of the American idea of state sovereignty, the conception of states as self-constituted, self-sufficient, and autonomous political communities. In practical, institutional terms, the invention of state sovereignty marked the final stage in the rise of the assemblies. Facing an increasingly uncertain future in the last years of imperial rule, the representatives gained expansive new powers under the first new state constitutions.[20]

But it would be a mistake to conclude that securing assembly rights was Jefferson's sole, or even primary, concern in the Declaration. Justifying Congress's assumption of the authority to declare independence constituted his most formidable challenge. Anglo-Americans always had had a well-developed sense of their rights as individuals, and the corporate claims of the new states grew out of their colonial experience. But the Continental

Congress had no such legitimating pedigree. Its pretensions were most revolutionary, and therefore most in need of justification.[21]

Jefferson justified himself, and Congress, by demonstrating that George III sought to establish "an absolute tyranny over these states." This "long train of abuses & usurpations" was directed immediately at the colonial assemblies, and ultimately at the "inalienable rights" of the people themselves. According to Jefferson's version, resistance moved in the opposite direction, beginning with the people—whose "rights" were "self-evident"—proceeding through colonial governments whose "just powers" were based on their "consent," and culminating with Congress itself. In other words, Congress sought to take the king's place. But this pretension could not be openly asserted: Congress's rule would be seen as legitimate only as long as it made no claims on its own behalf.[22]

Jefferson pulled out all the rhetorical stops as he showed George III unkinging himself. In striking contrast, the Declaration is totally silent about Congress's succession to royal authority. Jefferson recognized that saying anything would be saying too much. For Congress could only assume the king's prerogatives—most notably and pressingly over the conduct of war and diplomacy—if it was seen as completely different from the George III depicted in the Declaration. George, the bad father, was Congress's reverse image: congressmen would never violate the trust of their constituents by pursuing their own interests at the people's expense. This identification between governors and governed was, of course, the premise and design of republican governments. But it also evoked—and, in the Declaration, much more powerfully—the myth of the "good" king, the true father to his people. Congress would be so completely and transparently identified with "the people" that they would dissolve into one another. Significantly, this identification was not assured by the elaborate constitutional mechanisms favored by radical republicans: the government of the United States only became republican after a protracted series of constitutional crises and reforms. In 1776 the implicit model for Congress was an idealized conception of kingship. George III "has abdicated government here by declaring us out of his protection, and waging war against us." Congress must take his place.[23]

Congress could present itself as the legitimate successor to the British monarchy as long as it was seen to be faithfully representing the new state governments, and through them the American "people." This meant, as we have seen, that the rights of the states, the predicate of congressional legitimacy, had to be established first. This is why the congressional resolution of May 10 and 15, 1776, authorizing the rebellious colonies to institute new governments, was so crucial.[24] Congressmen feigned surprise that thirteen colonial clocks should strike as one when the United States declared independence. But the clockwork had long since been set in motion by the concerted efforts of patriot leaders. It was important, however, that the mechanism be concealed and that the revolting colonists believe—or, perhaps, in the case of Adams, Jefferson, and other prime movers, convince themselves—that resistance was the spontaneous and simultaneous expression of popular grievances and popular will throughout the colonies.

This myth of spontaneous resistance was a crucial prop to congressional legitimacy. Exploiting an early burst of popular enthusiasm for the war effort, Congress quickly and successfully assumed a quasi-monarchical authority. Congress's dilemma was that any effort to institutionalize its authority inevitably jeopardized it. Set against the legitimating myth of spontaneous resistance—"popular sovereignty" in action—any formal assumption of authority was bound to generate suspicion. This may help explain why it proved to be so difficult to draft acceptable Articles of Confederation and why Congress's prestige plummeted after 1781, when the Articles were finally ratified and Congress finally became a "constitutional" government.

There are many plausible explanations for Congress's sorry history. The recalcitrance of the states, intoxicated by visions of their own sovereignty, is everybody's favorite. But I would suggest that efforts to bolster congressional authority so often proved counterproductive because Congress was not an ordinary legislature, and the United States was not an ordinary republic. The "monarchical" authority of Congress depended on sustaining the myth of its faithful representation of the "people," and of the people's commitment to the common cause. Any attempt to fix the actual representation of different states, regions, or interests gave the lie to the myth, unleashing a competition for relative advantage—the factionalism that so disturbed contemporary commentators—that was the antithesis of a true and affectionate union. The template for that union was offered in the Declaration of Independence. When, according to Jefferson's formula, congressmen "pledge[d] to each other our lives, our fortunes, & our sacred honor," they were not negotiating a contract or drafting a constitution. They were instead invoking sacred ties of honor and friendship, the moral equivalent for liberty-loving republicans of the allegiance owed to a good father, or a good king. The pledge was all the more sacred and compelling because it was entered into by equals, and was not offered in weakness or fear to a superior power.[25]

Most commentators on the Declaration focus on the tension between the claims of individual and society implicit in the natural rights doctrine of the second paragraph. They overlook Jefferson's conception of union, a fundamental premise in his political and social theory that mediates between these polarities. Union was grounded in man's natural sociability, and was constructed and extended through ties of friendship, the most durable and efficacious "political bands." As a republicanized and sentimentalized gloss on the monarchical principle of allegiance, Jefferson's idea of union facilitated the transfer of legitimate authority from king to Congress. This was the Declaration's most revolutionary implication.

Jefferson linked the consent of individuals—the source of legitimate authority—to the rights of the new states as political communities and then to a yet higher level of association, the federal union, embodied in Congress itself. This is what I call the myth of federalism. The Declaration's implicit scheme—citizens, states, union—constituted the paradigm, or framework, for elaborations of the federal idea in succeeding decades. The highest level, the union of American republics, represented the most radical departure from conventional theory and practice. Real Whig republicanism offered little guidance in constructing a federal regime. Jefferson turned instead to an idealized version of monarchy and a sentimental notion of Revolutionary brotherhood for a new conception of union, "political bands" among the states that would never be "dissolved."

We generally think of federalism in negative terms, as a constitutional division of power and a strict constructionist jurisprudence that enables entrenched local interests to resist the encroachments of a "despotic" central government on states' rights and individual liberties. But there is another, more positive and forward-looking face to Jeffersonian federalism as it was first developed in the *Summary View* and Declaration of Independence. The end of British tyranny would not dissolve or destroy all social ties or "political bands," thus preparing the way for a possessive individualist millennium. Instead, Jefferson believed, the corruption and despotism of the imperial regime obstructed the natural and consensual ties of affection, principle, and common interest that were bound to draw Americans into ever closer union. Jefferson's federalism proceeded from this fundamental, hopeful premise.

It was—and is—easy enough for critics to mock Jefferson's vaulting hopes for the American union and to emphasize the fearful and self-regarding libertarianism and localism that were left in their wake.[26] But when

Jefferson said "we are all federalists" in his first inaugural address, he did not mean to sanction or foster this suspicious defensiveness, or to obstruct the continuing progress of the American experiment in self-government. To the contrary, the promise of 1776—including the promise of an evermore perfect federal union—would be at last redeemed. Jefferson's project may have been a great failure, based on an illusory premise; he may have been betrayed in the end by his profound aversion to politics and the exercise of power. But the vision of natural society, of free states in affectionate union, and of the nations of the world working toward harmony and peace continues to exercise a powerful appeal. If, as Joyce Appleby argues, Jefferson was the apostle of hope for a democratizing America, his conception of an expanding union of free states was his most hopeful and visionary—and elusive—legacy.[27]

Notes

This essay was originally published in *Essays in History* (Corcoran Department of History, University of Virginia) 35 (1993). It is available at http://etext.virginia.edu/journals/EH/EH35/onuf1.html.

1. Thomas Jefferson (hereafter TJ), First Inaugural Address, March 4, 1801, in Merrill D. Peterson, ed., *Thomas Jefferson Writings* (New York, 1984), 493. See Ralph Ketcham, *Presidents above Party: The First American Presidency, 1789–1829* (Chapel Hill, NC, 1984).

2. Richard Hofstadter, *The Idea of a Party System: The Rise of Legitimate Opposition in the United States, 1780–1840* (Berkeley, CA, 1970), 122–69.

3. See the essays collected in James Horn, Jan Ellen Lewis, and Peter S. Onuf, eds., *The Revolution of 1800: Democracy, Race, and the New Republic* (Charlottesville, VA, 2002).

4. Peter S. Onuf, *Jefferson's Empire: The Language of American Nationhood* (Charlottesville, VA, 2000), chap. 3. See also Lance Banning, *The Jeffersonian Persuasion: Evolution of a Party Ideology* (Ithaca, NY, 1978); and Richard Buel Jr., *Securing the Revolution: Ideology in American Politics, 1789–1815* (Ithaca, NY, 1972).

5. For a good introduction to this literature, see Robert Shalhope, "Toward a Republican Synthesis: The Emergence of an Understanding of Republicanism in American Historiography," *William & Mary Quarterly* (hereafter *WMQ*) 22 (1972): 49–80; and idem, "Republicanism in Early American Historiography," *WMQ* 34

(1982): 334–56. For a provocative, possibly premature, postmortem, see Daniel T. Rodgers, "Republicanism: The Career of a Concept," *Journal of American History* 79 (1992): 11–38.

6. See my discussion of federalism, with citations to recent work, in "Reflections on the Founding: Constitutional Historiography in Bicentennial Perspective," *WMQ* 46 (1989): 341–75, esp. 356–64. See also Peter B. Knupfer, *The Union as It Is: Constitutional Unionism and Sectional Compromise, 1787–1861* (Chapel Hill, NC, 1991), 22–55. Recent work, published since this essay originally appeared, suggests that such a synthesis may now be emerging. See particularly the following: Lance Banning, *The Sacred Fire of Liberty: James Madison and the Founding of the Federal Republic, 1780–1792* (Ithaca, NY, 1995); Andrew Lenner, *The Federal Principle in American Politics* (Madison, WI, 2000); and David C. Hendrickson, *Peace Pact: The Lost World of the American Founding* (Lawrence, KS, 2003).

7. Neither Richard K. Matthews nor Garrett Ward Sheldon discusses the Kentucky Resolutions in their explications of Jeffersonian political thought; see Matthews, *The Radical Politics of Thomas Jefferson: A Revisionist View* (Lawrence, KS, 1984); and Sheldon, *The Political Philosophy of Thomas Jefferson* (Baltimore, 1991). David N. Mayer's *Constitutional Thought of Thomas Jefferson* (Charlottesville, VA, 1994) is the only major study that devotes much space to Jefferson's federalism. But Mayer, whose libertarian predilections are apparent, is primarily interested in federalism as a mode of constitutional interpretation.

8. Merrill D. Peterson, *Thomas Jefferson and the New Nation: A Biography* (New York, 1970), 608–25, quotations on 609. For a good treatment of the Virginia and Kentucky Resolutions, see Drew R. McCoy, *The Last of the Fathers: James Madison and the Republican Legacy* (New York, 1989), 131–50.

9. TJ, First Inaugural Address, March 4, 1801, in Peterson, ed., *Jefferson Writings*, 493–94.

10. See the discussion in Peter Onuf and Nicholas Onuf, *Federal Union, Modern World: The Law of Nations in an Age of Revolutions, 1776–1814* (Madison, WI, 1993), 19–20.

11. *A Summary View of the Rights of British America* (July 1774), in Peterson, ed., *Jefferson Writings*, 105–22, quotations on 121. See the editorial apparatus and commentary in Julian P. Boyd et al., eds., *The Papers of Thomas Jefferson*, 32 vols. to date (Princeton, NJ, 1950–), 1:105–36. My reading of the *Summary View* relies heavily on Stephen A. Conrad, "Putting Rights Talk in Its Place: The *Summary View* Revisited," in Peter S. Onuf, ed., *Jeffersonian Legacies* (Charlottesville, VA, 1993), 254–80. See also Anthony M. Lewis, "Jefferson's *Summary View* as a Chart of Political Union," *WMQ* 5 (1948): 35–41. On Wilson and Adams, see Peter S. Onuf,

The Origins of the Federal Republic: Jurisdictional Controversies in the United States, 1775–1787 (Philadelphia, 1983), 26. The best introduction to the problem of federalism in the British Empire is Jack P. Greene, *Peripheries and Center: Constitutional Development in the Extended Polities of the British Empire and the United States, 1607–1788* (Athens, GA, 1986).

12. On Britain's "holding the balance," see Felix Gilbert, *To the Farewell Address: Ideas of Early American Foreign Policy* (Princeton, NJ, 1961), 19–43. See also Onuf and Onuf, *Federal Union, Modern World,* chap. 4; and Thomas Paine, *Common Sense,* Feb. 14, 1776, in Eric Foner, ed., *Thomas Paine: Collected Writings* (New York, 1995), 5–59.

13. On the peace plan tradition, see F. H. Hinsley, *Power and the Pursuit of Peace: Theory and Practice in the History of Relations between States* (Cambridge, UK, 1963). The importance of this tradition for American constitutional development is briefly discussed in Cathy D. Matson and Peter S. Onuf, *A Union of Interests: Political and Economic Thought in Revolutionary America* (Lawrence, KS, 1990), 145–46.

14. These themes are elaborated in Onuf and Onuf, *Federal Union, Modern World,* intro., chaps. 4–5.

15. Garry Wills, *Inventing America: Jefferson's Declaration of Independence* (Garden City, NY, 1978); Matthews, *Radical Politics of Thomas Jefferson,* 25–27.

16. For an explication of the "politics of feeling," see Jay Fliegelman, *Declaring Independence: Jefferson, Natural Language, and the Culture of Performance* (Stanford, CA, 1993). My understanding of the importance of affective ties in Jeffersonian thought has been enormously enriched by Fliegelman's brilliant book.

17. The text of the Declaration is in Peterson, ed., *Jefferson Writings,* 19–24, all quotations on 19, including references to "colonies" and "states."

18. Ibid., 22–23; the corresponding passage in the *Summary View* is in ibid., 118–19. See also TJ's "original Rough draft" and Declaration of Independence as Adopted by Congress, July 4, 1776, in Boyd et al., eds., *Jefferson Papers,* 1:423–28, 429–33. On Jeffersonian historiography, see Trevor H. Colbourn, *The Lamp of Experience: Whig History and the Intellectual Origins of the American Revolution* (Chapel Hill, NC, 1965), 158–84. For a trenchant discussion of expatriation theory, see John Phillip Reid, *Constitutional History of the American Revolution: The Authority of Rights* (Madison, WI, 1986), 114–31.

19. On the "rise of the assemblies," see Jack P. Greene, *The Quest for Power: The Lower Houses of Assembly in the Southern Royal Colonies, 1689–1776* (Chapel Hill, NC, 1963); and Greene, *Peripheries and Center,* 83–97.

20. The literature on this subject is vast. For a review and synthesis, see Peter S. Onuf, "The Origins and Early Development of State Legislatures," in Joel H. Silbey,

ed., *Encyclopedia of the American Legislative System,* 3 vols. (New York, 1994), 1:175–94.

21. The best treatment of this dilemma is Jack N. Rakove, *The Beginnings of National Politics: An Interpretive History of the Continental Congress* (New York, 1979), 87–110. See also Peter Onuf, "The First Federal Constitution: The Articles of Confederation," in Leonard W. Levy and Dennis J. Mahoney, eds., *The Framing and Ratification of the Constitution* (New York, 1987), 82–97.

22. Declaration of Independence, in Peterson, ed., *Jefferson Writings,* 19.

23. Ibid., 21 (TJ's original draft). On Congress's "succession" to crown powers, see Onuf, *Origins of the Federal Republic,* 12–17; and Jerrilyn Greene Marston's excellent *King and Congress: The Transfer of Political Legitimacy, 1774–1776* (Princeton, NJ, 1987).

24. Worthington C. Ford, ed., *Journals of the Continental Congress,* 34 vols. (Washington, DC, 1904–37), 4:342, 357–58.

25. Declaration of Independence, in Peterson, ed., *Jefferson Writings,* 24. See the discussion in Fliegelman, *Declaring Independence,* 21–25, passim.

26. See the discussion in Peter Onuf, "The Expanding Union," in David T. Konig, ed., *Devising Liberty: The Conditions of Freedom in the Early American Republic* (Stanford, CA, 1995), 50–80; and in Onuf and Onuf, *Federal Union, Modern World.*

27. Joyce Appleby, *Capitalism and a New Social Order: The Republican Vision of the 1790s* (New York, 1984); and Appleby, "Jefferson and His Complex Legacy," in Onuf, ed., *Jeffersonian Legacies,* 1–16.

THE REVOLUTION
OF 1803

If there was one thing the United States did not seem to need in 1803, it was more land. The federal government had plenty of acreage to sell settlers in the new state of Ohio and throughout the Old Northwest, as did New York, Pennsylvania, and other states. New Englanders were already complaining that the western exodus was driving up wages and depressing real estate prices in the East.

The United States then consisted of sixteen states: the original thirteen, strung along the Atlantic seaboard, and three recent additions on the frontier: Vermont, which had declared its independence from New York during the Revolution, was finally recognized and admitted in 1791; and Kentucky (1792) and Tennessee (1796), carved out of the western reaches of Virginia and North Carolina, extended the union of states as far as the Mississippi River. The entire area east of the Mississippi had been nominally secured to the United States by the Peace of Paris in 1783, although vast regions remained under the control of Indian nations and subject to the influence of neighboring European imperial powers.

Many skeptical commentators believed that the United States was already too big, that the bonds of union would weaken and snap if new settlements spread too far and too fast. "No paper engagements" could secure the connection of East and West, Rufus King wrote in 1786, and separatist movements and disunionist plots kept such concerns alive in subsequent years.[1] The American negotiators in Paris had not even dreamed of acquiring an area as vast as the Louisiana Territory. Why would anyone welcome the vast accession, doubling the size of the United States, with enthusiasm?

It is hard for us today to recapture the decidedly mixed feelings of that time and place. However much some modern Americans may bemoan the patriotic passions and imperialistic excesses of "manifest destiny" and its "legacies of conquest," the expansion of the United States has the retrospective feel of inevitability. Expansionists had a penchant for naturalistic language—at best, the "surge" or "tide" of white settlement might be channeled, but it was ultimately irresistible—and it's almost impossible for us now to imagine any other outcome. But President Thomas Jefferson and his contemporaries understood that they stood at a crossroads, that the American experiment in republican self-government and the fragile federal union on which it depended could also easily fail. They understood that the United States was a second-rate power, without the "energy" or military means to project—or possibly even to defend—its vital interests in a dangerous world almost constantly at war. And, finally, they understood all too well that the loyalties of their countrymen—even, if they were honest with themselves, their own loyalties—were volatile and unpredictable.

There were very good reasons for such doubts about American allegiances. Facing an uncertain future, patriotic (and not so patriotic) Americans had only the dimmest notions of who or what should command their loyalty. The union had nearly collapsed on more than one occasion: during the succession crisis of 1800–1801, which saw a tie in the electoral college and thirty-six contentious ballots in the House of Representatives before Jefferson was elevated to the presidency; under the Confederation (1781–89), when the central government ground to a virtual halt and the union almost withered away before the new constitution saved the day; and during the 1790s, a tumultuous decade of partisan political strife between Federalists and Jefferson's Republicans. Of course, everyone professed to be a patriot, dedicated to preserving American independence. But what did that mean? Federalists such as Alexander Hamilton preached fealty to a powerful, consolidated central government capable of doing the people's will (as they loosely construed it); Republican oppositionists championed a strictly construed federal constitution that left power in the hands of the people's (or peoples') state governments. Each side accused the other of being subject to the corrupt influence of a foreign power: counterrevolutionary England (Federalist "aristocrats" and "monocrats") or revolutionary France (Republican "Jacobins").

In Jefferson's mind, and in the minds of his many followers, the new Republican dispensation initiated by his ascension to power in "the Revolution of 1800" provided a hopeful answer to all of these doubts and anxieties. In their eyes, Jefferson's first inaugural address, which the soft-spoken fifty-eight-year-old president delivered to Congress in a nearly inaudible whisper in March 1801, heralded a new epoch in American affairs. Jefferson's inspiring vision of the nation's future augured something "new under the sun," as he told the English radical Joseph Priestley, then a refugee in republican Pennsylvania. "We are all republicans, we are all federalists," he insisted in his inaugural; "let us, then, unite with one heart and one mind."[2]

While Jefferson's conciliatory language famously helped to heal the partisan breach—and, not coincidentally, to cast Hamilton and his High Federalist minions far beyond the republican pale—it also anticipated the issues that would come to the fore during the period leading up to the Louisiana Purchase.

First, he addressed the problem of size: Could an expanding union of free republican states survive without jeopardizing the liberties won at such great cost by the Revolutionary generation? The president reassured the rising, post-Revolutionary generation that it too had sufficient virtue and patriotism to make the republican experiment work and to pass its beneficent legacy on to succeeding generations. "Entertaining a due sense of our equal right to the use of our own faculties" and "enlightened by a benign religion, professed, indeed, and practiced in various forms, yet all of them inculcating honesty, truth, temperance, gratitude, and the love of man; acknowledging and adoring an overruling Providence, which by all its dispensations proves that it delights in the happiness of man here and his greater happiness hereafter," we are bound to be "a happy and a prosperous people."

Jefferson congratulated his fellow Americans on "possessing a chosen country, with room enough for our descendants to the thousandth and thousandth generation," a vast domain that was "separated by nature and a wide ocean from the exterminating havoc of one quarter of the globe." Jefferson's vision of nationhood was inscribed on the American landscape: "an overruling Providence" provided this fortunate people with land enough to survive and prosper forever. But Jefferson knew that he was *not* offering an accurate description of the nation's present condition. Given the frenzied pace of westward settlement, it would take only a generation or two—not a thousand—to fill out the new nation's existing limits, still marked in the west by the Mississippi. Nor was the United States as happily insulated from Europe's "exterminating havoc" as the new president suggested. The Spanish remained in control of New Orleans, the key to the great river system that controlled the continent's heartland, and the British remained a powerful presence to the north.

Jefferson's vision of the future was, in fact, the mirror opposite of America's present. The nation was encircled by dangerous enemies and deeply divided by partisan and sectional differences. The domain he envisioned was boundless, continent-wide, a virgin land waiting to be taken up by virtuous, liberty-loving American farmers. In this providential perspective, Indian nations and European empires simply disappeared from view, and the acquisition of new territory and the expansion of the union seemed preordained. It would take an unimaginable miracle, the Louisiana Purchase, to consummate Jefferson's inaugural promise.

Jefferson's expansionist vision also violated the accepted axioms of contemporary political science. In his *Spirit of the Laws* (1748), the great French philosopher Montesquieu taught that the republican form of government could only survive in small states, where a virtuous and vigilant citizenry could effectively monitor the exercise of power. A large state could only be sustained if power were concentrated in a more energetic central government: Republicanism in an expanding state would give way to more "despotic," aristocratic, and monarchical regimes. This "law" of political science was commonly understood in mechanical terms: Centrifugal forces, pulling a state apart, gained force as territory expanded and could only be checked by the "energy" of strong government. Montesquieu's mechanical model of politics enjoyed broad acceptance in the United States.[3]

James Madison had grappled with this problem in his famous "Federalist No. 10," where he argued that an "extended republic" would "take in a greater variety of parties and interests," making it "less probable that a majority of the whole will have a common motive to invade the rights of other citizens."[4] Modern pluralists have embraced this argument, but it was not particularly persuasive to Madison's generation—or even to Madison himself a decade later. During the struggle over ratification of the Constitution, anti-Federalists effectively invoked Montesquieu's dictum against Federalist "consolidationism," and in the 1790s, Jeffersonian defenders of states' rights (including Madison) offered the same arguments against Hamiltonian High

Federalism. And Jefferson's "Revolution of 1800," vindicating the claims of (relatively) small state-republics against an overly energetic central government, seemed to confirm Montesquieu's wisdom.

At the same time, however, Montesquieu's logic posed a problem for Jefferson. How could he imagine a continental republic in 1801 and then negotiate a land cession that doubled its size in 1803? To put the problem somewhat differently, how could Jefferson overcome his own disunionist tendencies?—He had, after all, drafted the controversial Kentucky Resolutions of 1798, which threatened state nullification of federal authority.

Jefferson's response in his inaugural was to call on his fellow Americans to "pursue our own federal and republican principles, our attachment to union and representative government" with "courage and confidence." In other words, a sacred regard for states' rights ("federal principles") was essential to the preservation and strength of a "union" that depended on the "attachment" of a people determined to secure its liberties ("republican principles"). This conception of states as republics would have been familiar and appealing to many Americans, but his vision of the United States as a *powerful* nation, spreading across the continent, was breathtaking in its boldness. How could he promise Americans that they could have it both ways, that they could be secure in their liberties yet have a federal government with enough "energy to preserve itself"? How could he believe that the American government, which had only recently endured a near-fatal succession crisis and had a pathetically small army and navy, was "the strongest Government on earth"?

Jefferson responded to these questions resoundingly, by invoking—or perhaps more accurately, inventing—an American people or nation, united in devotion to common principles, and coming together, over the course of succeeding generations, to constitute one great family. The unity Jefferson imagined was thus prospective. Divided as they might now be, Americans would soon come to see that they were destined to be a great nation, freed from "the throes and convulsions of the ancient world" and willing to sacrifice everything in defense of their country. In Jefferson's vision of progressive continental development, the defensive vigilance of virtuous republicans, always ready to resist the encroachments of power from any and every source, would be transformed into a patriotic devotion to the transcendent community of an inclusive and expanding nation, "the world's best hope." "At the call of the law," Jefferson predicted, "every man . . . would fly to the standard of the law, and would meet invasions of the public order as his own personal concern." Jefferson thus invoked an idealized vision of the American Revolution, in which patriotic citizen-soldiers rallied against British tyranny, as a model for future mobilizations against internal as well as external threats. (It was an extraordinary—and extraordinarily influential—exercise in revisionist history; more dispassionate observers—including those who, unlike Jefferson, actually had some military experience—were not inclined to give the militias much, if any, credit for winning the war.)

Jefferson's conception of the American nation imaginatively countered the centrifugal forces, the tendency toward anarchy and disunion, that republicanism authorized and unleashed. Devotion to the union would reverse these tendencies, drawing Americans together even as their private pursuits of happiness drew them to the far frontiers of their continental domain. It was a paradoxical, mystifying formulation. What seemed to be weakness—the absence of a strong central government—was in fact strength. Expansion did not attenuate social and political ties, but secured a powerful, effective, and affective union. The imagined obliteration of all possible obstacles to the enactment of this great national story—the removal of Indians and foreigners—was the greatest mystification of all, for it disguised the ways in which the power of the federal state was deployed to clear the way for "nature's nation."

In retrospect, the peaceful acquisition of the Louisiana Territory—at the bargain basement price of fifteen million dollars—seemed to conform to Jefferson's expansionist scenario in his inaugural. The United States bought land from France, just as individuals bought land from federal and state land offices, demonstrating good intentions—to be fruitful and multiply, to cultivate the earth—and their respect for property rights and the rule of law. Yet the progress of settlement was inexorable, a "natural" force, as the French wisely recognized in ceding their claims.

The threat of force was, nonetheless, never far below the surface. When the chilling news arrived in America in 1802 that Spain had retroceded Louisiana to France under pressure from Napoleon Bonaparte, some Federalists agitated for a preemptive strike against New Orleans before the First Consul could land troops in New Orleans and begin to carry out his plan for a reinvigorated French empire in the western hemisphere. As if to provide a taste of the future, Spanish authorities in New Orleans revoked the right of American traders to store goods for export in the city, sending ripples of alarm and economic distress through farms of the Mississippi River valley. Americans might like to think, with Jefferson, that the West was a vast land reserve for future generations, but nature would issue a different decree if the French gained control of the Mississippi River system.

With Napoleon ensconced in New Orleans, Senator William Wells of Delaware warned the Senate in February 1803 that "the whole of your Southern States" would be at his "mercy." The French ruler would not hesitate to foment rebellion among the slaves, that "inveterate enemy in the very bosom of those States." A North Carolina congressman expected the Frenchman to do even worse: "The tomahawk of the savage and the knife of the negro would confederate in the league, and there would be no interval of peace."[5] Such a confederation—a powerful, unholy alliance of Europeans, Indians, and slaves—was the nightmarish antithesis of the Americans' own weak union. The French might even use their influence in Congress to revive the vicious party struggles that had crippled the national government during the 1790s.

Jefferson had no idea how to respond to the looming threat beyond sending his friend and protege James Monroe to join U.S. Minister to France Robert R. Livingston in a desperate bid to negotiate a way out of the crisis. At most they hoped that Napoleon would sell New Orleans and the Floridas to the United States, perhaps with a view to preempting an Anglo-American alliance. Jefferson dropped a broad hint to Livingston (undoubtedly for Napoleon's edification) that if France ever took "possession of N. Orleans . . . we must marry ourselves to the British fleet and nation."[6] For the Anglophobe Jefferson, this must have been a horrible thought to contemplate, even if it was a bluff. But then, happily for Jefferson—and crucially for his historical reputation—fortune intervened.

Napoleon's plans for the New World hinged on control of Saint Domingue (now Haiti), where a slave revolt led by the brilliant Toussaint L'Ouverture had complicated his plans. With a strong assist from yellow fever and other devastating diseases, the rebels had fought a French expeditionary force of more than twenty thousand to a standstill. Thwarted in his western design and facing the imminent resumption of war in Europe, Napoleon decided to cut his losses. In April 1803 his representative offered the entire Louisiana Territory to a surprised Livingston. By the end of the month, the negotiators had arrived at a price. For fifteen million dollars, the United States would acquire 828,000 square miles of land stretching west from the Mississippi River to the Rocky Mountains and from the Gulf of Mexico to the Canadian border. The nation was nearly doubled in size; thirteen states eventually would be carved from the new lands.

The news was met with general jubilation when it reached America in July. Still, this was a great deal more than anybody had been bargaining for. There was widespread agreement that national security depended on gaining control of the region around New Orleans. Spanish Florida, occupying the critical area south of Georgia and of the territory that state had finally ceded to Congress in 1802, was also prominent on the wish list of southern planters. But it was hard to imagine any immediate use for the trans-Mississippi region, notwithstanding Jefferson's inspiring rhetoric. There was some grumbling that the negotiators had spent more than Congress had authorized, and a few public figures, mostly New England Federalists, opposed the treaty on political and constitutional grounds.

The future of the West was *not* of paramount interest in 1803. The Lewis and Clark Expedition, authorized even before the Purchase was completed, testifies to the Americans' utter ignorance of the region. The two explorers were sent essentially to feel around in the dark. Perhaps, Jefferson mused, the trans-Mississippi region could be used as a kind of toxic waste dump, a place to send emancipated slaves beyond harm's way. Or, a more portentous thought, Indian nations might be relocated west of the river—an idea that President Andrew Jackson later put into effect with his infamous removal policy.

What gripped most commentators as they celebrated the news of the Purchase in 1803 was simply that the union had survived another awful crisis. They tended to see the new lands as a buffer. "The wilderness itself," Congressman Joseph Nicholson of Maryland exclaimed, "will now present an almost insurmountable barrier to any nation that inclined to disturb us in that quarter." We are now "insulated from the rest of the world," a Jeffersonian pamphleteer exulted.[7]

David Ramsay, the South Carolina historian and devout Republican, offered the most full-blown paean to the future of the "chosen country" as Jefferson had envisioned it. "What is to hinder our extension on the same liberal principles of equal rights," he asked, echoing Jefferson's first inaugural, "till we have increased to twenty-seven, thirty-seven, or any other number of states that will conveniently embrace in one happy union, the whole country from the Atlantic to the Pacific ocean, and from the lakes of Canada to the Gulf of Mexico?"[8] Jefferson himself would ask, in his second inaugural in 1805, "who can limit the extent to which the federative principle may operate effectively?" Gone were his doubts about the uses to which the new lands could be put. "Is it not better," he asked, "that the opposite bank of the

Mississippi should be settled by our own brethren and children, than by strangers of another family?"[9]

Jefferson's vision of the American future, eloquently articulated in his first inaugural and seemingly fulfilled in the Louisiana Purchase and later additions to the national domain, has ever since provided the mythic master narrative of American history. In the western domains that Jefferson imagined as a kind of blank slate on which succeeding generations would inscribe the image of American nationhood, it would be all too easy to overlook other peoples and other possibilities. It would also be all too easy to overlook the critical role of the state in the progress of settlement and development. In retrospect, effects would be confused with causes: War and diplomacy eliminated rival empires and dispossessed native peoples; an activist federal state played a critical role in pacifying a "lawless" frontier by privatizing public lands and promoting economic development. But in the mythic history of Jefferson's West, an irresistible westward tide of settlement appears to be its own cause, the manifest destiny of nature's nation.

Yet if the reality of power remains submerged in Jefferson's thought, it is never far below the surface. The very idea of the nation implies enormous force, the power of a people enacting the will of "an overruling Providence." In Jefferson's Declaration of Independence, Americans claimed the "separate & equal station to which the laws of nature and of nature's God entitle them."[10] The first law of nature, the great natural law writers of the day proclaimed, was self-preservation, and the first great mobilization of American power in the Revolution to secure independence was the defining moment in American history. President Jefferson's vision of westward expansion projected that glorious struggle into the future and across the continent. It was a kind of permanent revolution, reenacting the nation's beginnings in the multiplication of new, self-governing republican states.

Born in war, Jefferson's conception of an expanding union of free states constituted a peace plan for the New World. But until it was insulated from Europe's "exterminating havoc," the new nation would remain vulnerable and unable to realize its historic destiny. By eliminating the clear and present danger of a powerful French presence at the mouth of the Mississippi, the Louisiana Purchase guaranteed the survival of the union—for the time being, at least. By opening the West to white American settlers, it all but guaranteed that subsequent generations would look backward and see their own history in Jefferson's vision of their future. Yoking individual liberty and national power, promising a future of peace and security in a dangerous world, Jefferson's mythic, nation-making vision thus remains compelling to many Americans today.

Notes

This essay was originally published in *Wilson Quarterly* (Winter 2003): 22–29.

1. Rufus King to Elbridge Gerry, June 4, 1786, in Edmund Cody Burnett, ed., *Letters of the Members of the Continental Congress,* 8 vols. (Washington, DC, 1921–36), 8:380.

2. The quotations are all from Thomas Jefferson (hereafter TJ), First Inaugural Address, March 4, 1801, in Merrill D. Peterson, ed., *Thomas Jefferson Writings* (New York, 1984), 491–96; and TJ to Joseph Priestley, March 21, 1801, ibid., 1086.

3. Montesquieu, *The Spirit of the Laws* (1748), trans. and ed. Anne Cohler, Basia Miller, and Harold Stone (Cambridge, UK, 1989), bk. 8, chap. 16, 124.

4. James Madison, "Federalist No. 10," in Jacob E. Cooke, ed., *The Federalist* (Middletown, CT, 1961), 64.

5. Sen. William Wells, speech, Feb. 24, 1803, *Annals of the Congress of the United States, 1789–1824,* 42 vols. (Washington, DC, 1834–56), 7th Cong., 2d sess., 156; Rep. Samuel Purviance (NC), speech, Oct. 25, 1803, ibid., 8th Cong., 1st sess., 444.

6. TJ to Robert R. Livingston, April 18, 1802, in Peterson, ed., *Jefferson Writings,* 1105.

7. Rep. Joseph Nicholson, speech, Oct. 25, 1803, in *Annals of Congress,* 8th Cong., 1st sess., 466; "Sylvestris," *Reflections on the Cession of Louisiana to the United States* (Washington City, 1803), 13.

8. David Ramsay, *Oration on the Cession of Louisiana, to the United States* (Charleston, SC, 1804), 21.

9. TJ, Second Inaugural Address, March 4, 1805, in Peterson, ed., *Jefferson Writings,* 519.

10. TJ, Declaration of Independence, July 4, 1776, in Peterson, ed., *Jefferson Writings,* 19.

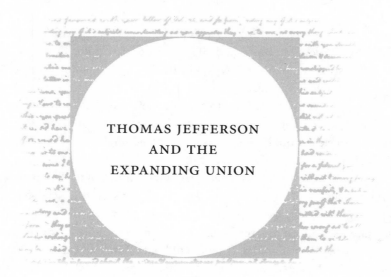

THOMAS JEFFERSON
AND THE
EXPANDING UNION

Thomas Jefferson exulted in prospects for western exploration, settlement, and economic development. Although he never traveled west himself, he was a voracious reader of travel accounts and an armchair natural philosopher with an insatiable thirst for new knowledge. For Jefferson the West was not a howling, dangerous wilderness but was instead what he called in his first inaugural address a "chosen country, with room enough for our descendants to the thousandth and thousandth generation."[1] Near the end of his life, Jefferson reaffirmed his faith in America's future. The progress of civilization was inscribed on the western landscape:

> I have observed this march of civilization advancing from the sea coast, passing over us like a cloud of light, increasing our knowledge and improving our condition, insomuch as that we are at this time more advanced in civilization here than the seaports were when I was a boy. And where this progress will stop no one can say. Barbarism has, in the meantime, been receding before the steady step of amelioration; and will in time, I trust, disappear from the earth.

This was what a later generation called "manifest destiny": civilization and empire inexorably moved westward as expansion across space recapitulated progress through time. In Jefferson's panoramic vista, the ascending stages of historical development could all be seen at once, from "the earliest stage of association" among the "savages of the Rocky Mountains" to the "most improved state in our seaport towns."[2]

Yet the story did not have to turn out this way. Jefferson knew all too well that different outcomes were possible: the fragile union of independent American states could collapse, as it nearly did on the eve of his election in 1800; without an effective union, the orderly expansion of westward settlement could be thwarted, as it had been during much of the colonial period, and perhaps even reversed. Or, more troubling still, the "semi-barbarous citizens" who swarmed across the frontiers could revert to savagery, subsisting all too easily on nature's bounty and turning their backs on civilization. Recognizing these realities, Jefferson did not hesitate to exercise the power of the federal state to shape and direct the progress of westward expansion.

Commerce

Fulfillment of Jefferson's prophetic vision depended on the expanding networks of trade that enterprising Americans sought to foster.[3] Without markets, why would settlers bother to produce surpluses? Without the reinforcement of common economic interests, how could political loyalties be sustained?

Jefferson's hostility to merchants is notorious—and hardly surprising for a tobacco planter who could never escape the thrall of debt to British creditors. For suspicious agrarians, merchants epitomized pure profit seeking; they lacked patriotic attachments to particular places, like Jefferson's "country," Virginia, and therefore any sense of public responsibility. Farmers therefore were, as he famously wrote in *Notes on the State of Virginia*, "the chosen people of God, if ever he had a chosen people, whose breasts he has made his peculiar deposit for substantial and genuine virtue." The independent husbandman relied on his "own soil and industry" for subsistence, while the dependence of all other classes begat "subservience and venality."[4] Jefferson did not equate independence with isolation, for it was the farmer's "virtue"—his unfettered, uncorrupted natural sociability—that constituted the most durable bond of union. But here was the crux of Jefferson's paradox: farmers could never escape market relations, for society itself was dependent on—if not synonymous with—"commerce" and "intercourse with the world."[5] It was hardly surprising, then, that the agrarian Jefferson should look *eastward*, toward "our seaport towns," for progressively higher forms of civilization. It was through these towns that Americans were connected to the centers of European civilization and to the commercial opportunities of the Atlantic trading system.

Of course, Jefferson believed Americans should certainly keep their distance from European vice and corruption: this was the animating impulse of his expansionist faith. At the same time, however, he recognized the need to improve and perfect commercial ties between Old World and New, to free trade from the distorting effects of mercantilist regulations and thus to bring American producers and European consumers closer together. Jefferson's agrarianism juxtaposed virtuous farmers to avaricious merchants, but the territorial expansion that would create a great "empire of liberty" depended on a synthesis of his antithetical terms. In Jefferson's paradoxical vision, enterprising Americans would come together by moving apart. Americans therefore would have to develop a transportation and communication infrastructure across their vast continental domain. Providentially, nature showed the way, in the great system of rivers that would link farmers to distant markets, transforming inland trading centers into bustling "seaports." The cement of union was man's sociable nature, the tendency of independent individuals to associate for mutual protection and improvement and to exchange the fruits of their labors. But "nature" would have to be mapped and surveyed, mastered and improved, if man's natural potential were to be fulfilled. The first challenge was to clear the field of rival claimants.

External Enemies

The West not simply a blank state during the early years of the republic. The Indian peoples who inhabited the region constituted formidable obstacles to the progress of American settlement. But they also possessed invaluable information about the continent and its resources that Jefferson and his fellow citizens sought to exploit. In return, Americans offered trade goods that were already familiar in Indian country and the less tangible promise of "civilization." In philanthropic moments, Jefferson looked forward to the assimilation of these native proprietors, imagining that one day they would "form one people with us, and we shall all be Americans."[6] But that prospect was distant at best, for the Indians were reluctant to give up their "barbarous" way of life—and the vast hunting grounds needed to support it. Too often they were abetted by the new nation's enemies. Pawns of corrupt European empires, Indians tragically resisted the spread of republican civilization, their only hope for survival in the modern world.[7]

In his inaugural address, Jefferson celebrated the happy fact that "a wide ocean" separated the New World from the "exterminating havoc" of the Old. But Europe was very much present in the American hinterland, and its influence was felt—or imagined—in the belligerent posture of the "merciless Indian savages." Jeffersonians conceived of conflicts along the frontier in ideological terms, imputing hostilities to the counterrevolutionary, anti-republican principles of European imperial rivals and their Indian proxies. War against the Indians—even a war that would lead to their removal or extermination—was thus seen as yet another phase of the republican revolution against Old World tyranny and despotism. That Europeans would deploy "savage" auxiliaries against the Americans merely confirmed their reactionary antipathy to the progress of civilization; that Indians would align with corrupt Europeans rather than with their true countrymen, the Americans, showed that there was no place for them on the continent.[8]

American Revolutionaries articulated the Enlightenment's faith in the progress of civilization in political terms. Adherence to republican principles, Jefferson's fundamental definition of Americanism, justified and disguised less exalted means and motives. The geopolitical rivalries in the West that would determine the republic's future do not seem, in retrospect—or to skeptical contemporaries—to have much to do with principles. The same enterprising impulses that attracted Americans—the fur trade, land speculation, the expansion of commercial agriculture—inspired European projects in the region. The great question was who would control the port of New Orleans, and with it the trade of the inland empire of the Mississippi River system. This was a central issue in American politics from the time of the Revolution onward. The Revolutionary generation understood that the continuing union of East and West ultimately depended on extending American jurisdiction across the Appalachian Mountains, and this in turn depended on diplomacy and power politics.

Because the new nation was surrounded by enemies, its continuing expansion was by no means assured. Visionaries like Jefferson might see the spread of republican institutions and the addition of new states to the federal union as inevitable, but no one expected the process to be smooth or peaceful. Patriotic Americans who celebrated the Louisiana Purchase were amazed and relieved that it came so cheaply, that war—the preemptive strike on New Orleans urged by Federalists or the mass mobilization of American settlers threatened by political adventurers upriver—had not been necessary after all. Jefferson hoped to avoid armed conflict, less because of his pacifistic principles than because he feared, with good reason, that the Americans might lose and the union collapse. One day, when American settlements spread thickly across the continent, the new nation would be impregnable. Once the landscape had been transformed and the patriotic attachments of an enterprising yeomanry were well secured, the United States would be, as Jefferson promised in his inaugural, "the strongest Government on earth."[9] But that day had not yet arrived at the time of the Louisiana crisis, and not even after the threat of a powerful French presence at the mouth of the river was miraculously averted by the Purchase. For the greatest threats to the survival of the union came from internal, not external, sources.

Centrifugal Tendencies

For many contemporary commentators, including the anxious governors of neighboring empires, the spread of American settlements seemed to be an irresistible, almost natural force. When Americans insisted that the United States had a "natural right" to New Orleans and the mouth of the Mississippi, they warned that rapidly increasing frontier settlements eventually would enforce their demand for free trade on the river, whatever diplomats might decide. There was a strong undercurrent of anxiety in this expansionist rhetoric, for the American government was itself powerless to control the tide of settlement. And Jefferson knew that settlers' loyalties were tenuous, that economic interest could lead them to pledge allegiance to whatever power could secure them access to the Atlantic trading system. Commerce might draw Americans together in a harmonious union of interests, but it might just as easily divide them. Just as nature had to be improved to facilitate the spread of republican civilization, so trade had to be directed into the right channels. Jefferson and his fellow agrarians railed against merchants, the "foreign and false citizens" without patriotic attachments to their country who infested "our sea ports" and "are planted in every little town and district of the interior country."[10] But it was equally, and more ominously, true that the loyalties of the "chosen people" themselves—the enterprising land speculators and commercial farmers who spearheaded expansion—were also for sale.

The problem of loyalties was central to the Revolution. Republicanism was a risky experiment, for a people who abjured allegiance to the king might also turn against the governors they had chosen for themselves. One revolution could lead to another, fearful conservatives worried, and the result would be anarchy. Their concerns were justified: there were separatist movements in frontier regions of almost every state, from the Maine District of Massachusetts to the new state of Franklin in the western region of North Carolina; and although most separatists proclaimed their fealty to the Revolutionary cause (even while challenging the authority of the original states in the union), they sometimes looked to Britain or Spain for support in their political enterprises. The renegade state of Vermont (formerly the northeastern counties of New York) was most successful in pursuing an independent, potentially counterrevolutionary "foreign" policy, entering into secret negotiations with the British while the Revolution was still in progress; political adventurers in Kentucky conspired with Spanish officials in New Orleans, even after their new state gained its independence from Virginia. Separatism was attractive because settlers had serious grievances against the states that claimed jurisdiction over them, but failed to establish effective legal and governmental institutions and offered little protection against Indian enemies. The most compelling issue in almost every case was conflict over land titles, as the old states sought to protect the interests of land speculators who acted under their authority from the challenges of "foreign" squatters and speculators. Kentucky remained a hotbed of political discontent throughout the early national period precisely because there was so much confusion over conflicting land claims.[11]

Conflicts of interest over land titles belied and inverted the Jeffersonian image of the virtuous and independent yeoman freeholder. The frontier farmer's patriotism could not be taken for granted, as the solid foundation of a stable republican edifice, but would instead be the *result* of the successful resolution of endemic jurisdictional conflicts. The future of the union was also jeopardized by sectional divisions among the old states. If separatist movements generally reflected east-west tensions, focusing immediately on land and Indian policy, incipient sectionalism grew out of controversy over national commercial policy between northern mercantile interests and southern staple producers. The ultimate question in both cases was: How would different sectors of the economy and sections of the country best fit into the Atlantic trading system?

Controversy over the future of the West and over the continuing union of North and South came to a head in the late 1790s and in the first years of Jefferson's presidency. Chafing under the domination of northern High

Federalists, Jeffersonian Republicans broached the possibility of secession in 1798; had the election impasse of 1800 not been resolved in their favor, they were prepared to jettison the federal Constitution and the union that it had created. Soon thereafter, Spanish threats to close the Mississippi and rumors that Napoleon meant to erect a new French empire in the American hinterland revived anxieties about the political future of settlements in the Northwest Territory (Ohio), in the new states of Kentucky and Tennessee, and in the far western reaches of Georgia.

Jefferson articulated his confident vision of America's future at a time when the new nation's prospects were more in doubt than they had been since the darkest days of the Revolution—or would again be until the eve of the Civil War. How could he say that this was "the strongest Government on earth," when its weaknesses were so manifest and divisions among Americans were so conspicuous?

Bonds of Union

It was the conventional wisdom of Jefferson's day, most influentially set forth by Montesquieu in his *Spirit of the Laws,* that republican government could only survive and prosper in small states.[12] The principle of consent operated most effectively in compact societies where virtuous citizens could share common values and interests. The preservation of a large state, by this logic, required a powerful, even despotic, government that could enforce its authority on distant provinces. How then could Americans hope to enjoy the benefits of republican self-government in a large, expanding federal union? Was "empire of liberty" a contradiction in terms?

For Jefferson the answer to the problem of size was not to be found in the kind of "energetic" central government Alexander Hamilton and his fellow High Federalists sought to create but, rather, in the patriotic attachments of citizens of who fully embraced "federal and republican principles." Jefferson believed that order emerged spontaneously in a self-governing people when traditional distinctions between rulers and ruled were obliterated and citizens were conscious of their rights and duties. In his apotheosis of popular patriotism, Jefferson was a precocious nationalist, homogenizing differences in a transcendent conception of nationhood that counteracted the centrifugal tendencies of expansion. Precisely because a despotic central government did not seek to impose order, "every man, at the call of the law, would fly to the standard of the law, and would meet invasions of the public

order as his own personal concern."[13] The American Revolution demonstrated the power of patriotic appeals in time of crisis: when the distinction
between "public" and "personal" was dissolved, the power of the people was
irresistible.

Jefferson was an astute political psychologist. He recognized that the
United States did not have the coercive resources to govern recalcitrant
and unruly frontier settlers: if they were to be governed at all, they would
have to govern themselves. But this did not mean that there was no place
for an active federal state in Jefferson's empire of liberty. To the contrary, it
was incumbent on the United States government to clear the way for settlement through diplomatic negotiations with imperial neighbors whose success depended on a credible threat of force. The goals of Jeffersonian diplomacy—to insulate the union from external danger and to provide space for
expansion—justified the resort to any means necessary, as the Louisiana crisis and subsequent efforts to extend American jurisdiction in West Florida
demonstrated. After all, the first law of nature was self-preservation: the
need to secure vital national interests preempted any moral or constitutional scruples. The future of the American nation depended on a statecraft
that could create the kind of homogenous, empty space Jefferson imagined
in his inaugural address, a "chosen country" for a "chosen people."

Jefferson's Indian policy also depended on the exercise of power, through
diplomacy and war, to achieve the same goals. Ever responsive to the agitation of land-hungry settlers, Jefferson always gave highest priority to acquiring new lands. In peacetime, the threat of force could be concealed, as
market pressures led indebted Indians to relinquish their property volun-
tarily. Federal negotiators also offered aid and assistance to Indian efforts to
become "civilized," often in collaboration with the philanthropic initiatives
of Christian missionaries. The net result, whether in war or peace, was to
speed the retreat and removal of Indian nations as distinct political societies
that could threaten the security of the federal republic or block its continuing expansion. If, in the process, a few civilized Indians blended into the
tide of white settlement, all the better. In any case, however, the federal state
played a central role, giving "nature" a powerful assist by clearing Indians
off the land.

The paradox of expansion in Jeffersonian America was that a supposedly
spontaneous, natural process depended so crucially on the exercise of state
power. Government played a key role in collecting and circulating useful
knowledge to facilitate settlement and economic development, in securing

property rights and promoting commercial exchange by extending republican institutions and rule of law, and in promoting the internal improvements that would enable farmers and planters to get their surpluses to distant markets. Federal land policy was the centerpiece of this orderly, state-directed process of settlement and development. By surveying and selling the national domain according to the provisions of the Congressional Land Ordinance of 1785 (based on a system proposed by Jefferson and fellow committee members the previous year), the land office provided critical information that enabled settlers to make informed choices about recouping their investments in an expanding system of market relations. The purchaser of federal lands thus represented the antithesis of the subsistence-oriented squatter, or "white savage," who would have been perfectly content to live off the land. Under the federal land system, enterprising and orderly settlers were selected from the larger stream of potential migrants; the government pledged to uphold their titles against all other claimants, including squatters. Grateful for this protection, citizens in the territories and new states would rally to "the standard of the law" in time of crisis.

Jefferson's faith in popular patriotism was thus not based on a naively optimistic conception of human nature. Americans in newly settled frontier regions would *become* good republicans as they sought to improve their condition within established systems of economic and political opportunity. As Jefferson suggested, individual choices provided the dynamic energy for expansion, but these choices were structured in ways that drew settlers together and thus strengthened the union. By guaranteeing the rapid introduction of institutions of self-government, the territorial system channeled political ambitions into statehood aspirations, thus preempting the appeal of separatist movements—and foreign alliances. The development of Republican party organizations in frontier areas rationalized the distribution of federal contracts and patronage in order to foster the emergence of local political elites loyal to the union. If the achievement of statehood eliminated some of this federal largesse, it also opened a wide new field for political ambition, both in state and federal politics. That new states, despite their small populations, should enjoy equal representation in the U.S. Senate constituted one of the strongest bonds of union. Far from being kept in a permanent state of colonial subjection, new western states would be guaranteed equal standing in the union. Just as republicanism obliterated the traditional distinction between rulers and ruled, so an expanding federal union collapsed the traditional distance between center and periphery, metropolis and provinces.

Jefferson's vision of republican empire, of an expanding union of self-governing republics, represented a bold departure from historic precedents. But the vision, by invoking the beneficent operations of "nature" in a vast, fertile, virgin landscape and by stipulating a virtuous, patriotic citizenry ready to exploit its gifts, was profoundly misleading. Both terms of Jefferson's equation were problematic: the "chosen country" had already been "chosen" by others, and the loyalties of American settlers were notoriously volatile. Any number of outcomes were possible: the "manifest destiny" of an expanding nation was only one of them, and not necessarily the most likely. To fulfill his vision, the continent would have to be explored, surveyed, sold, settled, integrated into expanding market relations, and incorporated into the union on an equal basis. In all of these areas, the federal government would play a decisive, continuing role.

Federal involvement in the development of the trans-Mississippi West grew out of diplomatic and scientific initiatives in Jefferson's first term. The Lewis and Clark Expedition helped open this vast domain to successive waves of adventurers, entrepreneurs, and settlers. To many contemporary commentators—and subsequent celebrants of America's "manifest destiny"—the rapid progress of republican "civilization" seemed spontaneous and inexorable, even "natural." Westward expansion, as Jefferson envisioned it in his first inaugural, could thus be seen as the ultimate vindication of his conception of minimal, limited government, the form of government that best conformed to nature's laws. Yet we can now clearly see that Lewis and Clark were enacting much more human designs, projecting federal power into a contested region where European empires sought to establish their own influence and authority and where native peoples sought to secure their ancestral lands. And the federal government would continue to play a critical, even essential, role in fostering expansion as it protected vulnerable settlements, founded civil governments, distributed resources, and promoted economic development. Nowhere else in the far-flung republican empire did the federal government exercise such extensive powers.[14] The mythology of popular sovereignty, limited government, and manifest destiny may indeed have been (and still be) so powerfully appealing to westerners, and to their countrymen generally, because it disguised and mystified the dependence of independent-minded, liberty-loving, self-governing Americans on the power of the federal state.

Notes

This essay was originally published in Alan Taylor, ed., *Lewis and Clark: Journey to Another America* (St. Louis: OASIS Institute and the Missouri Historical Society Press, 2003).

1. Thomas Jefferson (hereafter TJ), First Inaugural Address, March 4, 1801, in Merrill D. Peterson, ed., *Thomas Jefferson Writings* (New York, 1984), 494. On Jefferson's interest in the West, see Donald Jackson, *Jefferson and the Stony Mountains: Exploring the West from Monticello* (Urbana, IL, 1981).

2. TJ to William Ludlow, Sept. 6, 1824, in Peterson, ed., *Jefferson Writings,* 1497, 1496.

3. On the political economy of westward expansion, see Drew R. McCoy, *The Elusive Republic: Political Economy in Jeffersonian America* (Chapel Hill, NC, 1980). For a scathing indictment of expansionist ideology, see Albert K. Weinberg, *Manifest Destiny: A Study in Nationalist Expansionism in American History* (Baltimore, 1935).

4. TJ, Query 19 ("Manufactures"), in William Peden, ed., *Notes on the State of Virginia* (Chapel Hill, 1954), 165.

5. TJ to Justice William Johnson, Oct. 27, 1822, in Peterson, ed., *Jefferson Writings,* 1460.

6. TJ to Captain Hendrick, the Delawares, Mohicans, and Munries, Dec. 21, 1808, in Andrew A. Lipscomb and Albert Ellery Bergh, eds., *The Writings of Thomas Jefferson,* 20 vols. (Washington, DC, 1903–4), 16:452.

7. Jefferson's attitudes toward the continent's native proprietors are comprehensively treated in two excellent studies: Bernard W. Sheehan, *Seeds of Extinction: Jeffersonian Philanthropy and the American Indian* (Chapel Hill, NC, 1973); and Anthony F. C. Wallace, *Jefferson and the Indians: The Tragic Fate of the First Americans* (Cambridge, MA, 1999). See also Peter S. Onuf, *Jefferson's Empire: The Language of American Nationhood* (Charlottesville, VA, 2000), chap. 1.

8. TJ, Declaration of Independence, July 4, 1776, in Peterson, ed., *Jefferson Writings,* 21. The premises of Jeffersonian diplomacy are critically dissected in Robert W. Tucker and David C. Hendrickson, *Empire of Liberty: The Statecraft of Thomas Jefferson* (New York, 1990).

9. TJ, First Inaugural Address, March 4, 1801, in Peterson, ed., *Jefferson Writings,* 493.

10. TJ to Elbridge Gerry, May 13, 1797, in Lipscomb and Bergh, eds., *Writings of Jefferson,* 9:383.

11. The early history of separatist movements and early American land and territorial policy is recounted in Peter S. Onuf, *The Origins of the Federal Republic: Jurisdictional Conflicts in the United States, 1775–1787* (Philadelphia, 1983); and idem, *Statehood and Union: A History of the Northwest Ordinance* (Bloomington, IN, 1987).

12. Montesquieu, *The Spirit of the Laws* (1748), trans. and ed. Anne Cohler, Basia Miller, and Harold Stone (Cambridge, UK, 1989), bk. 8, chap. 16, 124.

13. TJ, First Inaugural Address, March 4, 1801, in Peterson, ed., *Jefferson Writings*, 493.

14. For a lively introduction to ongoing contests for control of the West, highlighting the crucial controversial role of the federal government, see Patricia Nelson Limerick, *The Legacy of Conquest: The Unbroken Past of the American West* (New York, 1987).

THE LOUISIANA
PURCHASE
AND AMERICAN
FEDERALISM

The United States began as a loose union of thirteen Anglo-American colonies that declared their independence in 1776. This first union was a kind of diplomatic and military alliance, as suggested by the use of the term "congress" to describe successive assemblies of delegates from the colony-states. Revolutionary Americans understood the crucial importance of sustaining and perfecting that union in order to make good on their claims to independence. Effective interstate cooperation was predicated on an "energetic" central government that could take the place of the former imperial government, mobilizing the resources of the continent on behalf of the common cause and presenting a single face to the "powers of the world."[1] The United States thus took on a novel, hybrid character that defied the logic of contemporary political science. The goal of most Revolutionary patriots was to establish a reformed, republican *empire*, purged of old regime corruption, that preserved the separate existence of its far-flung members; yet they also recognized the necessity of constituting themselves into a single *nation* in their relations with the larger world. The potential conflict between these conceptions of union, the logical conundrum of *"imperium in imperio,"* was played out in the subsequent history of American federalism.[2]

The separate states never aspired to full sovereignty and independence with respect to each other. To the contrary, the most compelling argument against the break with Britain was that these former provinces would be left in a "state of nature" that inevitably would degenerate into anarchic licentiousness. Thus when the states declared independence, they simultaneously pledged not to exercise the full array of powers sovereignties could claim. Yet that pledge implied a threat, that fealty to the union was conditional on its success in securing the essential rights and interests of its respective members. If the conditions were violated, the separate states would resume a sovereignty they had never actually exercised, thus fulfilling the direst prophecies of the imperial loyalists who had balked at independence in the first place. Disunion would unleash the "dogs of war," leaving the states far worse off than they had ever been under British rule.

No good American could countenance the collapse of a union that alone could guarantee a prosperous and peaceful future for the American people collectively. Thomas Jefferson eloquently articulated that promise in his first inaugural address: the new nation was "kindly separated by nature and a wide ocean from the exterminating havoc of one quarter of the globe; too high-minded to endure the degradations of the others; possessing a chosen country, with room enough for our descendants to the thousandth and thousandth generation."[3] Jefferson was inclined to take the long view in 1801, confident as he was that the union had been redeemed from the incubus of High Federalism in the "Revolution of 1800." But the author of the Kentucky Resolutions had been less sanguine about the prospects of union in 1798. Then Jefferson was acutely sensitive to the danger that the government of the union, as it was actually constituted and administered, could work to the advantage of some Americans (Anglophile "aristocrats" and "monocrats") and to the disadvantage of others (the silent, or silenced, majority of virtuous Republicans).[4]

Jefferson's flirtation with disunion set the stage for his apotheosis of union in the wake of his electoral "revolution." Union and disunion stood in a dialectical relation for Jefferson and his contemporaries: one defined and even invited the other. If peace and prosperity were so all important, then patriotic statesmen must be prepared to make any necessary compromise or concession to prevent aggrieved states from following through on threats to withdraw from, and thus destroy, the union. Although no state crossed that fatal threshold, with the exception of South Carolina in its abortive efforts to nullify the tariff in 1832, until the mass exodus of eleven Southern states in 1861, the possibility that a state or bloc of states could destroy the union always enhanced its bargaining power in the arena of federal politics.

The ratification of the federal Constitution did not preempt disunionist threats or establish a "more perfect union." At the time of the Louisiana Purchase in 1803, the character and future prospects of the federal union were as unstable and indeterminate as they had been either in 1776 or 1787. The Purchase exacerbated chronic tensions, most conspicuously in the growing alienation of Federalist New England over the next decade, even while seeming to resolve others. Controversy revolved around the great question of size: how much further could the "extended republic" Madison celebrated in Federalist No. 10 extend, without attenuating the ties of union and unleashing dangerously centrifugal forces?[5] Would a dynamic, expansive union jeopardize the complicated set of intersectional compromises incorporated in the federal Constitution? Or, to frame the same problem in different terms, would westward expansion ameliorate or exacerbate the sectional conflicts that had periodically surfaced during the party battles of the 1790s? And, finally, how well could the government of the enlarged union secure the collective interests of the American states and people against external threats? The danger in all cases was that a fragile American peace that depended on sustaining an effective union would give way to escalating conflict and war.

Jefferson's Louisiana diplomacy has gotten poor reviews by most diplomatic historians. "Realists" are inclined to diminish his active role in this epochal transaction and to emphasize his (undeserved) good luck—and the heroic efforts of Haitian revolutionaries in thwarting Napoleon's design for western empire. By contrast, political historians, noting popular enthusiasm for the Purchase throughout the union, are more inclined to grant the visionary Jefferson his due: anti-expansionist Federalists were, like the anti-Federalists during ratification, "men of little faith" who failed to grasp the dynamic genius of the federal system, reflected in a continuous process of new state creation that augmented national wealth and power. The two contrasting versions of Jeffersonian politics can be sustained because historians are too prone to distinguish diplomacy and domestic politics, and therefore to link federalism issues to ongoing party conflicts over the distribution of power within the union. But the distinction between foreign and domestic is by no means a neat one, at least until the Treaty of Ghent in 1814 and the end of the Napoleonic Wars, and perhaps not even then.[6]

The Louisiana Purchase should be seen as merely one aspect of a revolutionary realignment in American politics that began with the election of a Republican president and Congress in 1800. The Republican ascendancy strengthened the union in the short run, but it also exposed new threats to its long-term prospects. High Federalists had been hostile to states' rights, seemingly intent on diminishing the states to a clearly subordinate, dependent role in the federal system, if not on abolishing them altogether. By contrast, Republican receptivity to new state formation, beginning with Ohio (1803) and promised to other territories in the national domain under the terms of western land cessions to Congress—a promise now extended to citizens and settlers in the trans-Mississippi region under the terms of the Louisiana Treaty—represented a vindication of states' rights generally.

East-West

The paradoxical premise of Republican expansionism was that the union grew stronger as federal government's territorial regime gave way to statehood and republican self-government. This was the western equivalent of the Jeffersonian claim that Federalist measures to strengthen the union by concentrating power in the central government in fact constituted the greatest threat to the union's survival. Only when the federal balance was restored—and states' rights secured—would the union be truly powerful, for it was the broad consent of a patriotic and grateful people that made the government of the United States "the strongest Government on earth."[7] As long as frontier settlers were frustrated in their quest for statehood— and could not therefore consider the interests of the union as a whole as their "own personal concern"—they constituted potential enemies, allies of any foreign state that would respond more expeditiously to their legitimate demands. Outside of the union, frontier separatists and speculators were all too willing to entertain overtures from America's imperial rivals: future President Andrew Jackson was not alone in taking a loyalty oath to the King of Spain.

The Republican policy of co-opting frontier dissidence through new state formation thus combined an equal measure of political realism with its lofty appeal to republican principles. Challenging and inverting the axiom in contemporary political science—and Federalist policy—that expansion required the strengthening of central governmental power in order to offset its diminished effectiveness over increasing distances, Jeffersonians insisted that the rapid expansion of the union would transform potential enemies into patriots, thus diminishing the need to resort to coercive force. The states would, in turn, constitute a solid buttress against any future effort to consolidate power in the central government. "The true barriers of our liberty in this country are our State governments," Jefferson explained to the Frenchman Destutt de Tracy in 1811 in one of his most sustained commentaries on federalism. In France, by contrast, "republican government . . . was lost without a struggle," and Napoleon rose to power "because the party of 'un et indivisible' had prevailed; no provincial organizations existed to which the people might rally under authority of the laws, the seats of the directory were virtually vacant, and a small force sufficed to turn the legislature out of their chamber, and to salute its leader chief of the nation."[8]

The question of size in the political thought of Jefferson's day was dominated by Montesquieu's famous dictum that republican government could only survive in a small state and that monarchy was better suited to a unitary regime of continental dimensions. Jefferson's colleague James Madison countered Montesquieu during the debate over ratification of the federal Constitution by arguing that the proliferation of "factions" or interests in an "extended republic" would prevent any single interest from gaining a dominant position.[9] Jefferson's letter to Destutt built on Madison's pluralist analysis, but foregrounded the role of states rather than factions in maintaining an explicitly federal balance rather than the more complicated and diffuse system of countervailing forces envisioned by Madison. A history of party conflict since ratification had taught both Madison and Jefferson that struggles over the character of the federal union constituted the fundamental fault line of American politics. The challenge was to avoid a consolidation of authority at the center that would give rise to an American Napoleon while curbing dangerously centrifugal tendencies at the periphery and so secure a genuinely federal balance.

The extravagant language of Jefferson's first inaugural seemed to suggest that the patriotic loyalties of a grateful people were alone sufficient to sustain the union, and that these loyalties would be strengthened by curbing the power of the central government. Jefferson did believe that the division and diffusion of authority could facilitate political and military mobilization at a time of national crisis, translating the theory of popular sovereignty into something approaching political reality. But Jeffersonian federalism was not predicated on a libertarian fantasy that there could be union without government.[10] Jeffersonian policy toward new state creation reveals a much more complex, "realistic" understanding.

The key premise of Jefferson's approach was that settlers in frontier regions constituted potential enemies of the union—and counterrevolutionary tools of America's imperial rivals—until they were organized as states and incorporated in the union. Far from eschewing the use of force in foreign affairs, Jefferson did not hesitate to exercise executive authority on behalf of vital national interests: the first law of nature, self-preservation, might require him to lead the nation into another war—or it might justify the purchase and annexation of a vast new territory. Within strict constitutional limits, the president's authority to conduct foreign policy—like the monarch's prerogative—was absolute. The French had taken yet another wrong turn during the period of the Directory (1796–1800) when they created a plural executive, even as they fatefully centralized authority and abolished lesser jurisdictions. Jeffersonian federalism thus depended on "unity of action and direction in all the branches of the [federal] government" under a strong, unitary executive. The several states remained "single and independent as to their internal administration" and so stood ready to resist any encroachments on their legitimate rights, but as Jefferson explained to Destutt, were "amalgamated into one as to their foreign concerns." If the machinery of state government were ever turned against the union itself, if "certain States from local and occasional discontents, might attempt to secede from the Union" and thus make themselves foreigners, then the federal government could direct its full force against them.[11] Or, as Jefferson told another correspondent in 1814, when secessionist sentiment was rampant in New England, "I see our safety in the extent of our confederacy, and in the probability that in the proportion of that the sound parts will always be sufficient to crush local poisons."[12] The incorporation of new states would guarantee their "soundness," preempting tendencies to align with foreign enemies, and thus increase the ratio of "sound parts" to diseased in the federal body politic.

But why should new states be so eager to join the union? In the Revolutionary era, frontier separatists epitomized the selfish, calculating impulses that threatened to undermine the territorial integrity of the respective states and thus destroy the union; in subsequent decades, a tawdry history of land speculation and political adventurism on the periphery of the union only served to reinforce anti-expansionist skepticism. Although Jefferson might wax eloquent about the virtuous yeomanry, he had no illusions about their semisavage western cousins. Instead, he understood, interest was the pivot of western loyalty. Westerners would *become* good patriots if they calculated that the prospective advantages of membership in the union outweighed the risks—including the possibility that the federal government of the union might one day make war against them.

Preserving the peace thus constituted a leading motive for both the federal government and for frontier settlers in promoting new state formation. Other incentives naturally followed. First, statehood would enable an emergent political elite to consolidate its authority locally, shaking off the taint of complicity in a territorial regime that kept the citizenry in a condition of "colonial" subjection to congressional overlords while enhancing their access to the federal trough. In the Northwest Territory, for instance, Republicans who had railed against the "corruption" and "despotism" of Federalist Governor Arthur St. Clair leveraged partisan connections with the new Jefferson administration to accelerate statehood and secure control over both federal and state patronage. Simple political arithmetic guaranteed that the national administration would assiduously cultivate the new state leadership: lightly populated Ohio (with a population of 45,365, according to the 1800 census) would send the same number of senators to Washington as Virginia, the most populous state (807,557 in 1800). With the progress of settlement, the disparity would quickly disappear (by 1840, Ohio's population was approximately 50 percent greater than Virginia's), but in the meantime Ohio and other new states would enjoy disproportionate influence in federal councils. That influence could be used to distribute concrete rewards to the political elite, its clients, and constituents generally. The privatization of public (federal) lands was, in the case of most new states, the most lucrative bonanza, but much was to be gained as well from political appointments, government contracts, internal improvements, and other forms of federal expenditure.[13]

These appeals to self-interest constituted a solid foundation for the patriotic sentiments Jefferson invoked in his first inaugural. Jefferson understood that the same forces that had once jeopardized the survival of the states and the union could be redirected toward strengthening and perfecting the union. Preserving a balance between states and union that would secure their distinct spheres of authority was the great desideratum of Jeffersonian federalism, but this balance could only be sustained by a dynamic and expansive political system that made states and union functionally interdependent and promoted the constant circulation of men and resources between periphery and center. The Republican party mediated between theory and practice, linking political elites in the states to the central administration. The party therefore must avoid divisions, Jefferson told disgruntled editor William Duane in 1811, for it alone could sustain the union: "If we schismatize . . . our *nation* will be undone. For the republicans are the *nation*."[14]

Jeffersonian federalism was most successful in containing and redirecting the centrifugal tendencies of westward expansion by drawing political elites in frontier regions into a dynamic national political system. If the federal Constitution decentralized authority, thus making union depend on the uncoerced consent of sovereign states, the Republican party institutionalized that consent, directing political ambitions toward the center. Yet the balance resulting from these offsetting tendencies—centrifugal in the formal constitution, centripetal in the informal—proved highly unstable. As Jefferson's letter to Duane indicated, the national party had to preserve a common front on "men and measures" in order to "resist its enemies within and without." Party unity was essential "during the *bellum omnium in omnia* of Europe," at a time when a resurgent Federalist party exploited escalating divisions over foreign policy to recoup its fortunes. But what would the state of the Republican party be when the threat of foreign war diminished or when the Federalists ceased to act effectively as a national opposition party? Within only a few years, the end of the War of 1812 and the disgrace of the Federalists who had broached secession at the Hartford Convention (1814) would test the durability of the national Republican party—and therefore of the union itself.

Jeffersonian federalism worked most effectively on an east-west axis, preempting separatist impulses through new state creation and national party building. The ongoing struggle to secure the republican experiment against counterrevolutionary forces at home—the Federalists—and abroad—the British, the Spanish, or even, in the case of Louisiana, the French—provided the larger context for this dynamic, expansive concept of union. In his first inaugural address, Jefferson underscored the connections between the spirit of 1776 and its revival in 1800, between the Republican party and the American nation; he also suggested that westward expansion itself constituted the logical continuation and culmination of the American Revolutionary project. To later advocates of "manifest destiny," Jefferson's language seemed visionary, anticipating and legitimating vast annexations of territory. By 1815, however, the original context for Jefferson's paean to westward expansion—"the *bellum omnium in omnia*" in Europe and national partisan conflict in America—no longer existed. As party discipline eroded, new threats to vital state and sectional interests emerged. Opening up the West to rapid settlement and new state formation did not necessarily or obviously strengthen the union. A growing sense that slaveholding southern planters, the original core of the Republican party, were the chief beneficiaries of westward expansion exposed a "geographical line" of distinction, a more fundamental north-south axis that would define the subsequent history of American federalism.[15]

Federalist critics of Jefferson's Louisiana Purchase in 1803 presciently grasped this fundamental reorientation. The Federalists who later opposed Louisiana statehood in 1811 were powerless to resist the Republican juggernaut, signaling instead their own disgrace and ultimate demise. But they also glimpsed the new fault line on which the union would eventually collapse.

North-South

Federalist anti-expansionists dissented from every premise of Jeffersonian federalism. Beginning with their controversial Jay Treaty (1794), Federalists had long advocated closer relations with Britain, thus rejecting Jefferson's notion that American independence depended on a kind of permanent revolution against the former imperial metropolis. If the Federalists' advocacy of Anglo-American alliance reflected a realistic assessment both of the European balance of power and of America's relative weakness as a secondary power, it also suggested that there was no fundamental difference between the new nation's republican regime and that of monarchical Britain—and that the power differential would be overcome in due time through nation-building policies that concentrated authority in the central government. These were all "heresies" to orthodox Republicans like Jefferson, evoking Montesquieu's discredited dictum that the preservation of a state of imperial dimensions depended on the consolidation of power in a vigorous, potentially despotic central government. If the new nation simply aspired to be another Britain or if it submitted to the superior power of the old mother country in a counterrevolutionary alliance against republican France, what was the point of American independence?

Jefferson's election in 1800, the temporary cessation of the French revolutionary wars culminating in the Peace of Amiens (1802), and the Louisiana Purchase seemed to answer these questions definitively—at least for the time being. The United States, now miraculously extricated from European politics, could fulfill its continental destiny without betraying its republican ideals. The American union, as one enthusiastic Republican orator exclaimed, soon would be recognized as "the wonder of the world, and more formidable to the irruptions of tyranny, than were Chinese walls to Tartar hordes."[16] But what sort of union did these Jeffersonians envision? Could it be entirely impartial—to all states, sections, or interests—in the benefits it distributed? Was isolation from external threat the sufficient condition for the progressive perfection of the republican regime? Federalists' skepticism on all these counts proved amply justified.

Federalist concerns about the implications of rapid westward expansion reflected a prior history of interstate and intersectional controversy in the United States while anticipating future conflicts. When the Constitution was drafted in Philadelphia, delegates negotiated an elaborate series of interdependent compromises that at least temporarily assuaged the most conspicuous conflicts of interest, most notably between the staple-producing (and slaveholding) states to the south and the more diversified, commercial-oriented states of the Northeast. The coincidental resolution of the long-standing controversy over the western land claims of the large "landed" states that had jeopardized the union throughout the Confederation period constituted yet another crucial compromise. States with claims in the trans-Ohio region—Massachusetts, Connecticut, New York, and Virginia—ceded them to Congress under condition that land sales in the new national domain generate revenue for the union as a whole, while congressionally administered territories be prepared for statehood and eventual incorporation in the union. Subsequent cessions from North Carolina and Georgia gave Congress jurisdiction over the Southwest as well as the Northwest, setting the stage for the spread of settlement and expansion of the union throughout the original limits of the United States as defined in the Paris Peace Treaty of 1783.[17]

The creation of the national domain and the subsequent elaboration of Congress's western policy involved complicated calculations of their impact on state and regional interests. New Englanders could anticipate settlement opportunities for their surplus population in addition to the indirect benefits of national lands sales revenue; given the domination of Yankee settlers, the first new state formed in the Northwest Territory might well align itself with New England in the federal political arena. Virginians were equally persuaded that economic and geopolitical logic would draw all new states into their own expanding hinterland. These calculations were periodically recalibrated in subsequent decades, particularly as westerners began to articulate their own distinct interests—namely, in liberalizing land sales and promoting internal improvements. But the underlying concern with the impact of expansion on the existing balance of power in the union remained—and would remain—paramount. The Jeffersonian "Revolution of 1800" may have banished the specter of a high-toned, energetic national government, but it did not diminish the salience of conventional calculations of relative advantage within the union. Americans would continue to calculate the value of the union until the union itself finally collapsed.

Critics of the Louisiana Purchase charged that the annexation of this vast new territory subverted the compromises that secured vital sectional interests in the federal Constitution. These compromises were predicated on the new nation's 1783 boundaries, limits that Jefferson conspicuously overlooked in his inaugural. The intersectional balance negotiated at Philadelphia allowed for limited expansion: delegates understood that new states would be created in the national domain, and perhaps within the limits of some of the larger states. But expansion beyond the new nation's original boundaries was "unconstitutional," both from the perspective of the sort of "strict construction" Jefferson ordinarily favored and because the hard bargaining at Philadelphia that made union possible depended on respecting those limits. Would New Englanders have ever agreed to unlimited expansion, knowing that it would reduce them to an increasingly marginal place in the union?

Suppressing his own constitutional scruples, Jefferson insisted that the genius of American federalism was expansive. "Who can limit the extent to which the federative principle may operate effectively?" he asked in his second inaugural address. "The larger our association," he answered, echoing Madison's rejoinder to Montesquieu, "the less will it be shaken by local passions."[18] Jefferson's did not derive his "federative principle" from the Constitution but rather from the original "association" of Revolutionary republics in 1776. Union came first, then came the elaboration of constitutional provisions for its implementation. Strict construction of the Constitution was the means of securing states' rights and therefore preserving the union. Virginian John Page, one of Jefferson's dearest friends, thus summarized the Republican gospel in 1799: the federal Constitution "is the *Instrument* by which the people of the several *confederated states of America* meant to preserve to their respective states their *Independence.*"[19] The Constitution was the means, or "*Instrument*," of union, not an end in itself, particularly in a case where strict adherence to the constitutional text jeopardized the rights of future states. "A strict observance of the written laws is doubtless *one* of the high duties of a good citizen," Jefferson explained in 1810, "but it is not *the highest.* The laws of necessity, of self-preservation, of saving our country when in danger, are of higher obligation."[20]

Federalist anti-expansionists embraced strict construction at precisely the point Jefferson abandoned it. Disagreement hinged on the history and fundamental character of the union. For Jefferson's opponents, the ratification of the Constitution marked a fundamental break in American political history: the union itself was the product of specific, substantive constitutional compromises; it ceased to exist when those original understandings were violated. Because the federal government, the institutional embodiment and sine qua non of union, also derived its existence from the Constitution, "loose" constructions of the text that enhanced the administration's effective power were "constitutional." The Constitution—and therefore the union—were only at risk when Republicans subverted the balance of power within the union that the Constitution was meant to secure. Jefferson invoked "reason of state" and the law of national self-preservation when dealing with external enemies; his opponents invoked the same logic in the new nation's domestic affairs. Anti-expansionists thus insisted that the axioms of conventional political science continued to apply at home as well as abroad: peace among the American states depended both on maintaining a vigorous central government and on securing the vital interests of the union's original partners.

Conflicting interpretations of American federalism were fully rehearsed in congressional debates over admitting Louisiana, the first new state to be carved out of the Purchase. With Louisiana's admission, Massachusetts Federalist Josiah Quincy warned, "the bonds of this Union are virtually dissolved." The balance that the founders had so carefully constructed would be "destroyed" if Congress should "throw the weight of Louisiana into the scale."[21] Quincy's controversial speech reflected and anticipated a growing sense of sectional grievance in New England that would culminate in separatist rumblings and opposition to the Madison administration during the War of 1812. The disgruntled Federalists who met at Hartford in 1814 sought to restore the union, and the balance of power that sustained it, to its original state. Yet they also criticized original constitutional provisions—notably the three-fifths clause—that gave slaveholders disproportionate power in Congress, thus calling into question the union's legitimacy.

The Federalists' concerns about westward expansion and the waxing power of southern slaveholders survived their demise as a national political party. Their heirs, the antislavery Restrictionists who sought to bar Missouri's admission as a slave state in 1819, appealed to principle as well as interest in opposing the unfettered operation of Jefferson's "federative principle." The proliferation of new slave states made a mockery of the new nation's republican pretensions, even as it extended the influence and power of one section—the slaveholding South—at the expense of the others.

Conclusion

The history of American federalism at the time of the Louisiana Purchase can be conceptualized in terms of two geopolitical axes—east-west and north-south—and their ideological and interpretative concomitants.

Jefferson and his Republican coadjutors focused on the east-west axis, celebrating the capacity of a dynamic federal union to incorporate new members without the dangerous concentration of power in an overbearing central government. Rapid expansion preempted centrifugal tendencies in frontier regions, strengthening the union against external threats. The formation of new states under the sanction of Article IV, Section III of the federal Constitution, specific provisions of the Confederation Congress's Northwest Ordinance (1787), and subsequent congressional organic acts constituted a progressive, liberal alternative to the colonial rule of old regime empires. Republican administrations would pursue this enlightened, anticolonial policy in the vast region of the Louisiana Purchase.

Anti-expansionists instead focused on the north-south axis, emphasizing the implications of new state formation for the balance of power in the original union. From their skeptical perspective, Jefferson's appeal to the "federative principle" disguised and mystified the concrete interests—of land speculators, Republican politicos, and slaveholding planters—that expansion really served: these interests were not equally distributed throughout the union, notwithstanding the hopes of New Englanders who first promoted settlement in the Ohio country. Jeffersonians may have deemphasized the kind of strong central government Federalists favored, but they showed a genius for party and state building that successfully linked an expanding periphery to the centers of power. They thus showed that control of the federal government was vitally important for promoting the coalition of interests aligned under their party's banner. While Republicans celebrated the triumph of principle, they vigorously pursued their own interests. Union thus was not spontaneously consensual: the Republicans' success depended on their ability to mobilize consent by appealing to a wide array of interests. And the most important interest was always Jefferson's original core constituency, the staple-producing, slaveholding planters of the South.

Advocates of these opposing versions of federalism could easily see through their opponents' pretenses. Republicans persuasively argued that Federalists were out of step with history: an ambitious, enterprising people would not be restrained in their expansive pursuits; they would find ways of governing themselves that maintained order without concentrating power. But Federalists understood equally well that the new Republican order served some interests better than others and that territorial expansion under Jeffersonian auspices expanded the empire of slavery as well as the "empire of liberty." They recognized that the principles of federalism could never be fully extricated from the underlying question of the actual balance of power in the union.

Northern Federalists anticipated the ultimate rupture of the union between North and South in their early opposition to the Louisiana Purchase and westward expansion. In the years after the War of 1812, New Englanders and northerners generally overcame their misgivings about expansion, recognizing new ways in which they could enjoy its benefits and perhaps even direct its course. In an ironic reversal, southern Old Republicans who rejected any active role for the federal government in promoting economic development now embraced the separatist logic of northern High Federalists. Increasingly concerned about their diminishing power in Congress and their status as an endangered minority section, these southerners questioned the value of the union. Parting company with Jefferson, they no longer envisioned limitless expansion in a dynamic, harmonious union. They looked to the north, not to the west.

Notes

This essay was originally published in Peter J. Kastor, ed., *The Louisiana Purchase: Emergence of an American Nation* (Washington, DC: CQ Press, 2002), 117–28.

1. Declaration of Independence, in Merrill D. Peterson, ed., *Thomas Jefferson Writings* (New York, 1984), 19.

2. On the early history of federalism, see Forrest McDonald, *States' Rights and the Union: Imperium in Imperio, 1776–1876* (Lawrence, KS, 2000). David C. Hendrickson, *Peace Pact: The Lost World of the American Founding* (Lawrence, KS, 2003) is the definitive history of the origins and early development of American federal thought. See also Cathy D. Matson and Peter S. Onuf, *A Union of Interests: Political and Economic Thought in Revolutionary America* (Lawrence, KS, 1990);

Peter Onuf and Nicholas Onuf, *Federal Union, Modern World: The Law of Nations in an Age of Revolutions, 1776–1814* (Madison, WI, 1993); and James E. Lewis Jr., *The American Union and the Problem of Neighborhood: The United States and the Collapse of the Spanish Empire, 1783–1829* (Chapel Hill, NC, 1998).

3. Thomas Jefferson (hereafter TJ), First Inaugural Address, March 4, 1801, in Peterson, ed., *Jefferson Writings*, 494.

4. TJ's ideas about federalism are analyzed in Peter S. Onuf, *Jefferson's Empire: The Language of American Nationhood* (Charlottesville, VA, 2000), chap. 3; see also David N. Mayer, *The Constitutional Thought of Thomas Jefferson* (Charlottesville, VA, 1994), 185–221.

5. James Madison, Federalist No. 10, in Jacob E. Cooke, ed., *The Federalist* (Middletown, CT, 1961), 56–65.

6. For critical accounts of Jefferson's Louisiana diplomacy, see Alexander DeConde, *This Affair of Louisiana* (New York, 1976); and Robert W. Tucker and David C. Hendrickson, *Empire of Liberty: The Statecraft of Thomas Jefferson* (New York, 1990). The best study of the political, diplomatic, and constitutional history of Louisiana is Peter Kastor, *The Nation's Crucible: The Louisiana Purchase and the Creation of America* (New Haven, CT, 2004). Jon Kukla, *A Wilderness So Immense: The Louisiana Purchase and the Destiny of America* (New York, 2003), is particularly strong on European developments. The most perceptive study of New England's reaction to westward expansion is James M. Banner Jr., *To the Hartford Convention: The Federalists and the Origins of Party Politics in Massachusetts, 1789–1815* (New York, 1970).

7. TJ, First Inaugural Address, March 4, 1801, in Peterson, ed., *Jefferson Writings*, 493.

8. TJ to A. L. C. Destutt de Tracy, Jan. 26, 1811, in Peterson, ed., *Jefferson Writings*, 1245–46, emphasis in original.

9. Montesquieu, *The Spirit of the Laws* (1748), trans. and ed. Anne Cohler, Basia Miller, and Harold Stone (Cambridge, UK, 1989), bk. 8, chaps. 16–17, 124–25; Madison, Federalist No. 10, in Cooke, ed., *Federalist*.

10. This theme is developed in Peter Onuf and Leonard Sadosky, *Jeffersonian America* (Oxford, 2001), chap. 4.

11. TJ to Destutt, Jan. 26, 1811, in Peterson, ed., *Jefferson Writings*, 1244–46.

12. TJ to Horatio G. Spafford, March 17, 1814, in Andrew A. Lipscomb and Albert Ellery Bergh, eds., *The Writings of Thomas Jefferson*, 20 vols. (Washington, DC, 1903–4), 14:120.

13. On developments in Ohio and the Northwest, see Peter S. Onuf, *Statehood and Union: A History of the Northwest Ordinance* (Bloomington, 1987). For broad

surveys of the history of the territorial system, see Jack Ericson Eblen, *The First and Second United States Empires: Governors and Territorial Government, 1784–1912* (Pittsburgh, 1968); and Peter Onuf, "Territories and Statehood," in Jack P. Greene, ed., *Encyclopedia of American Political History*, 3 vols. (New York, 1984), 3:1283–1304. Andrew R. L. Cayton offers illuminating insights into the federal dimension of frontier politics in his essays: "'Separate Interests' and the Nation-State: The Washington Administration and the Origins of Regionalism in the Trans-Appalachian West," *Journal of American History* 79 (1992): 39–67; and "'When Shall We Cease to Have Judases?' The Blount Conspiracy and the Limits of the 'Extended Republic,'" in Ronald Hoffman and Peter J. Albert, eds., *Launching the "Extended Republic": The Federalist Era* (Charlottesville, VA, 1996), 156–89.

14. TJ to William Duane, March 28, 1811, in Lipscomb and Bergh, eds., *Writings of Jefferson*, 13:28–29, emphasis in original.

15. TJ to Hon. Mark Landon Hill, April 5, 1820, in Lipscomb and Bergh, eds., *Writings of Jefferson*, 15:243.

16. Orasmus Cook Merrill, *The Happiness of America: An Oration Delivered at Shaftsbury, on the Fourth of July, 1804* (Bennington, VT, 1804), 20.

17. Peter S. Onuf, *The Origins of the Federal Republic: Jurisdictional Controversies in the United States, 1775–1787* (Philadelphia, 1983).

18. TJ, Second Inaugural Address, March 4, 1805, in Peterson, ed., *Jefferson Writings*, 519.

19. John Page, *Address to the Freeholders of Gloucester County, at their Election of a Member of Congress . . . April 24, 1799* (Richmond, 1799), 19, emphasis in original.

20. TJ to John B. Colvin, Sept. 20, 1810, in Peterson, ed., *Jefferson Writings*, 1231, emphasis in original.

21. Rep. Josiah Quincy, speech, Jan. 14, 1811, in *Annals of the Congress of the United States, 1789–1824*, 42 vols. (Washington, DC, 1834–56), 11th Cong., 3d sess., 525, 540.

PART III

Religion and Education

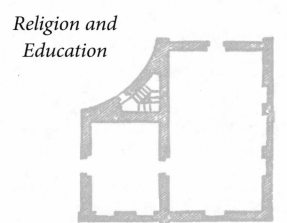

JEFFERSON'S RELIGION

Priestcraft, Enlightenment, and the Republican Revolution

Although Thomas Jefferson counted many devout Christians among his friends, allies, and followers, he hated and feared the organized clergy.[1] Where religion was established—and that was everywhere in the young Jefferson's world—"priests" upheld the hierarchy, unequal privilege, and despotic rule that in return supported and enriched them. The character of the church was defined by the unholy alliance the clergy formed with a corrupt state. During the "darker centuries," it had been mankind's "misfortune," Jefferson lamented when he launched his crusade against the Virginia establishment in 1776, that ambitious and avaricious "Xn priests" should combine "with the magistrates to divide the spoils of the people."[2] By mystifying power and fostering popular ignorance, the established clergy played a critical role in propping up corrupt old regimes. The clergy's mis-education of the people constituted the most formidable obstacle to the success of the new nation's republican experiment. Their success in preaching up hierarchy and promoting popular deference to superior authority called into question the "self-evident" axioms of self-government that Jefferson set forth in his Declaration of Independence.

It was one thing to overthrow the increasingly unpopular and illegitimate rule of a distant British imperial government, but quite another to uproot the deep popular prejudices that sustained unequal rule. The break from Britain shook religious establishments across the continent, particularly where those establishments were closely tied to the imperial metropolis. But the establishment principle proved surprisingly durable as clergymen of various denominations—including Anglicans—aligned with the Revolution and sought to secure a privileged position for themselves under the new republican dispensation. As long as the war continued, Jefferson believed, the popular commitment to equal sacrifice, equal rights, and the common good would keep the clergy at bay. "But is the spirit of the people an infallible, a permanent reliance?" he asked in his *Notes on the State of Virginia,* at a time (1781–82) when his campaign for disestablishment had stalled. "From the conclusion of this war," he predicted, "we shall be going down hill." When "our rulers" no longer had "to resort every moment to the people for support," the people "will be forgotten . . . and their rights disregarded." For their part, "our people" will become "careless," forgetting themselves "in the sole faculty of making money." It was crucial, therefore, to strike while the iron was hot, to secure religious liberty specifically and the people's rights generally before it was too late: "The shackles, therefore, which shall not be knocked off at the conclusion of this war, will remain on us long, will be made heavier and heavier, till our rights shall revive or expire in a convulsion."[3]

The draft of Jefferson's Bill for Establishing Religious Freedom eloquently epitomized his anxious ambivalence about the prospects for republicanism. If the people's rights were fully articulated and constitutionally defined, the progress of enlightened opinion ultimately would provide their secure foundation. "Almighty God hath created the mind free," Jefferson memorably intoned. But what God had created, man had corrupted.[4] As a result, and in stark juxtaposition to the political principles that the very process of revolutionary mobilization had made seem so obvious and compelling, the full implications of "the laws of nature and of nature's God" for the foundation and flourishing of republican society remained obscure.[5] Ordinary folk could readily grasp that predatory British tax gatherers and "standing armies" jeopardized their liberty and property and interfered with their "pursuits of happiness," but it was by no means clear to them that those who promoted unpopular and impious opinions also had "rights," or that, to use Jefferson's notorious example, "it does me no injury for my neighbour to say there are twenty gods, or no god. It neither picks my pocket nor breaks my leg."[6] After all, the war justified stigmatizing, ostracizing, sanctioning, and sometimes exiling political deviants. Assuming the connection between religious piety and republican virtue, as most Christian Revolutionaries undoubtedly did, Jefferson's believer in "twenty gods" might seem to threaten much more than a picked pocket or a broken leg.

Here was Jefferson's challenge: to link disestablishment, a generally popular cause, with a broad definition of religious liberty that would license unpopular sects, non-Christians, deists, and atheists "to profess, and by argument to maintain, their opinions in matters of religion."[7] Given the plurality of religious sects in Revolutionary America, the unwillingness of most Christians to see one group gain any advantage over others, and a reflexive popular hostility to tax-supported establishments, the prospects for disestablishment might have been bright in 1776. But Jefferson knew that few Americans would see any compelling reason why religious liberty should be universal and promiscuous. A whole-hearted, enlightened embrace of religious liberty would be the *result* of free competition in the marketplace of ideas, not its starting point or premise. The "truth is great and *will prevail* if left to herself," Jefferson insisted in his bill: "She is the proper and sufficient antagonist to error, and has nothing to fear from the conflict unless by human interposition disarmed of her natural weapons, free argument and debate; errors ceasing to be dangerous when it is permitted freely to contradict them."[8] Yet "human interposition" in religious affairs was everywhere the norm, and many patriots were convinced, with Jefferson's friend Benjamin Rush, that promoting popular Christian piety and virtue was all the more important in the wake of the Revolutionary demolition of the old political and social order. "I have always considered Christianity as the *strong ground* of Republicanism," Rush told Jefferson in 1800. "It is only necessary for Republicanism to ally itself to the christian Religion, to overturn all the corrupted political and religious institutions in the world." This, of course, was precisely the opposite of what Jefferson argued during the struggle for religious liberty: it was the "alliance" of church and state that was the ultimate and most dangerous source of corruption in a free state.[9]

Jefferson may have rued his unguarded comment about "twenty gods" (published in a book designed for limited circulation among the cognoscenti) when Federalists and their clerical allies led the assault on his heresies in the 1796 and 1800 presidential canvases.[10] But in his later retirement years, long after Federalism's demise, Jefferson told himself that the "great majority" in the Virginia Assembly that endorsed the Bill for Establishing Religious Freedom—the bill's true "authors"—had recognized the need to establish religious freedom in the fullest sense. By refusing to insert a reference to "Jesus Christ, the holy author of our religion," legislators showed "that they meant to comprehend, within the mantle of it's protection, the Jew and the Gentile, the Christian and Mahometan, the Hindoo, and infidel of every denomination."[11] Characteristically, Jefferson submerged his own identity here into that of the bill's putative authors, much as he modestly disclaimed any "originality" in drafting the Declaration, a mere "expression of the American mind."[12] But Jefferson did *not* claim that all Virginians agreed with the advanced position the bill staked out in 1779 and that the assembly affirmed in 1786—although many dissenters advocated a similarly capacious definition of religious liberty.[13] To the contrary, Jefferson was fearful that because the bill was only a statute it was vulnerable to emendation or repeal by a subsequent legislature—perhaps by the insertion of a reference to "Jesus Christ" that would have in some sense established Christianity. To guard against this outcome, the bill concluded with a bold and unequivocal statement that "the rights hereby asserted are of the natural rights of mankind, and that if any act shall be hereafter passed to repeal the present or to narrow its operation, such act will be an infringement of natural right."[14] Jefferson's separation of church and state had to be absolute so that "truth" would triumph; until the day when the people generally recognized that the domains of religion and politics must be kept distinct and inviolate, Jefferson relied on their deference to the enlightened authors of the bill and their unwillingness to violate "natural rights" that they had not yet fully grasped.

Priestcraft

Jefferson's animosity toward the clergy did not abate after the war was won and the Anglican Church was disestablished in Virginia. Because establishments survived in New Hampshire, Massachusetts, and Connecticut—in the heartland of Federalism—and because clergymen elsewhere sought to regain power, "priestcraft" remained a clear and present danger to the republican cause. The threat of clerical influence was exacerbated because the Revolution had driven aristocratic impulses underground. The piety of Godly Christians provided a new, ostensibly republican, "foundation" for hierarchy and privilege: even when they failed to capture the state, the clergy could shape public opinion to promote their own interests and those of their aristocratic allies. They could rally the Christian majority against unpopular individuals or groups, narrowing the ambit of religious liberty and thus preparing the way for dangerous new alliances between church and state.

Jefferson was particularly alert to the dangers of reestablishment in Virginia. Not surprisingly, he linked sectarianism with partisan politics: the eclipse of Anglicanism led other groups to jockey for preferential position. Presbyterians thus provided critical support for future Federalist Patrick Henry's nearly successful proposal for a multiple establishment in 1785.[15] As party divisions deepened in the 1790s, the alliance between Presbyterianism and Federalism grew stronger, culminating in the vicious assault on Jefferson's heresies in the 1800 presidential campaign. The subsequent Republican ascendancy scattered the forces of partisan and clerical reaction, at least for the time being: the little Federalism "we have," Jefferson reported to Postmaster General Gideon Granger, a Connecticut ally, "is in the string of Presbyterian counties in the valley between the blue ridge & North Mountain where the clergy are as bitter as they are in Connecticut."[16] But the Presbyterian clergy would rise again, during Jefferson's retirement, to block the appointment of the infamous deist Thomas Cooper at Jefferson's new university. "The Presbyterian clergy are loudest; the most intolerant of all sects, the most tyrannical and ambitious," Jefferson fulminated to William Short. If they could, they would burn heretics at the stake, as "their oracle Calvin consumed the poor Servetus" in Geneva: "they pant to re-establish, *by law,* that holy inquisition, which they can now only infuse into *public opinion.* We have most unwisely committed to the hierophants of our particular superstition, the direction of public opinion, that lord of the universe."[17]

Jefferson assumed that clergymen were always "ambitious" for political power, that the influence they exercised over their followers' spiritual lives was instrumental to these worldly purposes. Whatever their professions, priests as a class were harbingers of counterrevolution and enemies of republican government. The paradoxical dilemma was that disestablishment gave preachers extraordinary new opportunities to sway public opinion, and thus to subvert the foundations of republican government. If the republican experiment failed in America, it would not be because the people yearned for a return to monarchy and aristocracy, but because they were totally engrossed in their own private pursuits, tamely submitting to priestly power (presumably to save their souls) and failing to recognize and resist the new and insidious forms of hierarchy the priests promoted. Ultimately the impoverishment of public life would be fatal to republicanism, inaugurating a new era of spiritual darkness in which the exaltation of mysteries and miracles would eclipse science, reason, and moral progress.

Commentators have been struck with Jefferson's overheated, hyperbolic language in his indictments of "monocrats," "aristocrats," and "priestcraft" and the bad faith and evil motives he imputed to partisan and sectarian enemies. Of course, his bold generalizations did not apply to many individual cases—for instance, to his friend Charles Clay, an Anglican with evangelical tendencies—or even to whole groups he so glibly libeled, including the moderate Federalists he appealed to in his first inaugural address and the sectarians who embraced a broad Jeffersonian conception of religious freedom. In 1800 Jefferson himself acknowledged that the Virginia Constitution's "incapacitation of a clergyman from being elected" did not make sense, when, in the wake of disestablishment, they were no longer "ingrafted into the machine of government"—and when the practical effect of the ban was to exclude some of Jefferson's most fervent supporters from the legislature. "The clergy here *seem* to have relinquished all pretension to privilege" (Jefferson could not suppress his doubts that this was or always would be the case), and they "ought therefore to possess the same rights" as their counterparts in the other professions, "lawyers, physicians &c."[18]

Jefferson could distinguish individuals from groups serving legitimate social purposes, including religious associations; he could also distinguish between such groups and the religious establishments and other state-sanctioned corporate bodies with monopolistic privileges that had collectively constituted the old regime. For Jefferson the corporatism of the old regime was the very antithesis of republicanism; he believed, therefore, that republicanism was at risk even, and especially, when states supported religious establishments for the apparently benign and unexceptionable purpose of promoting popular piety and virtue. Jefferson's anticlerical rhetoric was proportional to the ultimate threat to republicanism of an organized clergy seeking corporate privileges, however disproportionate to any immediate threat preachers presented and however unfair his implicit characterization of their motives. Jefferson recognized that he had to overcome popular prejudices in favor of pastors who seemingly sacrificed self-interest to serve their flocks. Americans were reflexively suspicious and vigilant about the way their political leaders might abuse power; they needed to be equally vigilant about "tyrannical and ambitious" clergymen—wolves in sheep's clothing—who might also abuse the people's trust. The critical test for any clergyman was whether he faithfully upheld, as a sacred truth, the fundamental republican principle of religious freedom, conscientiously eschewing any political preferment or advantage and acknowledging, in the words of Jefferson's bill, "that our civil rights have no dependance on our religious opinions, any more than our opinions in physics or geometry."[19]

Jefferson's Christianity

Jefferson's anticlericalism demanded a "wall of separation" between church and state in order to secure the uncorrupted soul of the republic. Yet suspicions about the organized clergy's motives did not mean that Jefferson himself was not, or would not become, increasingly concerned with religious questions. As long as the danger of priestcraft remained paramount, in Virginia and later in France, Jefferson's concerns were largely negative: moral philosophers ancient and modern remained the best guides to the good life.[20] So, writing from Paris in 1787, he urged his nephew Peter Carr to "shake off all the fears and servile prejudices under which weak minds are servilely crouched" and "question with boldness even the existence of a god." Carr should read the Bible critically, including the New Testament "history of a personage called Jesus," who some say "was begotten by god, born of a virgin, suspended and reversed the laws of nature at will, and ascended bodily into heaven" but who Jefferson and other like-minded men of reason say "was a man, of illegitimate birth, of a benevolent heart, enthusiastic mind, who set out without pretensions to divinity, ended in believing them, and was punished capitally for sedition by being gibbeted according to the Roman law."[21] Jefferson's years in Paris reinforced his faith in reason and his hostility to the rule of "kings, nobles, or priests," the "abandoned confederacy" that waged perpetual war "against the happiness of the mass of the people."[22]

Jefferson's utterly conventional Enlightenment sentiments took a new, more self-consciously religious turn when he came back to the United States. In the wake of disestablishment, anticlericalism seemed beside the point: the "abandoned confederacy" had been routed everywhere; even in New England, church establishments appeared increasingly tenuous. Yet, as Jefferson soon recognized, partisan preachers posed a new, more insidious, threat to American republicanism as they shaped and, in some places, dominated public opinion in the turbulent 1790s. Rather than forging unholy alliances with secular authorities that disestablishment had preempted, the clergy now operated indirectly, through electoral manipulation, and their prime targets were the insufficiently "Christian" candidates of the Jeffersonian opposition, the closet deists, atheists, and infidels who threatened to bring God's wrath down on the United States.[23] In this context, separation of church and state took on new meanings transcending the constitutional and institutional questions that had once obsessed Jefferson. As he sought to deflect the barrage of attacks on his spiritual life, Jefferson increasingly emphasized the integrity and autonomy of the conscientious self: the highest, most impermeable "wall of separation" should separate the individual believer—or nonbeliever—from the tyranny of public opinion. As Jefferson's concern shifted from the institutional to the personal, from the rule of priests to more insidious, indirect forms of priestly influence, his own "religious pilgrimage" began in earnest.[24] Once he had staked out and defended his own private, spiritual domain, Jefferson became, by his own account, a true "Christian," indeed a better Christian—because he was truly disinterested—than any of his clerical critics. Jefferson's careful editing of the gospels, his "Philosophy of Jesus," proved (to his own satisfaction at least) "that *I* am a *real Christian,* that is to say, a disciple of the doctrines of Jesus, very different from the Platonists, who call *me* infidel, and *themselves* Christians and preachers of the gospel, while they draw all their characteristic dogmas from what it's Author never said nor saw."[25]

Jefferson's understanding of himself as a Christian was worked out through conversations and correspondence with Benjamin Rush, Joseph Priestley, and a few other luminaries and through many hours of painstaking Bible reading. Jefferson told Peter Carr to avoid religious study until "your reason" is sufficiently "mature," thus anticipating his own subsequent engagement with Christian scripture. Eschewing the hermeneutic shortcut of unquestioning "faith" and reading the Bible critically as history, not as revelation, Jefferson could situate Jesus and the Christian dispensation within a world historical context of progress and improvement. Jefferson's key breakthrough was to cast Jesus as a great reformer and thus to establish a genealogy for America's republican revolution—and for himself as a reformer in the Christian tradition. Jesus had sought to reform Judaism by bringing the Jews "to the principles of a pure deism, and juster notions of the attributes of God, to reform their moral doctrines to the standard of reason, justice & philanthropy, and to inculcate the belief of a future state."[26] His instinctive "benevolence" reached beyond the Jewish nation, embracing "with charity and philanthropy our neighbors, our countrymen, and the whole family of mankind."[27] But Jesus's teachings had been distorted and perverted by later expositors, and the delusions of an "enthusiastic mind" had been invoked as evidence of "divinity." In effect, the cult of the man, said to be mystically sprung from the Godhead, superseded the man's teachings;

this was the primal source of priestly authority in Christianity, for the real effect of Christ's apotheosis was to exalt the keepers of the faith. And this in turn explained why the history of Christianity was punctuated by periodic reformations, by efforts to peal away encrusted layers of self-serving mystification and "tradition" that sustained the institutional church and the power of the priests.

The reform impulse, according to Jefferson, represented the true spirit of primitive, unadulterated Christianity. It also, not surprisingly, seemed to anticipate—or, we might skeptically prefer, reflect—the Enlightenment emphasis on universal natural law, "reason, justice & philanthropy." Yet, as Jefferson noted, enlightenment took distinctive forms in different countries, depending on the power of institutional Christianity. "In Protestant countries," Jefferson observed to Thomas Law in his famous letter on the moral sense, "the defections from the Platonic Christianity of the priests is to Deism, in Catholic countries they are to Atheism."[28] Only in America, perhaps, could the rejection of Platonic mystifications—and priestcraft—lead to a popular, purified Christianity that would sustain the moral progress of republican governments. Jefferson understood that deists and atheists could lead good lives, but he also believed that the new nation was providentially blessed not only with "all the necessaries and comforts of life" but with a "union of sentiment . . . auguring harmony and happiness to our future course," a union that was grounded in an enlightened and thoroughly republicanized Christianity. Jefferson's own religious quest as a self-professed Christian anticipated the "entire union of opinion" that would enable Americans to fulfill their providential mission.[29] That union would only be perfected and republicanism and Christianity finally converge if freedom of conscience—Jefferson's freedom from censorious preachers and the tyranny of public opinion—were religiously upheld.

But what sort of "Christian" was Jefferson? The conventional view is that Jefferson's Christianity, if that is what it was, was completely idiosyncratic, a defensive adaptation to a pervasively Christian, increasingly evangelical culture. Certainly his faith in reason and his hostility to the "faith" of the preachers ("the more incomprehensible the proposition, the more merit in its faith") put him well out of the American mainstream.[30] If we could "live without an order of priests," he wrote John Adams, we could then "moralise for ourselves, follow the oracle of conscience, and say nothing about what no man can understand, nor therefore believe; for I suppose belief to be the assent of the mind to an intelligible proposition."[31] Jefferson, there-

[147]

fore, could never believe in the trinity, a three-in-one conception of the Godhead that was the "Abracadabra of the mountebanks calling themselves the priests of Jesus." If the doctrine "could be understood it would not answer their purpose," Jefferson wrote in 1816, for "their security is in their faculty of shedding darkness," in obscuring what a man of reason would make clear.[32] The priests' power depended on keeping their flocks in the dark: misguided people who could embrace such a logical absurdity as the trinity—the vast majority of the American people—could be made to believe anything. Jefferson preferred to rest comfortably on "that pillow of ignorance which a benevolent creator has made so soft for us knowing how much we should be forced to use it."[33] "Ignorance is preferable to error," he concluded in his *Notes,* "and he is less remote from the truth who believes nothing, than he who believes what is wrong."[34]

Jefferson's rejection of the blind faith of trinitarian Christians led him back to the historical Jesus, the great teacher whose "intention was simply to reinstate natural religion, & by diffusing the light of his morality, to teach us to govern ourselves."[35] Jesus's message was, of course, anathema to priests who taught that men were inherently sinful and therefore incapable of self-government. Jefferson met similar resistance in his own day. "I expect no mercy" from the clergy, he wrote Levi Lincoln in 1801, for "they crucified their Saviour, who preached that their kingdom was not of this world; and all who practise on that precept must expect the extreme of their wrath."[36] Jefferson's identification with Jesus, as a reformer who dared to challenge priestly power, led him to question the clergy's Christian credentials. "Christians" who "mangled" the gospel to serve their own earthly ends were in fact "Pseudo-Christians," "pseudo-followers" of Jesus who spread pernicious "fictions" that "exposed him to the inference of being an impostor," and "pseudo-priests" who perverted his "genuine doctrines."[37] Jefferson knew that Jesus was no imposter and that once his teachings had been restored to their "original purity" they would be embraced by all Americans. "This reformation will advance with the other improvements of the human mind," he predicted to Unitarian Jared Sparks late in his life, "but too late for me to witness it."[38]

The Sanctified Self

Jefferson's almost pathological determination to keep his own religious views private—in effect, to make them a mystery—reflected his awareness of the theological differences that separated him from the vast majority of Americans, differences that would only disappear after his death.[39] "I am of a sect by myself," he told Calvinist Ezra Stiles Ely, one of many correspondents who sought to draw Jefferson out—and into their various sectarian camps. The genuine theology of Jesus, "the benevolent and sublime reformer," was simplicity itself: he "has told us only that god is good and perfect, but has not defined him."[40] Misbegotten efforts to define the indefinable gave rise to the neo-Platonic mystifications of Athanasius, Calvin, and their spiritual descendants, thus promoting schism and the persecution of "heretics." Jesus preached peace and love, but his followers had made "Christendom a slaughterhouse." Had Jesus's "doctrines, pure as they came from himself, been never sophisticated for unworthy purposes," Jefferson lectured the Reverend Thomas Whittemore, "the whole civilised world would at this day have formed but a single sect."[41] Or, as he succinctly put it to Margaret Bayard Smith, "there would never have been an infidel, if there had never been a priest."[42]

There were many priests in Jefferson's day, and they still exercised a dangerous influence over public opinion; they did not hesitate to call him an "infidel." Yet Jefferson and the people, his "sect" of one and the proliferating, popular sects that were transforming the religious landscape, were not as far apart as the priests proclaimed. Ultimately, he believed, a progressively enlightened public opinion would loosen the "shackles" of priestly influence and so rise above the bigotry and ignorance that sustained the clergy's power. Jefferson's confidence was bolstered by his own popular mandate in the "Revolution of 1800": coming to their senses after the "reign of witches," a growing majority now embraced "federal and republican principles," coalescing in a transcendent, noncoërcive "union of sentiments." This popular enlightenment worked against the unholy alliance of church and state; in their revulsion against corrupt establishments, the American people generally would come to see, as Jefferson famously wrote the Danbury Baptists, "that religion is a matter which lies solely between man and his God."[43] "What an effort . . . of bigotry in Politics & Religion have we gone through!" he exclaimed to Priestley.[44] But the "dominion of the clergy" was now shattered, Jefferson explained to Vermonter Moses Robinson: they "had got a smell of union between Church and State, and began to indulge reveries which can never be realised in the present state of science." The Republican triumph would restore Christianity "to the original purity and simplicity of its benevolent institutor," showing it to be the "religion of all others most friendly to liberty, science, and the freest expansion of the human mind."[45]

A revolution in sentiment on church-state issues reflected and promoted the institutional transformation of the various sects as they adapted to the exigencies and opportunities of a free and competitive religious market-place. The people would demand more control over their churches and better performance from their pastors, thus undercutting authoritarian hier-archies that commanded the obedience of subservient flocks. Worshipers might too easily be misled when priests monopolized religion and exploited the credulity of the faithful, but the people's good sense would always be vindicated when they enjoyed real freedom of choice: after all, Jefferson would sooner rely on the "ploughman" to decide a "moral case . . . as well, and often better than . . . a professor," because "he has not been led astray by artificial rules."[46] The problem under the old regime, even in its attenuated American forms, was that "ploughmen" did not get to make choices as long as priests—the quintessential "professors"—enjoyed a state-sanctioned mo-nopoly over opinion. Ultimately nature would triumph over artifice under the new republican dispensation. As Americans embraced and exercised religious freedom, religious institutions and beliefs would adapt accord-ingly: priestcraft, the unnatural union of religion and politics that propped up the old regime, would be superseded by a thoroughly republicanized Christianity. Jefferson, the lonely "Christian," would be the prototype for his progressively enlightened countrymen. The autonomous self that Jefferson cultivated as a refuge from a benighted and bigoted public opinion would then be recognized as the ultimate source and foundation of morality and religion.

Jefferson's faith in the progress of an enlightened, republicanized Chris-tianity stood in sharp contrast to his pessimism about the future of Spanish-American independence movements. The power of the church was so deeply entrenched in the Spanish Empire, he told the great German naturalist Alexander von Humboldt, that however much Revolutionaries there fol-lowed the North American lead, they would in the end "bow the neck to their priests, and persevere in intolerantism."[47] The benighted peoples of Spanish America had not progressed beyond "the lowest grade of ignorance" and were thus doomed to be exploited by "their civil as well as religious lead-ers." "History," he concluded, "furnishes no example of a priest-ridden people maintaining a free civil government."[48] Jefferson's skepticism about the prospects of republicanism to the south reflected his conception of the stages of historical development that made the highest "grade" of political civilization possible: Anglo-Americans were sufficiently enlightened before their Revolution to make the success of their "experiment" much more likely. Yet priestly influence remained potent enough in the United States to shake Jefferson's complacency, as his repeated professions of faith in the future (and his continuing reticence to make his own religious beliefs public) suggest.

Jefferson believed that the theological differences that divided Americans in his lifetime ultimately would disappear. But as long as preachers exploited popular credulity, he was determined to protect his privacy, keeping secret his advanced beliefs on the divinity of Jesus and the trinity in order to avoid alienating his allies and followers. The preachers would depict these differences as fundamental, defining Jefferson apart from the great majority of American Christians. Jefferson, nonetheless, was convinced that religious reform was already spreading in the wake of the republican revolution and that an eventual "union of sentiments" would transcend sectarian divisions. Disestablishment initiated institutional changes in the churches that would in turn transform popular beliefs. Once Americans began acting like republicans, they would begin to think like republicans and no longer allow an "interested aristocracy of priests" to "think for them."[49] Until then, however, Jefferson would remain silent, thinking for himself and carefully not "disturbing the tranquility of others by the expression of any opinion on the innocent questions on which we schismatize." Throughout Christian history, Jefferson told clerical correspondent James Fishback early in his retirement, "oceans of human blood have been spilt, & whole regions of the earth have been desolated by wars & persecutions" over "unimportant" and "mischievous" questions that were in any case "insoluble" to "minds like ours." When Americans fully internalized religious liberty, recognizing each other's moral and spiritual autonomy, they would consign trivial theological questions "to the sleep of death."[50]

The contrast between Jefferson's robust anticlerical polemics and his self-imposed silence on controversial theological issues is striking. He did not hesitate to challenge the worldly ambitions of the priests and therefore to make powerful enemies (although he carefully modulated his attacks in order not to offend the sensibilities of ordinary folk). But because his own beliefs did not affect anyone else directly, remaining silent about them was for Jefferson "a matter of principle." The people should judge Jefferson and other public officials by their deeds—in theological terms, by their "works"—not by their professed "faith" on controversial theological questions. Any religious test was an encroachment on the sacred domain of personal privacy and thus a fundamental violation of religious liberty. Yet why should Jefferson, as a private individual, remain silent about his beliefs when other Americans exercised their undoubted right to freely "profess, and by argument to maintain, their opinions in matters of religion"?[51] Scruples about exploiting his public influence to promote his own private beliefs were understandable but could hardly apply when he returned to private life in his retirement. Why shouldn't the eloquent Jefferson do what he could to bring on the postsectarian republican millennium?

Jefferson's reticence on the question of racial slavery offers some clues. Jefferson's fundamental commitment as a republican was to majority rule, but the majority of Virginians was not yet sufficiently enlightened to take steps, beyond liberalizing manumission in 1782, to dismantle the institution. Nor was it clear that a majority had fully embraced the broadest implications of religious liberty, notwithstanding James Madison's brilliant success in winning the Assembly's endorsement of Jefferson's bill in 1786. In both cases, "public opinion" needed to be more fully enlightened, whether to prevent backsliding on religious liberty or to prepare the way for emancipation. Yet this enlightenment could not be forced or coerced, but must instead spring from below, becoming manifest in the emergence of a new, more fully republican majority. To dictate to the people, even for the most enlightened and progressive purposes, was to violate the most fundamental principle of republican self-government. Republican means should never be sacrificed to ostensibly republican ends.[52]

The discrepancy between the present state of public opinion and its progressive potential constituted the greatest challenge to Jefferson's democratic faith, requiring patience and forbearance in the enlightened vanguard. Of course, the majority in every "sovereign" generation had the right to legislate its will, regardless of the progress of opinion. Any self-appointed leader who moved out too far ahead of his fellow citizens on an issue like slavery, where powerfully entrenched interests were at stake, would render himself useless to the cause. The perfection of the republic ultimately required an end to slavery, but a premature movement for emancipation could put the republic itself at risk. Jefferson, therefore, would bide his time, waiting for an enlightened majority to emerge. So, too, Jefferson would await the enlightened reformation of religious opinion before exposing his own advanced, unorthodox views—a moral reformation that, not coincidentally, would lead to slavery's demise. Jefferson underscored the link between these two great reformations, ending slavery and promoting Christian enlightenment, in his famous letter to Edward Coles in 1814 explaining why he remained unwilling to take a public stand against slavery. Jefferson urged his young neighbor to "reconcile yourself to your country," to "come forward in the public councils" as an apostle of antislavery, to "*become the missionary of this doctrine truly christian*; insinuate & inculcate it softly but steadily, through the medium of writing and conversation; associate others in your labors, and when the phalanx is formed, bring on and press the proposition perseveringly until its accomplishment."[53]

Jefferson's advice to Coles shows that he did not believe in the spontaneous generation of progressive opinion: like any other "missionary," Coles should seek to persuade and convert his countrymen. As a member of the older, Revolutionary generation, Jefferson could only remain on the sidelines, "fervently and sincerely pray[ing]" for Coles's success (prayer, of course, was a private activity, appropriately confined to the closet). Jefferson's generation may have passed from the stage—"I have overlived the generation with which mutual labors & perils begat mutual confidence and influence"—but at the same time he imaginatively linked himself with a glorious future, without slavery, which he would not live to see.[54] Most readers of this letter are understandably impatient with Jefferson's "patience," his counsel of procrastination to Coles and unwillingness to put himself on the line by endorsing Coles's antislavery initiative.[55] And they are certainly right to emphasize Jefferson's paramount concern with himself, with protecting and securing his autonomy and privacy and excusing himself from action by distancing himself from Coles's generation. But the "self" was by no means a trivial, merely selfish issue for Jefferson or for his conception of republican government. In the Coles letter, Jefferson defined the same distinction between self and society and between private belief and public opinion that characterized his religious life. If he prayed for the success of Coles's antislavery crusade, he also must have prayed for a general religious and moral reformation. Simultaneously living in the past and in the future, Jefferson erected a "wall of separation" around his autonomous self in the present while reaffirming his republican faith in progress and improvement.

The generational division of labor Jefferson described to Coles illuminates Jefferson's republican faith. The Revolutionary fathers created the republic, destroying an old regime that oppressed and exploited the people while retarding their moral progress. Coles's generation now had the opportunity to build on this solid foundation and fulfill republicanism's promise.

Enjoying the great boon of free institutions, younger Virginians could take their bearings from the dictates of their own moral sense. Jefferson would banish the priests from the republican temple, so that "error" would flee before "reason and experiment," "truth" would "stand by itself," and Virginians would begin to think for themselves.[56] To provide a vigilant people the tools they needed to secure their liberties, Jefferson promoted publicly supported education.[57] The Revolutionaries thus equipped their successors for the pursuits of a free people, confident that they would achieve progressively higher levels of material improvement and moral development. But the older generation could only glimpse the outlines of these great changes. The younger generation, acting and thinking like republicans, must chart their own path to a brighter future. Jefferson's reticence on religious and ethical issues thus reflected not only the self-protective impulses of a sensitive old man but also a principled solicitude for the freedom of inquiry and action of his fellow Virginians. Jefferson's self-restraint made it possible for Coles and his generation to discover within themselves the moral imperative of emancipation. And Jefferson could only sustain his faith in Virginia's ultimate moral redemption as long as enlightened young men like Coles reconciled themselves to their country and did not "lessen its stock of sound disposition by withdrawing your portion from the mass."[58]

Democratic Christianity

In one of his last letters, Jefferson justified his silence on slavery to James Heaton, insisting that "a good cause is often injured more by ill-timed efforts of its friends than by the arguments of its enemies." The cause of emancipation required a "revolution in public opinion," and this was "not to be expected in a day, or perhaps in an age; but time, which outlives all things, will outlive this evil also." In the meantime, "persuasion, perseverance, and patience are the best advocates on questions depending on the will of others."[59] Jefferson, a "friend" of emancipation, thus distinguished himself from the "others" who remained attached to the peculiar institution, a "public" that still groped in the darkness. Nearing his death, he would be patient, keeping the faith that others would take up the challenge, persuading their benighted countrymen, persevering until the end of time. Jefferson's antislavery "sentiments have been forty years before the public," he told Heaton. In *Notes on the State of Virginia*, the young Revolutionary expected more immediate results ("I think a change already perceptible"), but counseled a similarly indirect approach. In a republic, it was the sentiments of the people, not those of a few enlightened leaders, that gave rise to moral reformation: "we must be contented to hope," therefore, that "the various considerations of policy, of morals, of history natural and civil" that made emancipation imperative "will force their way into *every one's* mind."[60]

By the end of his life, Jefferson must have been disappointed in the progress of emancipation. If Virginians failed to see the light and act accordingly, he had predicted portentously in his *Notes*, "supernatural interference" would be the result. "Indeed I tremble for my country when I reflect that God is just," he wrote, for the resulting "revolution of the wheel of fortune" would mean nothing less than the failure of the great republican experiment.[61] But Jefferson's horizon may have been less clouded in 1826 than we might assume, particularly in view of the cataclysmic war that would finally lead to slavery's destruction a generation later—surely the judgment of a just God on a nation of sinners, if there ever was one. In his later years, Jefferson had good reason to believe that a more enlightened, republicanized Christianity was making extraordinary progress throughout the land. The main obstacle to popular enlightenment—and the long-awaited "revolution in public opinion" that would lead to slavery's demise—was the entrenched power of the priests, whether in their remaining establishment strongholds or in their continuing ability to promote bigotry and superstition among their followers. But the people were now beginning to overpower the priests, and when priestcraft was finally uprooted, all hierarchies, including slavery, would collapse.

It was unthinkable to Jefferson that either republicanism or Christianity, stripped of their worldly corruptions, could provide fertile ground for the consolidation and expansion of the institution of slavery, although this is the overwhelming verdict of the best recent historiography.[62] The longer slavery survived—and prospered—the more natural it seemed to many Virginians, though few were yet prepared to call it a "positive good." The reformist impulses that were increasingly conspicuous among faithful Christians of Coles's generation thus were directed more at the amelioration of the condition of slaves (or the colonization of free blacks) than at large-scale emancipation. Intentionally or not, Christian reformers thus helped to strengthen rather than eradicate the institution, and, with Jefferson, they could assuage lingering misgivings with a misplaced confidence "that the hour of emancipation, is advancing, in the march of time." But a "revolution in public opinion" must come first.[63]

Yet Jefferson would never abandon his faith in the ultimate, if long-delayed, triumph of an enlightened public opinion that would lead to slavery's demise. Jefferson's republican faith was holistic: under a republican regime, enlightenment would spread from one domain to another, building on the fundamental truths that were self-evident to ordinary citizens. Republicanism, the system of self-government that gave fullest scope to man's innate moral sense, constituted the necessary means to achieve moral progress; the Christianity that Jesus taught—and that "pseudo-Christians" had perverted and corrupted throughout history—enabled republicans to grasp the deeper meanings and broader ethical implications of their various self-initiated pursuits. Republicanism and Christianity were perfectly complementary, as Americans who were caught up in the excitement of the Second Great Awakening seemed to be discovering.

It is a commonplace among historians that the deistic Jefferson was profoundly out of touch with the development of popular, evangelical Christianity in his own day.[64] His famously misguided belief, expressed in a letter to Dr. Benjamin Waterhouse of Harvard, "that there is not a *young man* now living in the United States who will not die an Unitarian" epitomizes his failure to grasp powerful contemporary developments.[65] But Jefferson's misjudgment seems less laughable if we put ourselves in his position. Far from being distressed by the extraordinary growth of evangelical sects, Jefferson applauded their democratic potential. Believing that the priests who fostered an unholy alliance of church and state were responsible for conflict between enlightened science and popular piety, Jefferson was confident that the rout of the priests would lead to the ultimate reconciliation of reason and religion. Because, for Jefferson, ecclesiology ultimately shaped theology, the democratization of the churches would inevitably give rise to a common democratic theology, to expressions of faith that were more congenial to the popular appetite for enlightenment and improvement. The pronounced Arminian tendencies of the most popular sects—their emphasis on the efficacy of individual choice and importance of good works—was particularly encouraging to Jefferson, the avowed enemy of Calvinistic mystifications. For growing numbers of Christians, continuing belief in the trinity constituted a kind of atavism, not the bedrock of a vital, practical this-worldly faith. With him, the Disciples of Christ and other self-consciously democratic and forward-looking Christians harked back to the "primitive church," rejecting the institutional corruptions of the churches that predatory priests had fostered. From Jefferson's perspective, Unitarianism did not represent an elite reaction to the evangelical surge, but rather the precocious fulfillment of its ultimate theological tendencies.

Jefferson's assessment of the religious landscape does not comport with the genealogy of modern denominations. Our culture wars are not those of Jefferson's time, and not only because the real threat of religious establishments then still loomed so large. Faithful Christians of Jefferson's day did not cherish a sense of alienation or victimhood in the larger, "secular" culture, nor did they define "faith" against "science." The common ground Jefferson imagined for republican Christians was not one defined by subscription to a (modern) evangelical faith, but one that instead accommodated, and would be shaped by, enlightened denominations that rejected archaic, exclusive tests and best showed how republicanism and Christianity could work together. "Evangelical" and "Christian" were not synonymous terms for Jefferson. Preachers of the Second Awakening expressed the same democratic tendencies that characterized the Jeffersonian movement in politics, downplaying the doctrinal tests of the established churches: as they diverged from Calvinism, the most rapidly growing, evangelical churches seemed most "liberal" and inclusive. Unitarianism represented the culmination of these tendencies.[66] Jefferson urged leaders of the new denomination, with their "doctrines truly evangelical," to send "missionaries from Cambridge" to Virginia, where ordinary folk were well prepared to accept their enlightened gospel. "A bold and eloquent preacher would be no where listened to with more freedom than in this state," Jefferson told Benjamin Waterhouse, "nor with more firmness of mind." "The preacher might be excluded by our hierophants from their churches and meeting houses, but would be attended in the fields by whole acres of hearers and thinkers."[67]

The key issue for Jefferson was always the reciprocal corruption of religion and politics in church establishments. As a result, he focused obsessively on the governance of particular denominations, emphasizing their tendencies toward unholy alliances with the state. In the national churches of England and Scotland, as well as in church establishments in British America, the identity of church and state was complete. Where these churches were not established but retained institutional ties to the national churches, Anglican and Presbyterian church hierarchies reflected their strong affinity for the old regime. The congregational churches of New England were in theory the most "republican," but were fatally compromised by their alliance with civil authority. In Jefferson's view, the Congregational establishments of Connecticut, Massachusetts, and New Hampshire were effectively Presbyterian. The congregational principle of self-government was much better represented by antiestablishment dissenters in New England, most notably Jefferson's great allies the Baptists, and by their coreligionists to the south. Most democratic of all were preacherless Quaker congregations, where the anti-institutional impulses of radical Protestantism were institutionalized. But just as the alliance with civil authority compromised New England congregationalism, Quakers' ties to the "Mother-society" in Britain—not to mention their peace testimony—belied their republican credentials: "their attachment to England is stronger than to their principles or their country," Jefferson told Madison in 1798.[68]

The ecclesiological tendency Jefferson observed throughout the new nation was progressively toward more democratic forms and away from authoritarian church hierarchies. He was heartened by the successes of the Baptists and of splinter groups like the Disciples of Christ who jettisoned traditional creedal tests and preached free choice and good works. These popular, democratic churches repudiated the Calvinists' conception of original sin; their hierarchical, state-supported churches; and the persecution of dissenters. Even where churches continued to cherish the exclusive beliefs and practices that once had led to the spilling of "oceans of human blood," the practical effect of religious liberty was to modulate doctrinal differences and encourage Christians to think for themselves.[69]

Jefferson had little interest in the theological mystifications that required leaps of faith, the renunciation of reason, and the abnegation of self. He was intellectually and temperamentally hostile to the revivalists' conception of the new birth and their celebration of the "enthusiastic," delusional promptings of disordered psyches. As a result, Jefferson undoubtedly exaggerated the enlightened, rational, and democratizing tendencies of popular religion, but he did not mistake them altogether. In the ferment of the religious marketplace, traditional Christian beliefs and practices were rethought and reformed to meet the demands of popular audiences. Belief in the trinity, the most conspicuous symbol of old regime priestcraft, would inevitably erode as ordinary Christians recognized the ways this absurd test of faith undergirded the clergy's social and political power. Of course, Jefferson would be proven wrong about the place of faith in the future of popular religion. Yet there were powerful "liberal," democratizing tendencies in church government and popular theology that warranted his optimism.

Jefferson's misplaced hopes for Unitarianism illuminate the extent—and limits—of his understanding of popular Christianity. He exaggerated the significance of the progress of liberal religion in eastern Massachusetts because this is where resistance to republicanism was most deeply entrenched.[70] If the clergy's political power rested on the credulity of the faithful, the assault on trinitarianism would necessarily topple the establishment and liberalize, if not revolutionize, public opinion generally. Jefferson could not see how religious liberalism and social and political conservatism could possibly co-exist, as they did with Timothy Pickering and other Unitarian Federalists, and his hopes that Boston Unitarians would send missionaries southward to proselytize Virginia can only seem bizarre in view of Jefferson's career-long efforts to spread the Republican gospel in the Federalist heartland. In imag-ining a great Unitarian revival in his own neighborhood, Jefferson conflated and confused the spread of liberal, enlightened religion in New England and its assault on trinitarianism with the democratizing Christianity of the Second Great Awakening. Yet if Jefferson was mistaken about the Unitarians' vanguard role in the American reformation, he was right to include them within this broadly democratizing movement. Jefferson had good reason to believe that a more practical, ethical, and democratic version of Protestant Christianity would come to dominate the new nation, wrong only to be-lieve that he and his fellow Unitarians anticipated its ultimate theological (or posttheological) destination.

Christian Nation

The modern conception of the United States as a "Christian nation" would have appalled Jefferson, the "apostle of reason" and sworn enemy of un-reasoning faith. But it is, nonetheless, true that Jefferson himself can in some measure be held responsible for the modern version of this idea. Notwithstanding his strictures against "uniformity" and his advocacy of di-versity, Jefferson believed that religious differences in America would be progressively mitigated and ultimately disappear.[71] Jefferson was most fun-damentally committed to securing the autonomy of the self, not to a plural-ity of sects, because his republican faith was predicated on the individual's free and enlightened consent. In Jefferson's republic, free citizens would participate in a process of moral development and progressive enlighten-ment that drew them closer together in a "union of sentiments" even as it showed them the way toward a better future. Over time, as this union was perfected, the new nation would become more homogenous.

Far from being indifferent to questions of character and belief—in the modern civil libertarian mode—Jefferson believed that the moral and religious progress of the republic was essential to its very survival. Jefferson's obsession with the unholy alliance of church and state under the mystifying rule of priestcraft reflected this conviction: by establishing religious liberty, the new republican dispensation would lead to the synthesis of enlightened popular religion with republican institutions of self-government. The most critical "separation" was not between religion (morality, or ethics) and politics, for they were inextricably linked, but, rather, between the private domain of the self, where virtue was cultivated and self-mastery achieved, and the public world that virtuous individuals collectively constituted. Following the lead of the moral sense philosophers, Jefferson embraced a conception of the self that was compatible with—and constitutive of—an all-embracing conception of the "people" or "nation."[72] It is this idea of American nationhood that makes it possible for modern Christians to imagine the United States as a "Christian nation."[73]

"Accommodationists," who argue that the founders did not erect a high "wall of separation" between religion and politics, can also draw ample evidence from the career of Thomas Jefferson, the author of that influential formulation.[74] Jefferson came to see himself as a Christian at a time when more disestablished, democratic, and enlightened forms of Christianity were spreading across the land. The Second Great Awakening made this reformed, Americanized religion more conspicuous, and Jefferson (at least in more optimistic moments) thought this a benign and hopeful development. He was certainly scrupulous about not endorsing particular Christian beliefs or practices that might in any way point toward the inevitably corrupting alliance of church and state, and his reticence about his own beliefs reflected not only an obsession with his own privacy but also his solicitude for the privacy of others. But this did not mean that all religious expression should be banished from the "public square" or even from the halls of Congress, where a succession of chaplains held forth during the Jeffersonian era (including a Unitarian from Baltimore, a most encouraging augury to Jefferson).[75] After all, public expressions of a generic Christianity required, and modeled, emerging forms of intersectarian civility that would have an enlightening effect on all the sects.

Jefferson sanctioned what would now be seen as violations of a strict church-state separation. In his private life, he participated in and celebrated the promiscuous worship of Christians in Charlottesville, who alternated services in the county courthouse and "mix in society with perfect harmony."[76]

Jefferson also "accommodated" sectarians—including Presbyterians, whose motives he questioned to the end of his life—at the University of Virginia, where they were invited to establish seminaries on the border of his "academical village."[77] As long as the university itself did not have a chair in theology, and therefore did not officially sanction religion in any way, the mixture of sectarians (and enlightened deists and nonbelievers) in the life of the university would have positive effects for everyone involved. The best practical guarantee for religious liberty was to teach the multiplicity of religious sects not only to coexist peaceably but to learn from one another, discovering and internalizing the common political, moral, and religious principles that bound them together. Most fundamental was the principle of religious liberty itself: separation of church and state guaranteed the autonomy of the consenting, virtuous individual citizen, the predicate of progressively higher degrees of union.

Yet if Jefferson's life and thought seems to offer inspiration and justification to modern advocates of the "Christian nation," it can only do so by ignoring and rejecting Jefferson's republican faith and his abiding belief in the inexorable progress of reason and science. Jefferson may have envisioned the future United States as an enlightened "Christian nation," but not one in which the mysteries and mystifications of unreasoning "faith" continued to exercise such an extraordinary sway over the minds and hearts of the people. That America today would be more Christian than the historically Christian nations of Europe would come as no surprise to Jefferson. But he would be ambivalent at best about the wealth, power, and influence amassed by religious teachers, and he would he would be surprised—even amazed—that Americans under their ministrations should be so much more likely than their European counterparts to believe in miracles and reject the wisdom (while enjoying the material benefits) of scientific inquiry.

Yet again, Jefferson, the self-professed "Christian" who rejected the faith of the fathers, speaks to us in (at least) two voices, one ebulliently confident in a glorious Christian future, the other chronically anxious about assaults on individual liberty and autonomy, ever alert about the dangers of priestcraft. But Jefferson's supposedly split personality is nothing more or less than a function of anachronism, of our continuing need to enlist him in our own enterprises. When we look closely at Jefferson (if we look beyond ourselves), we can begin to glimpse the many complex and ambiguous possibilities—the many futures—that were inherent in his world and that have played out, and are still playing out, in ours.

Notes

This essay was prepared for the "Symposium on Jefferson and Religion," School of Continuing and Professional Studies, University of Virginia, June 2005. Thanks to Charles F. Irons of Elon University and Johann Neem of Western Washington State University for their helpful comments. This essay is dedicated, with gratitude, to my colleague and friend Tom Dowd, formerly of the School of Continuing and Professional Studies.

1. The best introduction to Jefferson's (hereafter TJ) religious thought is Eugene R. Sheridan, *Jefferson and Religion* (Charlottesville, VA, 1998), originally published as the introduction to Dickinson W. Adams, ed., *Jefferson's Extracts from the Gospels: "The Philosophy of Jesus" and "The LIfe and Morals of Jesus"* (Princeton, NJ, 1983). See also Charles B. Sanford, *The Religious Life of Thomas Jefferson* (Charlottesville, VA, 1984); Paul K. Conkin, "The Religious Pilgrimage of Thomas Jefferson," in Peter S. Onuf, ed., *Jeffersonian Legacies* (Charlottesville, VA, 1993), 19–49; Edwin S. Gaustad, *Sworn on the Altar of God: A Religious Biography of Thomas Jefferson* (Grand Rapids, MI, 1996); and Andrew Burstein, *Jefferson's Secrets: Death and Desire at Monticello* (New York, 2005), chap. 9, "Disavowing Dogma," 237–63.

2. Notes and Proceedings on Discontinuing the Establishment of the Church of England (Oct. 11–Dec. 9, 1776), in Julian P. Boyd et al., eds., *The Papers of Thomas Jefferson,* 32 vols. to date (Princeton, NJ, 1950–), 1:548.

3. TJ, Query 17 ("Religion"), in William Peden, ed., *Notes on the State of Virginia* (Chapel Hill, NC, 1954), 161.

4. Bill for Establishing Religious Freedom (1779), in Boyd et al., eds., *Jefferson Papers,* 2:545.

5. Declaration of Independence, July 4, 1776, in Merrill D. Peterson, ed., *Thomas Jefferson Writings* (New York, 1984), 19.

6. TJ, in Peden, ed., *Notes,* 159.

7. Bill for Establishing Religious Freedom (1779), in Boyd et al., eds., *Jefferson Papers,* 2:546.

8. Ibid., emphasis added.

9. Benjamin Rush to TJ, Aug. 22, 1800, in Adams, ed., *Jefferson's Extracts from the Gospels,* 318, emphasis in original. See the discussions in Eugene R. Sheridan, "Liberty and Virtue: Religion and Republicanism in Jeffersonian Thought," in James Gilreath, ed., *Thomas Jefferson and the Education of a Citizen* (Washington, DC, 1999), 242–63; and Thomas E. Buckley, "The Political Theology of Thomas Jefferson," in Merrill D. Peterson and Robert C. Vaughan, eds., *The Virginia Statute of Religious Freedom: Its Evolution and Consequences in American History* (Cambridge,

UK, 1988), 75–107. Once religious freedom was fully secured in Virginia—as it was in Pennsylvania—the difference between TJ's and Rush's position disappeared. On the relation between politics and religion, see Robert M. Calhoon's provocative argument in "Religion, Moderation, and Regime-Building in Post-Revolutionary America," in Eliga H. Gould and Peter S. Onuf, eds., *Empire and Nation: The American Revolution in the Atlantic World* (Baltimore, 2005), 217–36, esp. 222–26. On the piety and virtue problem generally, see Peter Onuf, "State Politics and Republican Virtue: Religion, Education, and Morality in Early American Federalism," in Paul Finkelman and Stephen E. Gottlieb, eds., *Toward a Usable Past: Liberty under State Constitutions* (Athens, GA, 1991), 91–116.

10. Robert M. S. McDonald, "Was There a Religious Revolution of 1800?" in James Horn, Jan Ellen Lewis, and Peter Onuf, eds., *The Revolution of 1800* (Charlottesville, VA, 2002), 173–98.

11. TJ, *Autobiography,* Jan. 6, 1821, in Peterson, ed., *Jefferson Writings,* 40.

12. TJ to Henry Lee, May 8, 1825, ibid, 1501.

13. I am indebted here to John Ragosta's analysis of petitions to the Virginia Assembly in his "Between a Rock and a Hard Place: Negotiating Religious Freedom in Virginia during the Revolution" (unpublished paper in my possession).

14. Bill for Establishing Religious Freedom (1779), in Boyd et al., eds., *Jefferson Papers,* 2:546–47.

15. The standard account is Thomas E. Buckley, *Church and State in Revolutionary Virginia, 1776–1787* (Charlottesville, VA, 1977). See also the essays in Peterson and Vaughan, eds., *Virginia Statute for Religious Freedom,* particularly Lance Banning, "James Madison, the Statute for Religious Freedom, and the Crisis of Republican Convictions," 109–38.

16. TJ to Gideon Granger, May 20, 1803, transcript in Paul Leicester Ford, ed., *The Works of Thomas Jefferson,* Federal ed., 12 vols. (New York, 1904–5); also available online from the Library of Congress, American Memory Collection, Thomas Jefferson Papers, Series 1: General Correspondence: 1651–1827, http://memory.loc.gov/.

17. TJ to William Short, April 13, 1820, in Andrew A. Lipscomb and Albert Ellery Bergh, eds., *The Writings of Thomas Jefferson,* 20 vols. (Washington, DC, 1903–4), 15:246, emphasis in original. On the founding of the university, see Cameron Clark Addis, *Jefferson's Vision for Education, 1760–1845* (New York, 2002). See also my essay, "Thomas Jefferson's Military Academy: A Summary View," in this volume.

18. TJ to Jeremiah Moore, Aug. 14, 1800, transcript in Ford, ed., *Jefferson Works,* emphasis added; available online at Library of Congress, American Memory Collection, Thomas Jefferson Papers, Series 1: General Correspondence: 1651–1827, http://memory.loc.gov.

19. Bill for Establishing Religious Freedom, [1779], in Boyd et al., eds., *Jefferson Papers*, 2:545–46. The characterization of the clergy is in TJ to William Short, April 13, 1820, in Lipscomb and Bergh, eds., *Writings of Jefferson*, 15:246.

20. On Jefferson and classical philosophy, see Karl Lehmann, *Thomas Jefferson, American Humanist* (New York, 1947); and Jean M. Yarbrough, *American Virtues: Thomas Jefferson on the Character of a Free People* (Lawrence, KS, 1998).

21. TJ to Peter Carr, Aug. 10, 1787, in Boyd et al., eds., *Jefferson Papers*, 12:15–16.

22. TJ to George Wythe, Aug. 13, 1786, ibid., *Jefferson Papers*, 10:244–45.

23. Charles O. Lerche Jr., "Thomas Jefferson and the Election of 1800: A Case Study in the Political Smear," *William & Mary Quarterly* (hereafter *WMQ*) 5 (1948): 467–91; Constance B. Schulz, "'Of Bigotry in Politics and Religion:' Jefferson's Religion, the Federalist Press, and the Syllabus," *Virginia Magazine of History and Biography* 91 (1983): 73–91; McDonald, "Was There a Religious Revolution of 1800?" in Horn et al., eds., *Revolution of 1800*.

24. I am indebted here to Conkin, "Religious Pilgrimage of Thomas Jefferson," in Onuf, ed., *Jeffersonian Legacies*.

25. TJ to Charles Thomson (Jan. 9, 1816), in Adams, ed., *Jefferson's Extracts from the Gospels*, 365, emphasis in original. For an excellent analysis, see Susan Bryan, "Reauthorizing the Text: Jefferson's Scissor Edit of the Gospels," *Early American Literature* 32 (1987): 19–42.

26. TJ to Dr. Joseph Priestley, April 9, 1803, in Peterson, ed., *Jefferson Writings*, 1121.

27. TJ to Edward Dowse, April 19, 1803, in Lipscomb and Bergh, eds., *Writings of Jefferson*, 10:377.

28. TJ to Dr. Joseph Priestley, April 9, 1803, in Peterson, ed., *Jefferson Writings*, 1121; TJ to Thomas Law, June 13, 1814, in Lipscomb and Bergh, eds., *Writings of Jefferson*, 14:139–40.

29. TJ, Second Inaugural Address, March 4, 1805, in Peterson, ed., *Jefferson Writings*, 522–23.

30. TJ to Dr. Benjamin Waterhouse, June 26, 1822, ibid., *Jefferson Writings*, 1458.

31. TJ to John Adams, Aug. 22, 1813, in Lester J. Cappon, ed., *The Adams-Jefferson Letters: The Complete Correspondence Between Thomas Jefferson and Abigail and John Adams*, 2 vols. (Chapel Hill, NC, 1959), 2:368.

32. TJ to Francis Adrian Van der Kemp, July 30, 1816, in Adams, ed., *Jefferson's Extracts from the Gospels*, 375.

33. TJ to Rev. Isaac Story, Dec. 5, 1801, ibid., 325.

34. TJ, Query 6 ("Productions Mineral, Vegetable, and Animal"), in Peden, ed., *Notes,* 33.

35. TJ to Rev. James Madison, Jan. 31, 1800, in Peterson, ed., *Jefferson Writings,* 1077.

36. TJ to Levi Lincoln, Aug. 26, 1801, in Lipscomb and Bergh, eds., *Writings of Jefferson,* 10:275–76.

37. TJ to Francis Adrian Van der Kemp, July 30, 1816, in Adams, ed., *Jefferson's Extracts from the Gospels,* 375; TJ to William Short, Aug. 4, 1820, in Peterson, ed., *Jefferson Writings,* 1435; TJ to Jared Sparks, Nov. 4, 1820, in Lipscomb and Bergh, eds., *Writings of Jefferson,* 15:288.

38. TJ to Jared Sparks, Nov. 4, 1820, in Lipscomb and Bergh, eds., *Writings of Jefferson,* 15:288; TJ to Moses Robinson, March 23, 1801, in Peterson, ed., *Jefferson Writings,* 1087.

39. On TJ's obsession with privacy, see Conkin, "Religious Pilgrimage of Thomas Jefferson," in Onuf, ed., *Jeffersonian Legacies,* 35–36. I discuss TJ's self-fashioning in "Making Sense of Jefferson," this volume.

40. TJ to Ezra Stiles Ely, June 25, 1819, in Adams, ed., *Jefferson's Extracts from the Gospels,* 387.

41. TJ to Rev. Thomas Whittemore, June 5, 1822, ibid, 404. As he put it to Ely, "We should all be of one sect, doers of good and eschewers of evil" (TJ to Ezra Stiles Ely, June 25, 1819, ibid., 387).

42. TJ to Margaret Bayard Smith, Aug. 6, 1816, in Lipscomb and Bergh, eds., *Writings of Jefferson,* 15:60.

43. TJ to Messrs. Nehemiah Dodge and Others, a Committee of the Danbury Baptist Association, Jan. 1, 1802, in Peterson, ed., *Jefferson Writings,* 510. For the restored text of TJ's original draft and commentary, see James H. Hutson, "Thomas Jefferson's Letter to the Danbury Baptists: A Controversy Rejoined," *WMQ* 56 (1999): 775–90.

44. TJ to Joseph Priestley, March 21, 1801, in Peterson, ed., *Jefferson Writings,* 1085.

45. TJ to Moses Robinson, March 23, 1801, ibid., 1087–88.

46. TJ to Peter Carr, Aug. 10, 1787, in Boyd et al., eds., *Jefferson Papers,* 12:15.

47. TJ to Alexander von Humboldt, April 14, 1811, in Lipscomb and Bergh, eds., *Writings of Jefferson,* 13:34–35.

48. TJ to Alexander von Humboldt, Dec. 6, 1813, ibid., 14:21. "Another great field of political experiment is opening in our neighborhood, in Spanish America," TJ wrote Dupont de Nemours, but "I fear the degrading ignorance into which their priests and kings have sunk them, has disqualified them from the maintenance or

even knowledge of their rights, and that much blood may be shed for little improvement in their condition" (TJ to P. S. Dupont de Nemours, April 15, 1811, ibid., 13:40).

49. TJ to Thomas Seymour, Feb. 11, 1807, transcript in Ford, ed., *Jefferson Works* (also available online from the Library of Congress, American Memory Collection, Thomas Jefferson Papers, Series 1: General Correspondence: 1651–1827, http://memory.loc.gov/), referring to the unaccountable tyranny of "priests & lawyers" over the "intelligent people" of Connecticut.

50. TJ to James Fishback, Sept. 27, 1809, in J. Jefferson Looney, ed., *The Papers of Thomas Jefferson,* Retirement Series, 2 vols. to date (Princeton, NJ, 2005–), 1:564.

51. Bill for Establishing Religious Freedom (1779), in Boyd et al., eds., *Jefferson Papers,* 2:546.

52. This theme is elaborated in Ari Helo and Peter Onuf, "Jefferson, Morality, and the Problem of Slavery," in this volume.

53. TJ to Edward Coles, Aug. 25, 1814, in Peterson, ed., *Jefferson Writings,* 1346, emphasis added.

54. Ibid., 1345–46.

55. The most eloquent indictment is in Paul Finkelman, "Jefferson and Slavery: 'Treason against the Hopes of the World,'" in Onuf, ed., *Jeffersonian Legacies,* 181–221.

56. TJ, in Peden, ed., *Notes,* 160.

57. See my essay "Liberty to Learn," in this volume. See also Harold Hellenbrand, *The Unfinished Revolution: Education and Politics in the Thought of Thomas Jefferson* (Newark, DE, 1990); and Addis, *Jefferson's Vision for Education.*

58. TJ to Edward Coles, Aug. 25, 1814, in Peterson, ed., *Jefferson Writings,* 1346.

59. TJ to James Heaton, May 20, 1826, ibid., 1516.

60. TJ, Query 18 ("Manners") in Peden, ed., *Notes,* 163, emphasis added.

61. Ibid.

62. Charles F. Irons, "The Spiritual Fruits of Revolution: Disestablishment and the Rise of the Virginia Baptists," *Virginia Magazine of History and Biography* 109 (2001): 159–86; idem, "'The Chief Cornerstone': The Spiritual Foundations of Virginia's Slave Society, 1776–1861" (Ph.D. diss., University of Virginia, 2003).

63. TJ to Edward Coles, Aug. 25, 1814, in Peterson, ed., *Jefferson Writings,* 1345; TJ to James Heaton, May 20, 1826, in ibid., 1516.

64. This conventional view is effectively challenged in Nathan O. Hatch, *The Democratization of American Christianity* (New Haven, CT, 1989). My indebtedness to Hatch's work will be apparent in the discussion that follows.

65. TJ to Dr. Benjamin Waterhouse, June 26, 1822, in Peterson, ed., *Jefferson Writings,* 1459, emphasis in original.

66. On TJ's "surprisingly irenic" view of religious developments in the era of the Second Great Awakening, see Conkin, "Religious Pilgrimage of Thomas Jefferson," in Onuf, ed., *Jeffersonian Legacies,* 41–45, quotation on 41.

67. TJ to Dr. Benjamin Waterhouse, July 19, 26, 1822, in Adams, ed., *Jefferson's Extracts from the Gospels,* 407.

68. TJ to James Madison, March 28, 1798, in Lipscomb and Bergh, eds., *Writings of Jefferson,* 10:18. The "Mother-society" reference is in TJ to William Baldwin, Jan. 19, 1810, in Adams, ed., *Jefferson's Extracts from the Gospels,* 346. After his election, TJ generally expressed more positive attitudes toward the Friends. "They have no priests, therefore no schisms," he wrote Elbridge Gerry in 1801. "They judge of the text by the dictates of common sense & common morality" (TJ to Gerry, March 29, 1801, in Peterson, ed., *Jefferson Writings,* 1090). For similar sentiments, see TJ to John Adams, Aug. 22, 1813, in Cappon, ed., *Adams-Jefferson Letters,* 2:368.

69. TJ to James Fishback, Sept. 27, 1809, in Looney, ed., *Papers of Thomas Jefferson,* 1:564.

70. On TJ's misunderstanding of New England Unitarianism—and the Federalism of many of its leading exponents—see Conkin, "Religious Pilgrimage of Thomas Jefferson," in Onuf, ed., *Jeffersonian Legacies,* 42–43.

71. "Uniformity of opinion" is no more "desireable . . . than of face and stature," TJ wrote in Query 17 ("Religion"), in Peden, ed., *Notes,* 160.

72. See my *Jefferson's Empire: The Language of American Nationhood* (Charlottesville, VA, 2000).

73. As Thomas E. Buckley concludes, "Jefferson bears conspicuous responsibility for the development of an American civil religion, a complex of ideas, images, and symbols related to and dependent upon a transcendent reality we call God. Through his public writings and statements, he deliberately crafted this civic faith to bind the nation together" (Buckley, "The Religious Rhetoric of Thomas Jefferson," in Daniel Dreisbach, Mark D. Hall, and Jeffry H. Morrison, eds., *The Founders on God and Government* [Lanham, MD, 2004], 53–82, quotation on 74). But see also Mark Douglas McGarvie, *One Nation Under Law: America's Early National Struggles to Separate Church and State* (DeKalb, IL, 2004). McGarvie persuasively argues that "Christian organizations" in the new constitutional order were "protected in their rights to convert the nation to Christianity only because they assumed the form of private entities divorced from the institutions of public political power. . . . Protected as dissenters, the achievement of their goal—a Christian nation—became inconsistent with their continued viability to pursue it" (19).

74. The most comprehensive and persuasive work on this theme is Daniel L. Dreisbach, *Thomas Jefferson and the Wall of Separation between Church and State*

(New York, 2002); see also Philip Hamburger, *Separation of Church and State* (Cambridge, MA, 2002), 144–89.

75. TJ to Dr. Benjamin Waterhouse, July 19, 26, 1822, in Adams, ed., *Jefferson's Extracts from the Gospels*, 407.

76. "The court-house is the common temple" where "Episcopalian and Presbyterian, Methodist and Baptist, meet together, join in hymning their Maker, [and] listen with attention and devotion to each others' preachers" (TJ to Thomas Cooper, Nov. 2, 1822, in Peterson, ed., *Jefferson Writings*, 1464). For a good discussion of the local religious landscape, see Mark Beliles, "The Christian Communities, Religious Revivals, and Political Culture of the Central Virginia Piedmont, 1737–1813," in Garrett Ward Sheldon and Daniel L. Dreisbach, eds., *Religion and Political Culture in Jefferson's Virginia* (Lanham, MD, 2000), 3–40.

77. Minutes of the Board of Visitors, University of Virginia, Oct. 7, 1822, in Peterson, ed., *Jefferson Writings*, 477–79; TJ to Thomas Cooper, Nov. 2, 1822, ibid., 1465.

LIBERTY TO LEARN

Public education was a central concern of Thomas Jefferson's public career. Jefferson understood the American Revolution in generational terms, as the liberation of the "living generation" from the despotic rule of its predecessors.[1] Aristocracy, the dominion of privileged families whose estates were preserved across the generations through the legal devices of primogeniture and entail, had to be uprooted and destroyed if republican citizens were to enjoy the genuine equality that made government by consent possible.

It was natural for parents to provide for their children, passing on property they had inherited and enlarged through their own productive efforts. But when the founders of great families sought to buttress their superior position through unequal legal privilege and political power, their solicitude for their children—and children's children—became unnatural and destructive. The state should play no part in securing the preeminence of the privileged few over the mass of citizens, for such inequality inevitably would weaken and destroy the commonwealth. The state should instead treat all of its children equally, teaching them to be conscious of their equal rights as individuals and of their collective rights as a generation that would one day govern itself.

Conceiving of the Revolution as a moment when Americans suddenly became conscious of themselves as a people and grasped the "self-evident principles" that justified their claims to independence and self-government, Jefferson saw public education as the essential means of preserving republican government. The patriotic movement against British tyranny that culminated in resistance and revolution had been a sustained exercise in popular political education. Yet for Jefferson and other anxious Revolutionaries, the end of British rule was not a sufficient guarantee of republicanism, for ambitious individuals would always seek to use public authority to advance selfish private purposes while everyone else, absorbed in their own private pursuits, looked the other way. Public education thus would serve to sustain the Revolutionary spirit, the patriots' consciousness of themselves as a free people, bound together by the fraternal ties so eloquently articulated in Jefferson's Declaration of Independence.

Jefferson and his fellow patriots urged the "sons of liberty" to overthrow George III, a tyrannical father figure who had shown himself "unfit to be the ruler of a free people."[2] The British king was the antitype of the good republican father, always solicitous of his children's welfare. As Jefferson had written in his famous pre-Revolutionary pamphlet *A Summary View of the Rights of British America* (1774), "kings are the servants, not the proprietors of the people."[3] Because political authority was a kind of trust, its continuing exercise was conditional on the fulfilment of its original purpose: the people's welfare and happiness. It was finally up to the people themselves, after "a long train of abuses & usurpations," to judge whether the king had violated his trust, for they were the ultimate source of all legitimate authority.[4] But deposing the king and instituting a republican form of government were not sufficient safeguards of popular rights.

Jefferson understood that every generation began its career in a dependent, childlike condition, necessarily reliant on its predecessors for nurture and development. His own generation of patriots had come of age in the hard school of familial betrayal. George III had disowned the Americans, treating them as foreigners, not as free-born Britons, his own legitimate children. His most unnatural crime was to divide one people into two, turning the British—"these unfeeling brethren"—against the Americans. The royal father betrayed his trust by elevating some of his "children" over the rest, denying the colonists their birthright. In George III's betrayal—and in the fratricidal betrayal of their British "brethren"—Jefferson thus conjured up a compelling narrative about the fall of once enlightened Britons from a golden age of peace and prosperity. Had the British king not been "deaf to the voice of justice & of consanguinity," he exclaimed, "we might have been a free & a great people together."[5] Instead, George III sought to destroy the Americans' liberty and property in order to raise up a corrupt and subservient aristocracy, a sorry colonial caricature of the metropolitan social order.

The notion that the British king and his wicked ministers were solely responsible for all of America's afflictions was an attractive one, but not one that thoughtful Revolutionaries could long sustain. Before the imperial conflict turned to war in April 1775, many native-born Americans had resisted the patriot juggernaut, and growing numbers of loyalists and neutrals thereafter reflected the Revolutionaries' poor performance on the battlefield. Lack of enthusiasm for the war effort, insufficient public virtue, and an unwillingness to make necessary sacrifices all suggested that the people's education was not yet complete, that it was not enough to subscribe to the "self-evident . . . truths" of Jefferson's Declaration.[6] Ignorant and credulous Americans were all too vulnerable to the seductive wiles of would-be aristocrats happy to pose as popular leaders. If the people had shown great political maturity in the moment of national crisis, they also revealed a distressing tendency to revert to childlike ignorance and indifference.

With other educational reformers such as Benjamin Rush and Noah Webster, Jefferson saw publicly sponsored education as the great engine of republican enlightenment.[7] Constitutional machinery might check and balance dangerously powerful interests and dangerous ambitions, but a vigilant electorate alone could keep the republican experiment on track. Jefferson proposed his famous three-tier education system in 1779, when he served as chair of a committee to revise Virginia's laws to make them compatible with the new republican dispensation. Unable to take a significant role in writing the new state constitution in 1776 because of responsibilities in Congress (most notably drafting the Declaration), Jefferson saw the revisal of the laws as his opportunity to reinforce and complete Virginia's republican revolution. Of the 126 bills reported by the committee, he considered four most crucial: those abolishing primogeniture and entail; his celebrated bill for religious freedom (passed in 1786); and "A Bill for the More General Diffusion of Knowledge" (never adopted).[8] Together, Jefferson recalled in his *Autobiography* (1821), these bills were designed to form "a system by which every fibre would be eradicated of antient or future aristocracy; and a foundation laid for a government truly republican." Without legal provisions for keeping landed estates intact (entail) and "for making one member of every family rich, and the rest poor" (primogeniture), aristocracy could not take root in Virginia; freedom of conscience meant that taxpayers would no longer have to support the established "religion of the rich." But it was only through education that citizens of the commonwealth would be "enabled to understand their rights, to maintain them, and to exercise with intelligence their parts in self-government."[9] To preempt an aristocratic revival, the bill proclaimed, Virginians must "know ambition under all its shapes." Under Jefferson's proposal, young Virginians—boys and girls alike—would be entitled to three years of primary schooling; a select group of worthy boys would receive scholarships to pursue advanced studies, including Latin and Greek, at grammar schools scattered across the state; and, finally, one student each year would rise to the apex of this educational pyramid with state support to attend the College of William and Mary.[10]

Although Jefferson failed to gain passage of his general education bill, the final crucial element and capstone of his state-building project, he remained ever optimistic. The thrust of his proposal was broadly political, after all, and the citizenry could be aroused and enlightened by other means at a time when wary taxpayers considered a comprehensive public school system much too ambitious and expensive. Indeed, it was a nice irony that vigilant legislators in Virginia and other states manifested a characteristically Jeffersonian hostility to "energetic" (big) government in voting down school bills. It was yet another irony that antipartisan politicians such as Jefferson should have developed rudimentary party organizations and propaganda machinery to disseminate their views and educate the public. Jeffersonian Republicans' faith in the people's wisdom—and in their own ability to shape public opinion—was sorely tested in the 1790s, particularly when the Quasi-War with France and widespread prosperity boosted the popularity of the Adams administration. But the electoral cycle provided the most immediate and compelling sites for sustaining—or redeeming— the republican revolution by educating and mobilizing voters. As long as the future of the republic remained in doubt, as it did until Jefferson's election in the "Revolution of 1800," provision for schooling the rising generation would have to wait. And when the Republicans finally did ascend to power, the rapid decline and ultimate disgrace of the Federalists made popular political education seem less urgent.

Yet Jefferson never lost interest in public education. During his retirement, he campaigned vigorously for a state university, the top tier of the comprehensive system he had been advocating throughout his career. Following the recommendation of a commission headed by Jefferson, the general assembly voted to site the University of Virginia in Charlottesville, a few short miles away from Monticello. Jefferson set forth the new institution's rationale in the commission's report: "to form the statesmen, legislators and judges, on whom public prosperity and individual happiness . . . so much depend." The university could only fulfill its role, however, with the implementation of a comprehensive scheme of primary and secondary education that would enable "every citizen" to "understand his duties" and "know his rights."[11]

Though Jefferson acknowledged the value of literacy and numeracy for the business of everyday life, his interest in basic education was animated by his concern for sustaining the republic. He pinned his hopes for primary schools on a thoroughgoing reform of Virginia's constitution that would devolve authority on neighborhoods, or "wards," thus bypassing recalcitrant state legislators reluctant to invest in the rising generation. "In government, as well as in every other business of life," he wrote an advocate of constitutional reform in 1816, "it is by division and subdivision of duties alone, that all matters, great and small, can be managed to perfection."[12] Jefferson had long been a critic of Virginia's oligarchical system of county government, in which local voters played virtually no role. The commonwealth's republican promise would only be fulfilled, he told his trusted lieutenant Joseph C. Cabell, by instituting a "gradation of authorities," from "the elementary republics of the wards, the county republics, the State republics, and the republic of the Union." At the ward or township level, the chief responsibility of voters would be to run the local schools: "if it is believed that these . . . schools will be better managed" by functionaries of the state government "than by the parents within each ward, it is a belief against all experience."[13]

The educational benefits of local schools redounded both to neighborhood parents and children. Sharing "in the direction of his ward-republic," the once passive citizen who was only called into action "at an election one day in the year" would now feel that he was a "participator . . . every day."[14] Political participation was itself educational, teaching citizens to look beyond their immediate circumstances toward a larger public interest. But episodic voting in state or national elections too often played into the hands of self-aggrandizing elites who could frame the issues—and inflame popular passions—to promote their own interests. Jefferson's "gradation of authorities" would avert such dangers by establishing a hierarchy of republican governments that would link the most humble voter to the nation as a whole. By the continuous exercise of authority within his appropriate sphere, however modest and circumscribed, the republican citizen would form ever stronger attachments to the "federal and republican principles" Jefferson articulated in his first inaugural address (March 4, 1801) and therefore to the union. A nation that could appeal to such strong popular loyalties would be, as he said then, "the strongest Government on earth."[15] Or, as he put it to Cabell in 1816, the citizen who actively participated "in the government of affairs"— even the management of a small village school—"will let the heart be torn out of his body sooner than his power be wrested from him by a Caesar or a Bonaparte."[16]

The key figure in Jefferson's scheme for republican renewal was not therefore simply an idealized, public-spirited voter but rather a father or "parent." Indeed, the parent's solicitude for his children forced him to look beyond his immediate circumstances, to the time when the rising generation would come into its patrimony. Jefferson's scheme of "division and subdivision" thus did not end with the isolated, self-regarding individual but rather with the head of a family who followed the dictates of nature in providing for the future welfare of his children. For Enlightenment thinkers like Jefferson, this altruism or moral sense was the fundamental building block of a just republican social order. When parents acted together in their neighborhoods to provide for all their children, they would learn to think less of their own families' fortunes and more of the welfare of the whole younger generation. "Private interest" and the "public good" were therefore not antithetical terms; on the contrary, man was by nature altruistic and sociable, always capable of seeing himself as part of a larger whole. The challenge was to construct a constitutional order of ascending levels of political association—little republics, beginning with the family itself, that were imbedded within ever larger republics—and so give full scope to these civic impulses, thus transforming family feeling into true patriotism.

Jefferson's ward system would encourage the good republican father to provide not only for his own children but for the children of his neighbors. In seeing these children as a generation that would one day come into its collective estate and govern the commonwealth, republican fathers would come to recognize themselves as a generation, responsible for their country's future welfare. Every man's affectionate regard for his own family was thus the font of a more capacious public virtue. When the American Revolutionaries proclaimed the sovereignty of the people, they hoped to realign patriarchal impulses with a just and natural republican social order. The abolition of aristocratic privilege was the necessary precondition for the reign of good republican fathers. Not only would all the children of the commonwealth be treated as equals "endowed by their creator with inalienable rights" but the fathers collectively would cede their self-governing authority to the rising generation. The genius of republicanism was as much epitomized by the self-restraint of fathers who did not attempt to rule from beyond the grave—as did the founders of great aristocratic families—as by the more familiar doctrine that governments derived "their just powers from the consent of the governed."[17]

Jefferson's educational ideas grew out of his fundamental premise that good republican fathers should prepare the next generation for the duties and responsibilities of self-government. The role of mentor or teacher was one that Jefferson embraced enthusiastically in his own personal life. After the death of his father when he was fourteen years old, William Small at the College of William and Mary and law teacher George Wythe served as mentors—or father substitutes—for the young Jefferson.[18] In later years, Jefferson performed a similar role for a series of young men, exercising the sort of disinterested form of paternal authority—the temporary government of children in their own best interest—that the perpetuation of the republic required.[19] The mentor figure showed that family feeling need not take the selfish and destructive forms so characteristic of aristocratic society. A republican commonwealth would prosper and endure when the generation of the fathers thought of all its children, the generation that would one day take its place, in such disinterested terms.

Thomas Jefferson may have enjoyed only limited success as an educational reformer. But a narrow focus on schools does not do justice to his republican vision. The American Revolution was itself a great experiment in popular political education. When Jefferson and his fellow patriots accused George III of failing to discharge his responsibilities as the American people's political father, they fashioned a new conception of legitimate authority and therefore of an enlightened, vigilant citizenry capable of giving—or withholding—its consent to government.

By emphasizing the temporary, contingent character of authority, the Revolutionaries took the familiar idea of political rule as a kind of trust or stewardship in a radical new direction. The master fiction of a monarchical regime was that the king-father and his line were immortal, while the people, his children, remained in a perpetual state of dependency. In Jefferson's republic, by contrast, paternal authority was diffused through the whole living generation, but was only temporary. Conscious of their own mortality, republican fathers recognized the importance of preparing the next generation to govern itself—and to provide, in turn, for succeeding generations. Political participation was the chief spur to popular enlightenment, for liberty—the consciousness of rights and responsibilities—would inspire a republican citizenry to learn. This was the animating principle of Jefferson's scheme for ward republics. Jefferson believed that his wards would give full scope to the natural impulses of republican fathers to promote the welfare of their own and their neighbors' children and that provision for schools was sure to follow.

Jefferson eloquently articulated the fundamental transformation of generational relations that characterized the new American nation. The widespread establishment of tax-supported public schools would not take place for several generations, but private schools and academies catering to enterprising and ambitious young people of all classes flourished in every part of the country. Meanwhile, the democratization of the electorate and emergence of party organizations made ordinary citizens conscious of their political power. Under these dynamic circumstances, the aristocratic ethos of the old monarchical regime rapidly gave way to a new democratic way of life in which republican sons came into their own and "the earth belong[ed] in usufruct to the living."[20] Jefferson undoubtedly would have found many of the results of this great transformation disturbing and distasteful. But it was the logical expression and consequence of the republican principles he had so memorably set forth in the Declaration of Independence.

Notes

This essay was originally published in *Thomas Jefferson: Genius of Liberty* (New York: Viking Studio in association with the Library of Congress, Washington, DC, 2000), 138–43.

1. Thomas Jefferson (hereafter TJ) to James Madison, Sept. 6, 1789, in Julian P. Boyd et al., eds., *The Papers of Thomas Jefferson*, 32 vols. to date (Princeton, NJ, 1950–), 15:392–98. On the problem of generations in TJ's thought, see Herbert Sloan, "'The Earth Belongs in Usufruct to the Living,'" in Peter S. Onuf, ed., *Jeffersonian Legacies* (Charlottesville, VA, 1993), 281–315. On TJ's educational ideas, see Harold Hellenbrand, *The Unfinished Revolution: Education and Politics in the Thought of Thomas Jefferson* (Newark, DE, 1990); Lorraine Smith Pangle and Thomas L. Pangle,

The Learning of Liberty: The Educational Ideas of the American Founders (Lawrence, KS, 1993), esp. chaps. 6, 13; and Joseph F. Kett, "Education," in Merrill D. Peterson, ed., *Thomas Jefferson: A Reference Biography* (New York, 1986), 233–51.

2. Declaration of Independence as Adopted by Congress, July 4, 1776, in Boyd et al., eds., *Jefferson Papers*, 1:429–33, quotation on 431.

3. TJ, Draft of Instructions to the Virginia Delegates in the Continental Congress (manuscript text of *A Summary View of the Rights of British America)* [July 1774], ibid., 1:121–41, quotation on 134.

4. Declaration of Independence as Adopted by Congress, July 4, 1776, ibid., *Jefferson Papers*, 1:430.

5. TJ's "original Rough draft" and Declaration of Independence as Adopted by Congress, July 4, 1776, ibid., 1:423–28, quotations on 427, 426.

6. Declaration of Independence as Adopted by Congress, July 4, 1776, ibid., 1:429.

7. See Frederick Rudolph, ed., *Essays on Education in the Early Republic* (Cambridge, MA, 1965).

8. For a good discussion of TJ's career as a republican reformer in Virginia, see Merrill D. Peterson, *Thomas Jefferson and the New Nation: A Biography* (New York, 1970), 97–165. The bills reported by the revisors are reprinted in Boyd et al., eds., *Jefferson Papers*, 2:329–657.

9. TJ, *Autobiography,* Jan. 6–July 29, 1821, in Merrill D. Peterson, ed., *Thomas Jefferson Writings* (New York, 1984), 3–101, quotations on 44.

10. Bill no. 79, "A Bill for the More General Diffusion of Knowledge," in Boyd et al., eds., *Jefferson Papers*, 2:526–35, quotation on 526.

11. Report of the Commissioners for the University of Virginia, Aug. 4, 1818, in Peterson, ed., *Jefferson Writings,* 457–73, quotations on 459.

12. TJ to Samuel Kercheval, July 12, 1816, in Andrew A. Lipscomb and Albert Ellery Bergh, eds., *The Writings of Thomas Jefferson,* 20 vols. (Washington, DC, 1903–4), 15:32–44, quotation on 38.

13. TJ to Joseph C. Cabell, Feb. 2, 1816, ibid., 14:417–23, quotations on 422, 420–21.

14. Ibid., 422.

15. TJ, First Inaugural Address, March 4, 1801, in Peterson, ed., *Jefferson Writings,* 14:492–96.

16. TJ to Cabell, Feb. 2, 1816, in Lipscomb and Bergh, eds., *Writings of Jefferson,* 14:422.

17. Declaration of Independence as Adopted by Congress, July 4, 1776, in Boyd et al., eds., *Jefferson Papers*, 1:429.

18. The best account of TJ's early years is in Dumas Malone, *Jefferson and His Time*, 6 vols. (Boston, 1948–81), vol. 1, *Jefferson the Virginian*.

19. For TJ as mentor, see Andrew Burstein, *The Inner Jefferson: Portrait of a Grieving Optimist* (Charlottesville, VA, 1995).

20. TJ to James Madison, Sept. 6, 1789, in Boyd et al., eds., *Jefferson Papers*, 15:392. The best study of this transformation is Gordon S. Wood, *The Radicalism of the American Revolution* (New York, 1992). On the history of education in this period, see Lawrence A. Cremin, *American Education: The National Experience, 1783–1876* (New York, 1980); and Carl F. Kaestle, *Pillars of the Republic: Common Schools and American Society, 1780–1860* (New York, 1983).

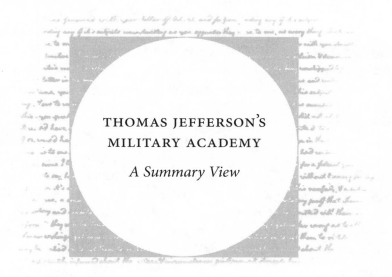

THOMAS JEFFERSON'S
MILITARY ACADEMY

A Summary View

As draftsman of the Declaration of Independence, Thomas Jefferson helped define the meaning of America. Unlike George Washington, the "father of his country," the civilian Jefferson was not an "indispensable" military man; nor was he a great law giver, like James Madison, author of the federal Constitution, or a great state builder, like his brilliant adversary Treasury Secretary Alexander Hamilton. Jefferson is instead remembered for the memorable language of the second paragraph of the Declaration— "all men are created equal . . . endowed by their creator with certain inalienable rights," including "life, liberty, and the pursuit of happiness." Jefferson's exalted status as democratic icon reflects the democratizing implications of a Declaration that enables Americans to see themselves as their own founders.[1]

To an envious and skeptical John Adams who took pride in his own heroic contributions to American independence, Jefferson's felicitous phrases—glittering generalities recycling the conventional, "self-evident" wisdom—seemed a slender foundation for his colleague's immortal reputation. What, after all, do they really mean? And what, after all, did Jefferson really contribute to the American founding? These questions have, throughout American history, shadowed Jefferson's bright image. Fervent believers in the ideals set forth in the Declaration have never tired—and will never tire—of charging Jefferson (and America) with failing to live up to its inspiring precepts; meanwhile, hardheaded "realists" warn that blind adherence to exalted principles too often leads to imprudent interventions in a dangerous and unpredictable "real" world.[2]

Not surprisingly, the realist tradition has flourished in military circles, where Jefferson's stock has historically been low. Yet Jefferson's image has never been fixed or static, and there are signs that even his severest critics are already taking a new look at their old nemesis. In 2002 Robert M. S. McDonald organized a scholarly conference to commemorate the bicentennial of the founding of the United States Military Academy; the essays subsequently published in McDonald's *Thomas Jefferson's Military Academy* offer us the opportunity to reassess Jefferson's role both as West Point's founder and as one of the nation's founders. Jefferson's legacy, we will discover, cannot be reduced to a few disconnected words or phrases.

As McDonald shows, Jefferson historically inspired little enthusiasm in a military establishment that was much more eager to assert the paternity of George Washington or to celebrate the great superintendent Sylvanus Thayer as its true founder. Yet the traditional bias against Jefferson is dissipating. Jefferson's hostility to "big government" has been ideologically resonant in a conservative military culture traditionally suspicious of civilian elites—and despite its own leading role in the vast expansion of the federal state during the twentieth century. The ratio of self-identified Republicans to Democrats among West Point cadets is now eight to one (64 percent to 8 percent), reversing, although certainly exaggerating, partisan preferences at elite colleges and universities preparing future civilian leaders. This ideological polarization, McDonald concludes, "probably constitutes good news for Jefferson's reputation within the army."[3] At the very least, custodians of institutional memory will no longer feel compelled to overlook Jefferson's crucial role in West Point's founding. But it remains to be seen if West Point will embrace Jefferson as a true founder, rendering him the same respect and reverence now claimed by Washington and Thayer.

Why does this matter? Americans have always had mixed feelings about the role of "great men," and particularly of military heroes. Jefferson and John Adams, Elizabeth D. Samet reminds us, were acutely self-conscious about the danger of exalting one great man, or an "aristocratic" elite, above the multitude, even in the case of Washington, the self-abnegating American Cincinnatus. Yet they also cherished their own reputations as founders of the republic, fearful that Americans might forget why the Revolutionaries had made such great sacrifices and what they hoped their bold experiment in republican self-government would achieve. They worried about how we would remember *them,* about the historical memory and civic consciousness of subsequent generations. In warning against the idolatrous apotheosis of founders, they hoped to keep alive a vital sense of a founding that must be constantly remembered and renewed.[4]

Of course, Jefferson did not worry specifically about his standing at West Point. If partisan and ideological enemies have conspired to obliterate his actual role in the academy's founding, it must be said that Jefferson himself contributed to this obliteration by saying so little on the subject. He was, as the inscription he ordered for his tombstone proudly recorded, "Father of the University of Virginia," but he made no corresponding claim for West Point.[5] I think Jefferson would agree with McDonald, however, that the real question has always been "not whether Jefferson made West Point, but what West Point makes of Jefferson."[6] This is simply a local specification of a larger question: What do Americans now make of Jefferson and the founding generation generally? West Point's answer to McDonald must also take into account—and, finally, must be shaped by—that larger question. The military has always to some extent, sometimes more, sometimes less, defined itself *against* the larger society, and particularly the civilian political establishment. Yet it has also defined itself in *subordination* to civil society, sublimating the ambivalence that fosters its corporate identity in unquestioning subscription to the values "Duty, Honor, Country."

Rethinking the founding of West Point requires us to rethink the nation's founding as well. Conditions in the military may now be propitious for a more favorable view of Jefferson. But to embrace Jefferson as the founder—or one of the founders—of the academy means to reconsider the Army's historic aversion to this quintessential civilian and to ask what role the military should now play in republican society. Jefferson's ideological appeal to contemporary Republicans is understandable. Yet the historical Jefferson cannot be reduced to the conservative—or, more accurately, classically liberal—precepts that make him so attractive to so many military people today. Indeed, I will argue, it is precisely because Jefferson's legacy is so complex, because he forces us to think about our history and about our present purposes, that he serves the American people so well as a "founder." Jefferson could be this kind of founder for West Point.

The civilian Jefferson played no direct personal role in winning the Revolution. Not surprisingly, in his celebration of the mass popular movement to overthrow British tyranny, he emphasized the patriotism of citizen-soldiers, not the skills of a professional military. Unlike Colonel Alexander Hamilton, who recklessly threw himself into the breach at Yorktown, Governor Jefferson kept himself out of harm's way, fleeing to safety when Benedict Arnold invaded Virginia. But if Jefferson was himself no hero, he was, in characteristic civilian fashion, eager enough that others should die. "The tree of liberty must be refreshed from time to time with the blood of patriots & tyrants," he told William S. Smith in 1787; in a letter to William Short six years later, he did not blink at mass slaughter: "I would have seen half the earth desolated" in the name of republican revolution. "Were there but an Adam & Eve left in every country, & left free, it would be better than as it now is."[7] Here, for skeptical military men, were the classic symptoms of civilian bloodthirstiness, justifying itself by appeal to the most exalted ideological principles.

Yet if republican ideology authorized massive sacrifices for the public good, it also encouraged vigilant civilians to keep professional soldiers on a short leash. For the British Real Whig thinkers whose radical ideas inspired Jefferson, a professional "standing army" was the most dangerous tool of despotic power. Jefferson juxtaposed the republican ideal of the good citizen, who in time of crisis "would fly to the standard of the law, and would meet invasions of the public order as his own personal concern," to the abject servility of the professional soldier who would obey any master.[8] But Jefferson most distrusted the officer corps, would-be aristocrats who commanded their troops and set themselves above the civilian population. Here was a class of courtiers without a king—although Washington might provide a plausible equivalent—anxious to advance their corporate and personal interests at the people's expense. Because war offered the greatest opportunity to fulfill these aristocratic ambitions, a professional army had an interest in fostering a never-ending cycle of conflicts. Not coincidentally, a state of war constituted the greatest threat to the survival of republican government, exaggerating the claims of arbitrary executive power and jeopardizing the lives, liberties, and property of taxpayers.

Jefferson expressed a pervasive Revolutionary ambivalence about war making. The determination of contemporaries—and most modern historians—to dissociate the Revolution from the war reflects this ambivalence. John Adams's assertion that "The Revolution was in the Minds of the People, and this was effected, from 1760 to 1775, in the course of fifteen Years before a drop of blood was drawn at Lexington" is the most famous and influential expression of this ambivalence.[9] Of course, this displacement of the actual war in accounts of the Revolution foregrounded the contributions of republican statesmen and ideologues who took a leading role in the imperial crisis and in the subsequent history of state making and constitution writing. But it also reflected a genuine conundrum. If patriotic revolutionaries rose up in resistance to the increasingly expansive pretensions of despotic imperial government, how could they avoid re-creating among themselves—by imposing unprecedented levels of taxation and concentrating power in strong governments—the very thing they meant to destroy? How could good republicans govern themselves effectively enough to win the war and secure the subsequent peace without jeopardizing their liberties? How could the army, the key institution of the old regime, be made safe for the new, republican regime?

The role of the military in American republican society remained a flashpoint for ideological and partisan conflict in the post-Revolutionary period. In these debates, Jefferson often took the role of civilian critic, warning against the concentration of power in an overly energetic federal government too eager to resort to military force. As leader of the emergent Republican opposition, Jefferson decried the militarism of Hamiltonian High Federalists as they prepared for war against Revolutionary France—the new nation's erstwhile "sister republic"—and, still more ominously, against their domestic enemies. Ideological polarization in the late 1790s thus reinforced the anti-Jeffersonian bias of military leaders, overwhelmingly Federalist appointees who became increasingly skeptical about Republican good faith and patriotism. Yet again, they charged, Republican ideologues were carried away by blind adherence to so-called principles, supporting a morally bankrupt French regime and risking the very survival of the republic by resisting preparedness measures and fomenting disunion.[10]

During the Quasi-War with France (1797–1800), Federalists had no doubt that the willingness to prepare for war was the true test for republican patriots. Preserving independence was the sine qua non of self-government, making Republican appeals to antistatist, libertarian sentiment profoundly dangerous. Jefferson's reputation in military circles thus sank to its all-time low as Republicans mobilized anti-administration forces in a great campaign to purge the republic of "monocrats" and "aristocrats." In Republican rhetoric, the mythic "citizen-soldier" was now recast as the patriotic partisan; real soldiers simply served as tools of a corrupt administration preparing to meet nonexistent external threats. Historians have been hard-pressed to take such "hysterical" rhetoric seriously, but it is clear that Jefferson and his allies were convinced that the future of the republican experiment was at stake in the war crisis.[11] They were also convinced that their High Federalist opponents meant to exploit the crisis to subvert states' rights and individual liberties. The Federalist administration could not be trusted to sustain civilian supremacy over the military. To the contrary, Republicans were convinced that the administration was powerless to control a move for military supremacy, masquerading as preparedness, masterminded by Hamilton and his allies.

Army leaders have always felt misunderstood. Indeed, a sense of alienation from an ungrateful and uncomprehending society is an essential prop to the military's corporate identity.[12] The Revolution itself provided the paradigm case of civilian obliviousness to the real costs of independence, and the same themes were rehearsed in the Republican campaign against the military in the late 1790s. From these experiences, the army developed a narrative of its own history, predicated on its quasi-adversarial role with the public and pivoting on its own patriotic dedication to sustaining the republic and submitting to civilian rule, however foolish and misguided it might be. Instead of setting themselves up as a distinct, privileged class, army officers struggled to develop an ethos of professionalism, or "regularity," that would demonstrate their unwavering fealty to republican principles. Far from seeking to promote counterrevolution and a monarchical revival, these self-sacrificing public servants would always exercise a conservative, moderating force, checking rather than abetting a bloodthirsty popular will.

The peaceful transition of power in 1801 shows that Republican fears of a counterrevolutionary coup were vastly exaggerated.[13] Instead, it was the Republican governors of Pennsylvania and Virginia who took steps to mobilize military force against the possibility of a "stolen election"; Federalists flirted with Aaron Burr, negotiating a deal with Jefferson's putative running mate that would *not* have violated any provision of the federal Constitution, but they never considered a military coup. However alienated from Jefferson they might be, army leaders could not imagine betraying their historic role as patriotic defenders of the republic—nor, to be practical, could they imagine that the tiny number of troops at their disposal could be put to any good use. Indeed, the image of Jefferson as pacifist and Francophile "philosopher" that emerged out of the partisan polemics of the late 1790s served to reinforce by juxtaposition the ethos of moderation in the military. In opposition to civilian "idealism," army leaders fostered a culture of "realism."

They would always be prepared to make the necessary sacrifices to preserve American independence, and they understood that any challenge to civilian supremacy would inevitably subvert the republican regime.

Jefferson played at best a minimal, even a negative, role in the army's narrative of its history and developing collective identity. He was the very embodiment of civilian foolishness, heedless about threats of war—even as his own policies threatened to bring it on—, too sanguine about the possibilities of commercial diplomacy, unwilling to invest in defensive measures that might have reduced the danger of conflict. There is much to be said for this narrative, most notably in the way it inculcates the fundamental premise of civilian supremacy, resolving the tension between army and society through the precepts of professionalism. Because Jefferson served as a foil for this emerging ethos, it is hardly surprising that he would be West Point's "lost founder." The academy came of age as an institution despite, even in opposition to, a Jeffersonian and then Jacksonian society that failed to grasp or appreciate the need either for a truly professional army or for an effective, energetic federal government.

Yet it is nonetheless true that Jefferson *was* West Point's founder. The Jefferson image that emerged during the 1790s was in many ways a misleading caricature, the product of partisan polemics during a period of profound crisis in the history of the union when no one could predict the future. For Federalist critics, Jefferson's policy failures as president seemed to confirm the caricature. But Jefferson was no pacifist, and his decision to establish the academy in 1802 was no aberration. He may have been suspicious of military men—given their partisan proclivities, he had every reason to be so—but he had no delusions about enjoying the benefits of peace without preparedness. If he remained somewhat skeptical about the army's self-restraint and professionalism, he was no less determined to achieve a civil-military balance that would protect the republic from internal as well as external threats.

Military critics, priding themselves on their "realism," charge Jefferson with being a pacifist ideologue, unable to grasp the necessity for energetic government capable of projecting effective power in a dangerous world. Jefferson may in fact be accurately called a "half-way pacifist," inspired by an Enlightenment vision of eventually eliminating the causes of war by dismantling the corrupt institutions of the old regime, including "standing armies."[14] But Jefferson never believed that American independence would instantly lead to a republican millennium of peace and prosperity. In 1787, after three years of diplomatic frustration in Paris, Jefferson would agree with Hamilton that the new nation had not yet achieved "the happy empire of perfect wisdom and perfect virtue." Fantasies of "perpetual peace" and spontaneous union among the states were predicated on the false premise that "the genius of republics . . . is pacific," the "deceitful dream of a golden age."[15] Jefferson knew that there was a fundamental difference between declaring independence and forcing the powers of the world to recognize it; he also knew that conflicts of interest among the states could easily destroy an increasingly fragile union, thus unleashing counterrevolutionary forces and Europeanizing American politics. Jefferson had misgivings about the new Constitution drafted at Philadelphia, but he was convinced that a fundamental reform of the confederation was absolutely necessary.[16]

Peace was a problem for Jefferson, the ultimate goal of his republican constitutionalism, not its premise or point of departure. Where he differed from Hamilton, a much more conventional state builder and geopolitician, was in his complex and comprehensive view of the potential sources of conflict that jeopardized peace. The first requirement for a durable republican regime in the New World was constitutional reform in the respective states. The American state-republics might not be naturally peaceful, as Hamilton warned, but at least they could be freed from the despotic rule of predatory ruling classes that, in effect, made "war" on their own peoples. Yet this happy outcome did not follow inevitably from destroying the old imperial regime; it depended instead on drafting proper constitutions according to the precepts of enlightened political science. So, too, Jefferson believed, perpetual peace among the states depended on an effective central government, potent in its own sphere but constitutionally restrained from encroaching on the reserved rights of the states or the liberties of the people. Such a government, he concluded, could promote peace in the world at large, advancing American interests by working toward a regime of free trade and rising prosperity throughout the commercial world.

Because he believed threats to peace were so pervasive, potentially proceeding from internal as well as external sources, Jefferson was reflexively hostile to claims by the executive—or its military minions—for unchecked prerogative powers that would enable it to "prepare" for war or make it without regard to civilian authority. War constituted the greatest challenge to the new nation, Jeffersonian Republicans agreed, for the exigencies of mobilizing men and resources in the cause of national independence and self-preservation—the first and highest duty of any government according to the law of nature—tended to obliterate constitutional distinctions among warring powers, thus transforming republics into monarchies with powerful, irresponsible governments—even when they pretended to preserve their republican forms. For the future founder of the military academy at West Point, the Federalists' Quasi-War with France raised these problems to the fore, giving urgent point to well-developed prior concerns about the pernicious implications of loose construction of the federal Constitution and the resulting expansion of the administration's powers for the preservation of the union and peace among the states.

The party conflicts of the 1790s culminated in the Federalists' efforts to suppress the Republican opposition through repressive legislation. The Alien and Sedition Acts of 1798 launched a broad-ranging assault on the administration's domestic enemies even as it prepared for a full-scale war against France. In response, Jefferson and his allies sought to rally their troops against the Federalist juggernaut, calling on American patriots to reenact the Revolutionary struggle against a tyrannical central government. This deepening political crisis made the warnings of Republican ideologues about pervasive threats to peace seem prophetic. The "perpetual union" that had secured peace among the states and their collective security in a dangerous world was poised on the brink of collapse. In the dark days leading up to the 1800 presidential canvas, an increasingly anxious Jefferson was nearly driven to despair. When, thanks to John Adams's diplomacy, the war crisis dissipated and public opinion recoiled against the administration's mobilization measures, Jefferson believed a new day had dawned. Patriotic voters finally came to their senses in the "Revolution of 1800," returning to Revolutionary first principles and securing their precious union.[17]

The crisis of 1800–1801 was emphatically *not* politics as usual. Jefferson's mandate was not as a party leader—he had not "campaigned" for office—but rather as the mere instrument of the people's will. As David N. Mayer argues, Jefferson's constitutionalism was "contextualist," changing over time "as background political circumstances changed." Jefferson's inauguration signaled a radical change in circumstances that cast executive authority in an entirely new light. Suspicious of Federalist intentions, Jefferson had previously opposed establishing a military academy on strict constructionist grounds. Now that the administration was safely ensconced within its proper sphere of authority, such constitutional scruples could be laid aside.[18] Instead, writes Theodore J. Crackel, Jefferson initiated a "carefully modulated program of reform" of both civil and military establishments that "would ultimately bring them into line with the broad aspirations and goals of the new Republican regime."[19]

Jefferson's many critics, then and now, have made much of his alleged "inconsistency" and "hypocrisy" on constitutional issues: as long as he was in opposition, Jefferson was a strict constructionist; once in power, he was prone to looser, self-serving constructions. Mayer notes, however, that Jefferson's constitutional contextualism always "permitted a broad latitude for the exercise of federal powers within the sphere assigned to the national government under the Constitution, particularly with regard to foreign affairs."[20] Defense of the republic justified any "necessary and proper" measures, as the first law of nature enjoined, but the same elasticity did not apply to relations between the federal government and the states or individual citizens. Given the Federalists' tendency to interpret the principle of federal supremacy as a license to consolidate all authority in the central government, it was incumbent on Republican oppositionists to raise the alarm at any initiative—including the founding of the National Bank, or even the proposal to establish a national military academy—that threatened to expand the ambit of federal authority. But once the administration was fully "republicanized"—that is, once it was purged of the "aristocratic," "monocratic" tendencies toward "consolidation" that characterized Federalist administrations—the federal government could be trusted to exercise more expansive powers. "*Federalism* to Jefferson meant far more than the 'states rights' caricature," Mayer concludes, for it led him "to interpret federal powers under the Constitution quite liberally in matters involving foreign affairs." In this respect, he "could be fairly described as a 'nationalist.'"[21]

For fearful Republicans, the internal threat of a consolidationist federal administration seemingly bent on obliterating the states eclipsed external threats from hostile foreign powers in the late 1790s. They could not take the war scare seriously: could the "sister republic" really want a war with its Revolutionary ally—unless goaded to it by Anglophile Federalists? The strategic horizon altered dramatically as Jefferson assumed office. With the union now secure against internal threat, Jefferson could envision a new epoch of territorial expansion, economic development, and collective security. His claim in his first inaugural address that the United States was "the strongest Government on earth" heralded his new conception of national defense. By any conventional reckoning of military preparedness, the claim was absurd on its face. But Jefferson was underscoring the crucial importance of revolutionary mass mobilization for national security: this was the only regime "where every man, at the call of the law, would fly to the standard of the law, and would meet invasions of the public order as his own personal concern." Jefferson's formulation conflated the military mobilization of the American Revolution with the political mobilization that saved the republic and led to his own election, thus conjuring up the iconic figure of the citizen-soldier as the embodiment of patriotic virtue.[22]

Jefferson's rhetorical resolution of civil-military tensions offered a mythic, justificatory narrative of the Revolution (in which, in fact, the relation between "citizen" and "soldier" was profoundly problematic) and of the just concluded political and constitutional struggle (in which so many benighted voters failed to understand their own true interests). Jefferson was hardly unaware of these discrepancies. His paean to the citizen-soldier and to the transcendent unity of the American people—"We are all republicans, we are all federalists"—was instead meant to articulate his administration's goals. "Sometimes it is said that man can not be trusted with the government of himself," Jefferson wrote. "Can he, then, be trusted with the government of others? Or have we found angels in the forms of kings to govern him?" Republicanism was a glorious experiment, an effort to vindicate human nature itself. Its ultimate success depended on the enlightenment of the people, their choice of good leaders, and their willingness to submit to legitimate authority. Everything hinged on the fundamental republican principle, that leaders must be drawn from—and responsible to—a vigilant citizenry, determined to preserve its liberties. It was precisely for this reason that it was so essential to Jefferson to "republicanize" the military establishment, to create an institutional structure and officer corps that could command the loyalties of citizen-soldiers and so make the United States the "strongest Government on earth."

A military academy purged of its monarchical and aristocratic tendencies was crucial to Jefferson's goal of republicanizing the officer corps. Notwithstanding his ideological hostility to a professional army, Jefferson had no illusions about dispensing with a military establishment. For a self-governing people to defend itself in time of crisis, a thoroughly republican officer corps must be prepared to lead. The Military Peace Establishment Act of 1802 was not intended to reduce the army, Crackel writes, but it did allow "Jefferson to rid himself of some of his most vociferous detractors in the army" and create "a force that would come to reflect the republican society from which it was drawn." The new military academy "established a source of future Republican officers."[23]

The critical role of a Republican military academy would be to draw future officers from society at large and to inculcate in them a principled commitment to patriotic service. The great danger was that the military establishment would become a quasi-aristocratic caste. The formation of the Society of the Cincinnati, a hereditary association of Revolutionary War officers, pointed ominously in this direction, as did the High Federalism of prominent veterans in the 1790s. For the republic to survive, Jeffersonian Republicans believed, it was necessary to root out the superstitious awe of the better sort that sustained social hierarchy. Crackel shows that reform of the army was part of a broader campaign to recruit Republicans to all branches of the federal administration and make them more representative of the people. Federalists were most deeply entrenched in the military establishment, a "standing army" whose very existence seemed to jeopardize republican liberty. The new administration's challenge, Elizabeth D. Samet writes, was to "weaken the pull of organizations such as the Cincinnati by giving future officers something other than the crucible of Revolutionary combat to unite them as disciplined professionals."[24]

War and peace presented a conundrum to practical Republicans. The Revolution itself demonstrated the central importance of an effective military force in vindicating American independence. Yet that same force could easily take a counterrevolutionary turn: a powerful army with a well-developed esprit de corps and a sense of its own distinctive, corporate interests could seize power at any time. Armies also thrived in a constant state of war that enhanced and rewarded their effectiveness while jeopardizing the liberty, property, and lives of ordinary citizens. How could a republic prepare for war without risking the peace? Aristocratic regimes reproduced themselves, perpetuating privilege and power among ruling families across the generations. Eschewing aristocratic succession, the new republic had to foster new forms of social solidarity, the "brotherhood" of fellow citizens, and a new conception of intergenerational relations. The new nation must find a way to produce "a long line of American Washingtons willing to subordinate themselves to civil power."[25]

The republican obsession with the problem of generational succession was most apparent in ambitious proposals for public education. Educational reformers struggled to overcome formidable resistance from war-weary taxpayers who suspected, with some reason, that publicly financed schools would serve elite interests at their expense. The training of army officers raised particularly acute problems. If American arms had triumphed in the Revolution without benefit of formal military education, why should a military academy be necessary in peacetime? As Don Higginbotham notes, the "tutorial method" of officer training in the midst of the Revolutionary War "seems to have worked reasonably well," and a "great influx of foreign officers" also gave the army "added military experience and eighteenth-century style professionalism."[26] But Jefferson and his fellow Republicans were not confident that the Revolutionary experience would be replicated in the next war. On one hand, military skills would atrophy in a period of protracted peace; if, on the other, chronic warfare enabled the highly informal, personalistic "tutorial" system to flourish, the growing power of the military establishment would jeopardize the survival of republican government. The Republican solution to this dilemma was the establishment of a formal system of military education. A truly republican academy would recruit widely in the larger society, thus countering the aristocratic tendency of a military caste to reproduce itself, and it would also inculcate republican principles in future officers. The most critical of those principles, the subordination of the military to civilian direction, would be implicit in the very constitution of a federally sponsored academy, established by—and financially dependent on—the people's representatives in Congress.

Education was the republican answer to aristocratic privilege, substituting achievement for the accidents of birth in recruiting a new generation of leaders. Jefferson and other educational reformers were not "agrarian" levelers who would destroy social distinctions. To the contrary, they promoted a conception of what Jefferson called "natural aristocracy," a regime in which merit would be recognized and rewarded. Given Jefferson's meritocratic perspective, the ascendancy of High Federalist warmongers in the late 1790s was particularly disturbing, revealing crypto-aristocratic tendencies that would destroy the republican revolution. One crucial lesson from this crisis was that these tendencies must be countered, not only by the appointment of Republican officials but by the proper education of the next generation of leaders. Jefferson recognized that there was a paucity of qualified Republicans—particularly in the military—who were qualified for high office. Conscious of the partisan dimensions of this deficit, Jefferson's Revolutionary enthusiasm for educational reform was rekindled in the period leading up to his election.

Historians traditionally have minimized Jefferson's role as West Point's founder because he said so little about the establishment of the academy in his extensive correspondence. The historiographical problem is one of perspective. Because Jefferson was determined to republicanize the military—to integrate it thoroughly into the larger society and make it more clearly subordinate to civilian authority—his ambitions for the academy transcended a narrow definition of professional military training. Jennings L. Wagoner Jr. and Christine Coalwell McDonald provide the crucial context for understanding Jefferson's role in West Point's founding. As they write, "Jefferson was awash in educational ideas, plans, and proposals as the new century ushering in the Republican 'revolution of 1800' dawned."[27] The most progressive approach to military education increasingly emphasized the importance of science and technology, blurring traditional distinctions between professional training in different fields. Early proposals by Pierre Samuel Dupont de Nemours and Joel Barlow "shared the feature of having special schools, including a military academy, that would operate as components of a national university."[28] In 1806 Barlow recommended moving the academy from West Point to Washington for this purpose; Jefferson and Superintendent Jonathan Williams subsequently favored such a move in order to transform the academy into a "national school of engineering."[29] Jefferson's impulse in these projects was not to dilute military education, but to give it additional prestige and public support by linking it with modern scientific and technical training in a comprehensive educational establishment. That Jefferson took this goal seriously is apparent in his openness to military education at his University of Virginia: in 1817 he even proposed that the Society of the Cincinnati endow a professorship there![30]

Because the academy stayed at West Point and plans for a national university came to naught, the relevance of Jefferson's educational vision for the institution's history has remained obscure. That obscurity was reinforced by the academy's less than glorious early history. Samuel J. Watson underscores the irony of the belated reception of "Jeffersonian" ideas about democratic access, professionalism, and advanced technical education during Thayer's superintendency (1818–33). The major obstacle to the institution's success in the early years was the tendency of its leaders—including Republican Alden Partridge—to flout the canons of military professionalism. Military men who cherished the aristocratic values Jefferson sought to extirpate—an exaggerated sense of social superiority and personal honor—were prone to resign their commissions at the slightest provocation. An ethos of professionalism, or "regularity," only triumphed at West Point when Thayer's standards of discipline and order fostered "unprecedented uniformity, stability, and predictability."[31] The new professionalism may have constituted the fulfillment of Jefferson's vision, as Watson suggests, but Thayer and his followers did not therefore see themselves as Jeffersonians. Recoiling against the demagogic war hero Andrew Jackson, Jefferson's self-anointed heir, leading military men were drawn into the ranks of the new Whig party. Jefferson's reputation plunged accordingly.

Thayer and his colleagues were able to rebuff Jackson's interference in the academy's administration because they had successfully established a meritocratic institution that could contain and suppress the aristocratic tendencies of the old military establishment. Insulated from the "corruption" of party politics, an increasingly professionalized army identified itself with the nation as a whole and embraced the principle of subordination to civilian authority. In a period of mounting sectional tensions, Watson shows, "the West Point–educated officer corps was the closest thing to a national administrative . . . cadre" in the United States.[32] The academy thus fulfilled Jefferson's original vision of inculcating patriotic values and disseminating advanced technical and scientific knowledge—and did so much more effectively than the University of Virginia, the great project of his declining years. Of course, when he founded the university, an increasingly embittered Jefferson, hypersensitive about encroachments on states' rights, no longer thought in national terms. Fittingly, his new university emerged as a bastion of planter privilege and a hotbed of secessionist sentiment on the eve of the Civil War. As it turned out, however, West Point's "nationalism" proved a frail prop to a disintegrating union: a large number of academy graduates joined the rebellious Confederate forces.

As Merrill Peterson showed many years ago, the "Jefferson image" has been appropriated and reshaped by successive generations of Americans for a dizzying array of often conflicting purposes.[33] Jefferson should not be seen merely as the passive victim of this process of image construction. Although he strained to sustain an overarching commitment to the republican principles he articulated so eloquently in the heady days of the American Revolutionary crisis, his positions on many fundamental issues changed dramatically over the course of his career. Anxiety about preserving the proper balance between liberty and power—and, particularly, between states' rights and federal authority—would be the crucial pivot for many of these changes. When loyalties to state and union were in perfect accord, as they seemed to be in 1776 and again in 1801 when he ascended to the presidency in the wake of another "revolution," a progressive, optimistic, enlightened Jefferson could look forward to the coming republican millennium. But when reactionary forces jeopardized the federal balance—when, for instance, "restrictionists" sought to ban slavery in Missouri, thus subverting the principle of new state equality and dangerously enlarging the power of the federal government—a despairing Jefferson feared the worst. Perhaps the American Revolution itself had been a tragic mistake, not the herald of a new epoch in the progress of political civilization.

In his expansive, optimistic mode, Jefferson could envision the development of an energetic, powerful central government. National defense clearly fell within his conception of the federal government's legitimate authority, and there was no constitutional barrier to establishing a military academy that would help secure the nation as a whole from future threats. Jefferson also believed that the public had a broad responsibility to educate the rising generation generally, although the role of the federal government was in this case more ambiguous. But if there were scruples about federal sponsorship of a national university—as opposed to a military academy—or to other internal improvements of national significance, it should be easy enough to amend the federal Constitution accordingly. In any event, the caricature of Jefferson as an antistatist libertarian does not hold, either at the federal or state level.

The Jefferson who founded West Point believed that power and liberty could be harmonized in an expanding republican empire. His paradoxical project of republicanizing the state depended on making institutions of government that had embodied aristocratic power and privilege responsible and accessible to a self-governing people secure in its rights. For Jeffersonians, the "standing army" was the most dangerously aristocratic institution, the potential tool of the despotic power that Hamiltonian High Federalists had sought to exercise during the Quasi-War crisis. That made the "chaste reformation" of the military establishment such a crucially important component of the broader republican reform program.[34] A republicanized army would be capable of defending the nation against external threats, making the United States "the strongest Government on earth," but would no longer represent the kind of internal threat to the rights of the state-republics and the liberties of the people that had driven Jefferson to the brink of despair in the late 1790s.

The difference between Jefferson and the "realists" who command most respect in military circles is that he had a far more comprehensive vision of potential threats to peace. Where the realist prepares to resist the assaults of foreign powers or to project power abroad, the Jeffersonian "idealist" also seeks to curb dangerous exercises of power at home. Jefferson thus conceptualized the problem of war and peace in three, interdependent dimensions: to secure a peaceful, progressively improving international order, the federal government had to take the form of a sovereign power capable of exercising conventional military power; at the same time, however, it had to secure the states in the full ambit of their rights as self-governing republics, thus sustaining their "perpetual union" and preempting the possibility of interstate warfare; and, finally, government at every level should be curbed from making war on the sovereign people by encroaching on their rights and violating the fundamental principle of consent. Properly interpreted, the federal Constitution authorized Jefferson to take all appropriate measures to defend the states collectively, but it also functioned as a kind of "peace pact," or super-treaty, to secure the states against each other and against the federal government.[35] Bills of rights in the federal and state constitutions defined the rights of individual citizens that were secured through the ordinary operations of republican self-government.

Jefferson's image of the citizen-soldier represented the ultimate convergence of state and society in his republican vision. Evoking a mythic Revolutionary past, Jefferson looked forward to a time when the army would be so thoroughly identified with a self-governing people that civil-military conflict would be unthinkable. But the synthesis of citizen and soldier, like the vision of a more perfect union of sovereign states, was bound to be frustrated. Even in a Jeffersonian republic, citizens and soldiers have different interests and will see the world differently. The Revolution military men remembered bore little resemblance to Jefferson's: they instead recalled the disjunction of citizen and soldier, and their own thankless struggle to sustain the war in the face of civilian suspicion and neglect. Their future—and the future of the independent United States—depended on the willingness of taxpayers to sustain a peacetime military establishment that could effectively mobilize men and resources in the next war. Perhaps then, Jefferson's terms should be reversed: the soldier, not the citizen, should come first; citizens could only "fly to the standard of the law" if the military establishment was prepared to lead them.

But Jefferson did not have to be told that citizens and soldiers constituted distinct interests. As Crackel has shown, Jefferson understood that his great challenge was to republicanize the federal administration, including the army, so that "liberty" would no longer be jeopardized by "power." Only at the highest level of abstraction, in the idea of "popular sovereignty," could this fundamental tension be fully resolved. In the real world, Jefferson knew, government would have to be prepared to act energetically and decisively, sometimes far in advance of public opinion or legislative action. The executive had a clear constitutional mandate to conduct foreign policy, to command the nation's military resources to secure its vital interests. Without an effective military establishment, the president could not perform his most important duties. If the new nation's sovereignty and independence were not secured, the union would collapse, the republican experiment would fail, and liberty would be lost.

Many Federalists, even Jefferson's archrival Hamilton, recognized that Jefferson had no intention of jettisoning the federal administration that Washington and Adams had labored so hard to establish. What remained controversial was the new president's appointment policies: how many Federalist appointees would be purged? Would there be a place for moderate Federalists in the new regime? While Jefferson's appointments inspired some criticism, particularly among hidebound obstructionists who had no intention of cooperating with the new administration, Jefferson clearly meant to co-opt as many former opponents as possible. The appointment of Major Jonathan Williams, a moderate Federalist, as the first superintendent at West Point set the tone for a moderate program of military reform. To the extent he relied on the academy to produce a new generation of officers, Jefferson was willing to be patient, accepting the necessity of dealing in the meantime with a military establishment that remained overwhelmingly Federalist in sentiment.

What sort of founder does this make Jefferson? The answer is as complicated for the military academy as it is for the nation as a whole. Most obviously, Jefferson sponsored and signed the bill that established the academy: he was, in some sense then, the "author" of the founding document, just as he was the author of American independence in his famous Declaration. But if, notwithstanding the efforts of revisionist historians, Jefferson continues to get too much credit for launching the new nation, the army has traditionally minimized Jefferson's role in the academy's founding, making him a "lost founder." In contrast, the scholars who participated in the commemoration of West Point's bicentennial take a more capacious view, sketching the broad outlines of an intellectual and institutional history that recovers Jefferson's role. If it is so important to know what influences shaped Jefferson's Declaration—and now to question the extent to which it *is* "Jefferson's" Declaration—isn't it also important to know what he had in mind when he authorized West Point's founding?

There is no question that West Point's "other founders"—the contributions of George Washington (deceased, at this point) or Sylvanus Thayer (who arrived some years later, as a young cadet)—have been duly noted and celebrated—and no danger that Jefferson will displace them. After all, the corporate identity of a military caste, proud of its own contributions to winning and preserving American independence, demands heroes and founders who come up through the ranks and share its values and world-view. In his famous letter to Henry Lee, setting forth his modest conception of his role in declaring American independence, Jefferson disclaimed any "originality of principle or sentiment," concluding that the Declaration was simply "intended to be an expression of the American mind."[36] But Jefferson could not pretend to express the "military mind." Instead, he challenged the very notion that the military should have a mind of its own, insisting that soldiers were citizens first.

Military men and women would not quarrel with this premise, the foundational principle of civilian supremacy, but they would articulate it in their own language, the language of professional "regularity" and in "concepts of duty, honor, and integrity rooted in disinterested personal accountability" that underscored *differences* between citizens and soldiers.[37] Hostility to Jefferson, and later to Jackson, epitomized the army's almost tribal sense that civilians would never give soldiers the respect and understanding they deserved, that if the military establishment were to function effectively without jeopardizing liberty it was because the military had so thoroughly internalized professional values. In other words, it was military self-restraint, not the superior wisdom of civilian politicians, that sustained the republic. From this perspective, Jefferson symbolically functions as an antifounder, the classic embodiment of civilian foolishness.

The contributors to Robert McDonald's bicentennial volume point to a more significant role for Jefferson in the military academy's founding. In emphasizing the deeper affinities between the professional ethos of the officer corps trained at Thayer's academy with the enlightened, meritocratic values espoused by Jefferson and other Revolutionary reformers, Watson illuminates a complex, dialectical process in which an honor-prone quasi-aristocratic military establishment eventually became thoroughly republicanized. This accommodation between army and society may have been set in motion by Jefferson's reform efforts, but it was at least equally the product of the army's alienation from popular politics and partisan meddling. The irony is that, in their Whiggish contempt for the excesses of Jeffersonian and Jacksonian democracy, the officer corps embraced Jeffersonian values. Many of the graduates of West Point in its antebellum heyday may have despised Jefferson. But they were truer to the values Jefferson espoused in 1802, when the academy was founded, than were the first generations of students at Jefferson's own University of Virginia.

Notes

This essay was originally published as the introduction to Robert M. S. McDonald, ed., *Thomas Jefferson's Military Academy: Founding West Point* (Charlottesville: University of Virginia Press, 2004), 1–22.

1. Declaration of Independence as Adopted by Congress, July 4, 1776, in Julian P. Boyd et al., eds., *The Papers of Thomas Jefferson*, 32 vols. to date (Princeton, NJ, 1950–), 1:429–33. The best history of the Declaration's drafting and reception is Pauline Maier, *American Scripture: Making the Declaration of Independence* (New York, 1997).

2. The classic study is Merrill D. Peterson, *The Jefferson Image in the American Mind* (New York, 1960); on Jefferson's (hereafter TJ) image in his own lifetime, see Robert M. S. McDonald, "Jefferson and America: Episodes in Image Formation" (Ph.D. diss., University of North Carolina, 1998). For assessments of more recent historiography, see Peter S. Onuf, "Making Sense of Jefferson," and Jan Ellen Lewis and Peter S. Onuf, "American Synecdoche: Thomas Jefferson as Image, Icon, Character, and Self," both in this volume. On the discrepancy between popular and academic attitudes toward TJ, see Joseph J. Ellis, *American Sphinx: The Character of Thomas Jefferson* (New York, 1997), prologue ("Jeffersonian Surge, 1992–93"), 3–23. The most vigorous assault on TJ's iconic standing comes from a prominent conservative, Conor Cruise O'Brien, in *The Long Affair: Thomas Jefferson and the French Revolution* (Chicago, 1996).

3. R. M. S. McDonald, "West Point's Lost Founder: Thomas Jefferson Remem-

bered, Forgotten, and Reconsidered," in R. M. S. McDonald, ed., *Jefferson's Military Academy*, 182–206, quotation on 198. For further thoughts on the contemporary cultural divide, see Jean M. Yarbrough, "Afterword: The Role of Republican Virtues in Preserving Our Republican Institutions," ibid., 207–21.

4. Elizabeth D. Samet, "Great Men and Embryo-Caesars: John Adams, Thomas Jefferson, and the Figure in Arms," ibid., 77–98. On the founders' concern with their historic reputations, see Joanne B. Freeman, *Affairs of Honor: National Politics in the New Republic* (New Haven, CT, 2001), epilogue.

5. Epitaph, reprinted in Merrill D. Peterson, ed., *Thomas Jefferson Writings* (New York, 1984), 706.

6. McDonald, "West Point's Lost Founder," in McDonald, ed., *Jefferson's Military Academy*, 203.

7. TJ to William S. Smith, Nov. 13, 1787, and TJ to William Short, Jan. 3, 1793, in Peterson, ed., *Jefferson Writings*, 911, 1004.

8. TJ's First Inaugural Address, March 4, 1801, ibid., 493.

9. Adams to TJ, Aug. 14, 1815, in Lester J. Cappon, ed., *The Adams-Jefferson Letters: The Complete Correspondence between Thomas Jefferson and Abigail and John Adams*, 2 vols. (Chapel Hill, NC, 1959), 2:455.

10. The most thorough account of the period, written from a decidedly neo-Federalist stance, is Stanley Elkins and Eric McKitrick, *The Age of Federalism* (New York, 1993).

11. Marshall Smelser, "The Federalist Period as an Age of Passion," *American Quarterly* 10 (1958): 391–419; John R. Howe Jr., "Republican Thought and the Political Violence of the 1790s," *American Quarterly* 19 (1967): 147–65.

12. See Charles Royster, *A Revolutionary People at War: The Continental Army and American Character, 1775–1783* (Chapel Hill, NC, 1979).

13. See the essays collected in James Horn, Jan Ellen Lewis, and Peter S. Onuf, eds., *The Revolution of 1800: Democracy, Race, and the New Republic* (Charlottesville, VA, 2002).

14. Reginald C. Stuart, *The Half-way Pacifist: Thomas Jefferson's View of War* (Toronto, 1978).

15. James Madison, Federalist No. 6, in Jacob E. Cooke, ed., *The Federalist* (Middletown, CT, 1961), 35, 31. See the excellent discussion in Gerald Stourzh, *Alexander Hamilton and Republican Government* (Stanford, CA, 1970), 149–53.

16. The analysis here and in the following paragraphs draws heavily on Peter Onuf and Nicholas Onuf, *Federal Union, Modern World: The Law of Nations in an Age of Revolutions, 1776–1814* (Madison, WI, 1993).

17. Peter S. Onuf, *Jefferson's Empire: The Language of American Nationhood* (Charlottesville, VA, 2000), 80–108.

18. David N. Mayer, "'Necessary and Proper': West Point and Jefferson's Constitutionalism," in McDonald, ed., *Jefferson's Military Academy*, 54–76, quotation on 69.

19. Theodore J. Crackel, "The Military Academy in the Context of Jeffersonian Reform," ibid., 99–117, quotation on 100.

20. Mayer, "'Necessary and Proper,'" ibid., 55.

21. Ibid., 57, emphasis in original. For further discussion of Jefferson's views on federalism, see David N. Mayer, *The Constitutional Thought of Thomas Jefferson* (Charlottesville, VA, 1994), 185–221; and Onuf, *Jefferson's Empire*, 109–46.

22. All quotations in this and the next paragraph are from Jefferson's First Inaugural Address, March 4, 1801, in Peterson, ed., *Jefferson Writings*, 493.

23. Crackel, "Military Academy in the Context of Jeffersonian Reform," in McDonald, ed., *Jefferson's Military Academy*, 111–12. See also the more extensive treatment of this theme in Theodore J. Crackel, *Mr. Jefferson's Army: Political and Social Reform of the Military Establishment, 1801–1809* (New York, 1987).

24. Samet, "Great Men and Embryo-Caesars," in McDonald, ed., *Jefferson's Military Academy*, 85.

25. Ibid., 88.

26. Don Higginbotham, "Military Education before West Point," ibid., 23–53, quotation on 36.

27. Jennings L. Wagoner Jr. and Christine Coalwell McDonald, "Mr. Jefferson's Military Academy: An Educational Interpretation," iibid., 118–53, quotation on 131.

28. Ibid., 132.

29. Ibid., 132–33, quotation on 142.

30. Higginbotham, "Military Education before West Point," ibid., 42. See the discussion of this proposal, and its political motivations, in Cameron Clark Addis, *Jefferson's Vision for Education, 1760–1845* (New York, 2002), chap. 2.

31. Samuel J. Watson, "'Developing Republican Machines': West Point and the Struggle to Render the Officer Corps Safe for America, 1802–1833," in McDonald, ed., *Jefferson's Military Academy*, 154–81, quotation on 169.

32. Ibid., 156–57.

33. Peterson, *Jefferson Image in the American Mind*.

34. TJ to Nathaniel Macon, May 14, 1801, in Andrew A. Lipscomb and Albert Ellery Bergh, eds., *The Writings of Thomas Jefferson*, 20 vols. (Washington, DC, 1903–4), 10:261.

35. The quotation is taken from David C. Hendrickson's important study, *Peace Pact: The Lost World of the American Founding* (Lawrence, KS, 2003).

36. TJ to Lee, May 8, 1825, in Peterson, ed., *Jefferson Writings,* 1501.

37. Watson, "'Developing Republican Machines,'" in McDonald, ed., *Jefferson's Military Academy,* 167.

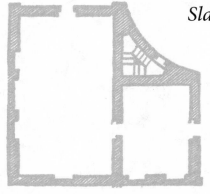

PART IV

*Race and
Slavery*

THOMAS JEFFERSON, RACE, AND NATIONAL IDENTITY

Getting to know Jefferson better can be a demoralizing experience. For many Americans today, a first exposure to his commentary on race in Query 14 of the *Notes on the State of Virginia* is sufficient to subvert his iconic standing in the pantheon of founding fathers.[1] Jefferson "suspected" that people of African ancestry were "inferior" to Europeans in their mental capacities and therefore not fit for citizenship in the new Revolutionary republics. The racial boundary he charted in his *Notes* between whites and blacks—a line that denied kinship ties and divided many Virginia families, including his own—strikes us now as arbitrary, unnatural, and undemocratic. Jefferson apparently did not recognize, and he certainly did very little to resolve, the contradiction between the American struggle for independence and the continuing enslavement of approximately a fifth of the total American population. Our recognition of this contradiction has tarnished—and for his bitterest critics, demolished—Jefferson's reputation as the "father of democracy."

Over the last half century, many Americans have come to believe that our nation's democratic promise will not be fulfilled until we have overcome the legacies of slavery, segregation, and racism. Jefferson embodies this American dilemma. The ringing phrases of his Declaration of Independence—"all men are created equal"—constitute our national creed, a promissory note that we have not yet fully honored. Jefferson defaulted on his own promise as the visionary professions of the democratic philosopher gave way to the prudent calculations of the slave-owning planter. When we learn that he freed only a handful of the many hundreds of enslaved African Americans he owned and that those few—including his children with Sally Hemings—had such strong personal claims on his solicitude, we begin to suspect that Jefferson himself is the problem. The discrepancy between practice and profession is a classic case of what the philosophers call "bad faith." And if Jefferson did not mean what he said, if those ringing phrases ring hollow, where does that leave us as a people?

We define democracy as inclusion. Jefferson defined slaves as aliens with no claim to membership in the new American nation. If his Declaration calls on a free people to burst the chains of despotism, his *Notes* tells black people that they will have to pursue *their* happiness elsewhere, anywhere but here. At the University of Virginia—"Mr. Jefferson's University"—African American students who read his words can feel like uninvited guests, or worse. In one of my seminar discussions, one young woman described suddenly feeling that she "did not belong here," that Jefferson was telling her that there was no place for her in his "academical village."

She had read that black was anything but beautiful. "The first difference which strikes us is that of colour," Jefferson explained. Whatever the source of that difference, it was clearly "fixed in nature" and was "the foundation of a greater or less share of beauty in the two races." Whites could express their finer feelings by "suffusions of colour," by "the fine mixtures of red and white" in a blushing countenance, while an "immoveable veil of black . . . covers all the emotions of the other race." Jefferson's color line was keyed to sexual attractiveness. Black men lusted after white women, just as the male orangutan favored "black women over those of his own species." There was a deeper, racial logic to sexual preferences that more squeamish observers might blush to acknowledge: "The circumstance of superior beauty, is thought worthy attention in the propagation of our horses, dogs, and other domestic animals; why not in that of man?"

Jefferson's ruminations on racial difference proceeded from the outside in, from skin color to internal organs—"they secrete less by the kidnies, and more by the glands of the skin, which gives them a very strong and disagreeable odour"—to emotional dispositions and mental capacities. Black men were "more ardent after their female," he observed, "but love seems with them to be more an eager desire, than a tender delicate mixture of sentiment and sensation." Once their appetites were satiated, they subsided into unfeeling lassitude: "their griefs are transient." This insensibility was directly linked to mental inferiority. Though "in memory they are equal to the whites," Jefferson acknowledged, blacks were "in reason much inferior, as I think one could scarcely be found capable of tracing and comprehending the investigations of Euclid." "In imagination they are dull, tasteless, and anomalous . . . never yet could I find that a black had uttered a thought above the level of plain narration; never see even an elementary trait of painting or sculpture." Among whites, suffering produced great art: "among the blacks is misery enough, God knows, but no poetry."

In conclusion, Jefferson "advance[d] it therefore as a suspicion only, that the blacks, whether originally a distinct race, or made distinct by time and circumstances, are inferior to the whites in the endowments both of body and mind." His defenders seize on the "suspicion," emphasizing the scientific stance of the natural philosopher who remained open to further evidence and argument. But the important thing about this passage is that Jefferson thought racial differences were fixed in nature, whatever their source and however they might be assessed. His comparative method focused on and therefore exaggerated racial differences. Where other observers invoked environmental conditions and cultural constraints to explain racial distinctions, Jefferson's approach worked in the opposite direction as "time and circumstances" conspired with nature to produce a natural racial hierarchy. Philanthropy thus decreed separation. "Will not a lover of natural history then, one who views the gradations in all the races of animals with the eye of philosophy, excuse an effort to keep those in the department of man as distinct as nature has formed them?"

Jefferson's defenders cannot say that he did not say these awful things. But they insist that his "racism" should not be allowed to overshadow his fundamental commitment to human rights and his great contributions to the history of freedom in the modern world. They have a point. Jefferson was certainly a great exponent of natural rights; his testimony against the injustice of slavery remains compelling, particularly in view of his "suspicions" about black inferiority. A later generation of proslavery ideologues would justify the institution as the most humane and civilized means of sustaining the racial order that Jefferson described in his *Notes*. But Jefferson was moving in the other direction, *from* the notion that slaves were subhuman and therefore as much "subjects of property as . . . horses and cattle" *to* the recognition of their fundamental, irreducible rights as fellow human beings. A friendly critic might even suggest that Jefferson's commentary on racial differences ultimately underscores his commitment to rights, for even if his conclusions were in fact all justified, they did not justify the tyrannical rule of one race over the other. We might further argue that Jefferson's anthropology, having raised enslaved African Americans from the status of barnyard animals to that of fellow human beings, however inferior their endowments, could have evolved still further to the more robust equalitarianism that we now embrace.

But this is where wishful thinking gets the better of historical understanding. Jefferson lived long enough for his racial thinking to evolve. It didn't.

My student got the point. Jefferson's commitment to racial separation was fundamental, not provisional: it was inextricably linked to his conception of American nationhood. She recognized instantly that she had no place in Jefferson's vision of the American future. Instead, Jefferson repeatedly insisted, black slaves should be emancipated and then "colonized to such place as the circumstances of the time should render most proper, sending them out with arms, implements of houshold and of the handicraft arts, feeds, pairs of the useful domestic animals." Only then would it be possible for slaves and their descendants to exercise their natural rights, as whites who had declared their own independence from Britain would in turn "declare" their former slaves "a free and independant people, and extend to them our alliance and protection, till they shall have acquired strength" sufficient to stand on their own in the family of nations.

Of course, we don't and shouldn't think of our nation as Jefferson envisioned it. We might pause a moment, however, before consigning him to historical oblivion. What we rightly honor in Jefferson's legacy is inextricably implicated in what we would deny or discard. Is there any way to unravel the knot?

The crucial concept for Jefferson was *nation,* a long familiar concept that was undergoing a profound transformation in his time. A "nation" was a "people," or race or ethnic group—synonymous terms that were not then clearly distinguished. During the Revolutionary era, Jefferson and other Americans began to think of themselves collectively as a nation in a more specifically political or legal sense derived from the "law of nations." Their Declaration of Independence was a plea for the recognition of that nationhood by other nations in the (European) family of nations. As many readers have noted, there is a profound circularity in the Declaration's logic. Before the Declaration, there was no "nation" capable of declaring its own existence, only a loosely affiliated union of disaffected British provinces seeking to renegotiate the imperial constitution. By solving—or rather, by disguising—this fundamental dilemma of new nationhood, Jefferson can be credited with "inventing America," to borrow Garry Wills's suggestive phrase.[2] The trick was to convince Americans themselves that they *were* a people entitled by "nature and nature's god" to exercise sovereign rights. "Popular sovereignty" was synonymous with national self-determination, or liberation.

These may strike us as bloodless abstractions, mere inventions of revolutionary propagandists. But they spoke powerfully to Jefferson and his contemporaries. Blood was already being shed, and these great sacrifices needed to be justified. And the Revolution would only succeed if Americans could imaginatively transcend the cross-cutting provincial, ethnic, religious, class, and even linguistic differences that traditionally separated them. The concept of nationhood, the idea that Americans were all members of a great family of families, provided a sentimental rationale for suffering and sacrifice.

Why couldn't racial differences be subsumed and obliterated in the same way? Of course, in some instances they were, particularly when slaves and freed people and Indian allies were mobilized in the Revolutionary War effort. Jefferson himself could occasionally imagine absorbing Indians (and their land) into the new American nation. But slavery itself presented fundamental problems, for slaves were by definition the enemies of masters who kept them unjustly in a state of bondage. Jefferson understood that slavery was an institutionalized state of war, a cold war that could turn hot whenever the balance of military power shifted against the Americans. For the thousands of slaves who declared their own independence by joining the British counter–Revolutionary War effort, the liberation of their captive nation meant defeating and destroying the ruling race. Jefferson's vision of a genocidal apocalypse was not the paranoid fantasy of a pathological racist, but a reasonable response to geopolitical realities: "Deep rooted prejudices entertained by the whites; ten thousand recollections, by the blacks, of the injuries they have sustained; new provocations; the real distinctions which nature has made; and many other circumstances, will divide us into parties, and produce convulsions which will probably never end but in the extermination of the one or the other." It was by no means clear that white Virginians would emerge victorious. With some help from the British, the slave "party" might very well turn Jefferson's world—and the racial hierarchy that supported it—upside down. This is why it was so critical for white Americans to get rid of slavery and their slaves. This is why they had to preempt a war of national liberation—a war between the races—by emancipating, expatriating, and declaring the independence of their former slaves. As the Haitian Revolution would soon show, it would be disastrous for white Virginians if the slaves did their own declaring, and vindicated their claims on the battlefield.

In a very practical and compelling way, race constituted a particularly vulnerable boundary of American nationhood. It was most obviously vulnerable during wartime, when slaves might look for outside support. We should keep in mind that the fledgling nation did not enjoy the luxury of isolation in the first four decades of its existence, but was constantly either making war itself or attempting to preserve its tenuous neutral status in a world that was almost continuously at war. But there was another, more insidious, threat, and this was that white and black Virginians would transgress the sexual boundaries that could alone sustain the distinction between their two nations or races. Jefferson's insistence on racial distinction, whether attributable to nature's original design or to "time and circumstances," stands in striking contrast to the real news from Virginia, that these two peoples were "amalgamating" into one. It is no accident that his most extended commentary on race—quoted above—is found in the Query on "Laws," for it would only be by the strict legal enforcement of racial separation that whites and blacks could be kept apart, or, more precisely, that the "boisterous passions" of white masters who exploited their female slaves could be restrained. The expatriation of the entire black population would require an extraordinary exercise of political will and entail a staggering cost. But perhaps this was the only way that the "lover of natural history" could be really sure that nature's will would be done.

Why was it so important to keep the races from mixing? There's much room for informed speculation here, particularly since we now know that Jefferson himself, later in life, moved freely across the sexual boundary and so helped to subvert the very racial distinctions he claimed to cherish. The simplest solution would be to recur to the now conventional image of Jefferson as a hypocrite, drawing a sharp boundary between his immortal words and all-too-mortal flesh. It's a bigger and better challenge, however, to eschew Jefferson's own boundary-marking impulses and try to reconcile word and deed. The answer can be glimpsed, I think, in Jefferson's conception of the nation as a kind of family.

Jefferson could see the new nation as a family only in futurity. With their diverse origins, the many would become one only as they forged real bonds of kinship, marrying across the many social and cultural boundaries that limited marital choice for colonial Americans. Here was a conception of union, beginning with the union of husband and wife and widening across space and time to connect succeeding generations in a common history. These were all consensual unions, perfecting ties of reciprocal obligation, interdependent interest, shared principles and affectionate feelings. Bound so closely to each other, Americans could dispense with the heavy-handed controls and restraints of an imperial state.

But there was trouble in Jefferson's paradise. The coercive relations that constituted the institution of slavery made a mockery of consent; the un-inhibited exercise of masters' sexual prerogatives produced illegitimate shadow families that straddled and subverted the ambiguous boundaries between slave and free, black and white. Slavery was a debilitating cancer on the American body politic. Jefferson recommended radical surgery.

Jefferson was a racist because he was a nationalist. But nationalism, as Lincoln recognized, is not simply another word for racism, the systematic exclusion and degradation of one part of the population for the benefit of another. And Lincoln could quite properly invoke the spirit of Jefferson in calling for national renewal, a "new birth of freedom," during the dark days of the American Civil War.[3] Jefferson's notion of the "people," we should not forget, was remarkably expansive and inclusive for its time. National feeling can be liberating and empowering, leveling traditional obstacles to pursuits of happiness among people who recognize each other—if not "all men"—as equal.

Still we are left with a feeling of Jefferson's limits and, if we are wise, of our own.

It's not just that Jefferson was simply "a man of his times" and could not rise above the customs and prejudices of his slaveholding class. Jefferson did not simply discover racial boundaries already inscribed and fixed in nature: he helped construct them, contributing significantly to the racial "science" that would in subsequent decades naturalize racial hierarchy. Jefferson was a nation maker who helped revolutionaries see themselves as a great people with an important role to play in world history. But he was also a race maker who defined enslaved Americans as a captive nation, an alien people who must be blotted from the face of the American earth.

Where does this all leave us in our ongoing quarrel with Jefferson's leg-acy, and with our own history? Perhaps in a place not unlike that of my alienated student. Sometimes we may feel that Jefferson would have considered us unwelcome aliens. More often, these days, those of us who have gotten to know Jefferson would be inclined to return the favor, to knock him off his lofty pedestal, to banish his tarnished memory from the great house that he helped build and we now inhabit.

But we cannot escape our connections with Jefferson. The anger many Americans now feel toward Jefferson testifies to the difficulty of our ongoing struggle to break the disastrous and destructive link he helped forge between race and nation. In the process, we have discovered that we are not the people he imagined and that he is not the man ancestor-worshiping patriots memorialize. But Jefferson will remain a touchstone for us as long as we continue to think of ourselves as a nation.

Notes

This essay was originally published in Jill Hartz, ed., *Siting Jefferson: Contemporary Artists Interpret Thomas Jefferson's Legacy* (Charlottesville: University of Virginia Press, 2003), 53–58.

1. The quotations are all from TJ, Query 14 ("Laws"), in William Peden, ed., *Notes on the State of Virginia* (Chapel Hill, NC, 1954), 137–43.

2. Garry Wills, *Inventing America: Jefferson's Declaration of Independence* (Garden City, NY, 1978).

3. Abraham Lincoln, Gettysburg Address, Nov. 19, 1863, in Roy Basler, ed., *The Collected Works of Abraham Lincoln*, 9 vols. (New Brunswick, NJ, 1953–55), 7:23.

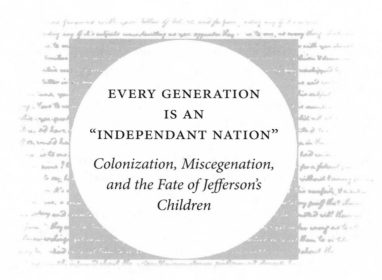

EVERY GENERATION
IS AN
"INDEPENDANT NATION"

*Colonization, Miscegenation,
and the Fate of Jefferson's
Children*

Thomas Jefferson never acknowledged his mixed race children with Sally Hemings. There is little evidence of any kind about how he might have thought or felt about these children. But Jefferson did have a great deal to say about the demoralizing implications of mixed-race relationships for Virginia's master class. His well-known concern, bordering on obsession, with generational sovereignty also suggests that he would be sensitive to the fate of his unacknowledged children with Hemings.

Knowing what we now know, it is time to take a fresh look at familiar themes in the Jefferson archive. I propose to reconsider Jefferson's lifelong advocacy of African colonization for clues about how he might have understood the history of his unacknowledged "shadow" family. By 1824, when in a letter to Jared Sparks, editor of the *North American Review,* Jefferson offered the fullest exposition of his thinking about the emancipation and expatriation of American slaves, his idiosyncratic approach was of little interest or relevance to the movers and shakers in the American Colonization Society (ACS).[1] But this fascinating letter does speak, though of course obliquely, to crucially important private as well as public issues.

Jefferson's ideas about colonization were first developed in an amendment to "A Bill concerning Servants" that he drafted when he was a member of the committee charged with revising Virginia's laws in 1779. Although, Jefferson recalled in his *Autobiography,* the committee endorsed "the principles of the amendment"—the "freedom of all born after a certain day, and deportation at a proper age"—the amendment was never submitted to the General Assembly: "It was found that the public mind would not yet bear the proposition."[1] Jefferson's discussion of this aborted proposal in his *Notes on the State of Virginia* (English edition, 1787) established his credentials as a precocious colonizationist. He subsequently had little to say on the subject, however, writing just a few weeks before his death that "his sentiments have been forty years before the public. Had I repeated them forty times, they would only have become the more stale and threadbare."[3]

Jefferson's letter to Sparks was the conspicuous exception to this self-imposed silence. As he later claimed, he remained true to the basic principles of his great panacea. Under his *post-nati* scheme, he told Sparks, slave children would be freed at birth, remaining with their mothers and laboring for their former masters until they were sufficiently mature to be expatriated to a colony under temporary American protectorate. But if the outlines of his colonization proposal had not changed, Jefferson offered a detailed plan for its implementation—focusing most conspicuously on the question of the costs of compensating slave owners for their property losses—that reflected a radically altered political landscape. In the wake of sectional divisions in the Missouri controversies (1819–21), Jefferson became increasingly convinced that antislavery agitation was a cynical pretext for northern neo-Federalist centralizers to reduce the southern slave states to provincial subjection. The burden was on Sparks and other northern colonizationists to demonstrate their good faith by a scrupulous regard for the honor, rights, and interests of the southern slave states. Under these circumstances, Jefferson's colonization proposal served primarily as a test of comity and good faith among the members of the union, while its original intention— the redemption of Virginia from the scourge of slavery—receded into the background. Americans must act now to heal the sectional rift, Jefferson urged, or risk the destruction of the union and their revolutionary legacy. But the slavery problem demanded patience. "The revolution in public opinion which this cause requires," he wrote resignedly in 1826, "is not to be expected in a day, or perhaps in an age."[4]

Jefferson's contemporaneous political concerns were clear in the Sparks letter. Yet for Jefferson the issue of colonization was also inextricably entangled with race mixing, a theme of compelling personal interest. When Jefferson wrote about race mixing in his *Notes,* he may have been reflecting in a general way about the threat it posed to the civic health of his beloved commonwealth. But miscegenation was already a fact of life at Monticello, apparent in the presence of Betty Hemings, alleged to have been the slave mistress of Jefferson's father-in-law, John Wayles, and her light-skinned children (including Sally). By the time he wrote Sparks in 1824, Jefferson had fathered a second family by Sally Hemings; two of their children had already "escaped" to freedom—evidently with his complicity—and the other two were now coming of age.[5] Of course, Jefferson had no intention of disclosing these personal implications to Sparks; it is even possible (though I think highly unlikely) that he could banish them from his mind when he held forth on the dangers of miscegenation and importance of colonization. But whatever Jefferson's gifts for denial, the distinction between the personal and the political would have been hard to sustain in this case. This was all the more true for a political thinker whose conception of republican social order was based on the virtue and integrity—and racial purity—of its constituent families.

Generations

The rupture of families was the price of freedom for the children of bondage. "The separation of infants from their mothers" under his *post-nati* colonization scheme "would produce some scruples of humanity," Jefferson told Sparks.[6] But the sufferings of mothers, genuine as they might be, did not amount to much in the greater, national perspective. Keeping families together was not an end in itself, but, rather, a foolish scruple of misplaced sentimentality, "straining at a gnat, and swallowing a camel." Rising above the selfish interests of particular parents, Jefferson insisted that family ties *must* be broken so that each new generation would be free to govern itself.

"*The earth belongs in usufruct to the living,*" Jefferson explained in his famous letter of September 6, 1789, to James Madison. "Between society and society, or generation and generation," he wrote, "there is no municipal obligation, no umpire but the law of nature." Every generation is a distinct and autonomous "society" or "nation." The "natural" relationship between the generations therefore was a state of war. Yet this was one of those "self-evident" principles that had eluded common understanding: "We seem not to have percieved that, by the law of nature, one generation is to another as one independant nation to another."[7]

The logic of generational sovereignty both justified the Americans' republican revolution and explained why the emancipation of enslaved Africans was morally imperative. But the circumstances of these two peoples were hardly comparable: the colonists declared their own independence while emancipated slaves would have theirs declared for them. Americans broke from Britain before they were reduced to bondage; in contrast, the captive nation of enslaved Africans had no civil capacity and therefore could declare nothing before it was released *from* bondage. Americans masters and their African slaves thus approached nationhood from opposite directions: Americans became conscious of themselves as a people when they confronted the danger of their own "enslavement"; at the same time, they could not help but see that their slaves also constituted a nation, forcibly held in bondage and unjustly denied its natural right to national self-determination.[8]

American nation making made the captive nation of enslaved Africans visible to Jefferson. At the same time, his identification of the new American nation with the "living generation" suggested a fundamental line of division within the captive nation as well. By emancipating and colonizing the rising generation, Americans could rectify the injustice done to their slaves and thus avoid the otherwise inevitable war between whites and blacks. The present generation of slaves would pay the price for their children's liberation, forgoing their own just claims to freedom and suffering the disruption of their families. The only alternative was "convulsions which will probably never end but in the extermination of the one or the other race."[9] Under a true republican regime, Jefferson imagined, there would be a peaceful succession of generations, with each generation acting as stewards of the collective estate, or "country," for those who followed. Of course, slave parents could pass no property to their children: they were a people without a country and without civil existence. Because slaves were property under the laws of republican Virginia, property-owning masters who stood in the place of slave parents alone could make provision for the rising generation of slave children. Yet the forbearance of slave parents who would themselves never enjoy the great boon of freedom was itself a form of the intergenerational altruism that would sustain a just republican regime.

The generational boundary was crucial for Jefferson's republican theory, however problematic it might be in practice.[10] If the composition of the "people" were constantly changing, the popular will could never be binding beyond the moment of its expression. Jefferson's conception of political generations froze time, extending the duration of a majority's rule until the moment when survivors were outnumbered by those subsequently born.

It was his imaginative effort to extrapolate the natural order of individual families, where the generations were clearly distinct, to society as a whole.

Jefferson faced a similar challenge in defining the boundary between blacks and whites, contemporaneous but distinct nations occupying the same country. Again, the idea that the two peoples should be kept apart was clear enough. "Will not a lover of natural history," Jefferson asked, "one who views the gradations in all the races of animals with the eye of philosophy, excuse an effort to keep those in the department of man as distinct as nature has formed them?" Nature decreed the boundary, though its integrity would depend on the "efforts" of philosophers and statesmen such as Jefferson: the "real distinctions which nature had made" between the two peoples, reinforced and institutionalized by slavery, were apparent to anyone who looked beyond particular cases to general patterns.[11] But it was necessary to police this frontier because individual slave owners, exercising their sexual prerogatives over female slaves, crossed the line so promiscuously. Just as boundaries between generations dissolved at the margins, black and white blended in proliferating shadow families on many Virginia plantations, including Jefferson's Monticello.

If Jefferson's theorizing about generations represented a problematic extrapolation of family to society, his thinking about race moved in the opposite direction, from the clear distinctions of natural philosophy to the complexities of race mixture in particular families. For Jefferson the family home was thus both the source of value, a domestic microcosm of virtuous republican society, and the place where the "perpetual exercise of the most boisterous passions" by masters threatened to complicate and subvert the natural racial order. The whites' despotic power over their slaves' labor and female slaves' bodies jeopardized the survival of the republic. The longer slavery persisted, the more likely was "a revolution of the wheel of fortune, an exchange of situation"; even if this day of judgment were postponed and black men remained incapable of repaying whites for the countless "injuries they have sustained," the sexual exploitation of black women would undermine the republic. As the "unfortunate difference of colour" became progressively harder to discern, it would be increasingly difficult for slaveholding fathers to deny that they held their own children in bondage.[12]

That one generation should exercise absolute power over the next, that fathers should own their own children, was the complete antithesis and negation of everything Jefferson said he stood for. Compared to slavery, the aristocratic features of the European old regime that Jefferson assailed throughout his career seem innocuous, even benign. Under aristocracy, the rising generation could never hope to exercise its rightful authority as a generation, but individual children would at least come into their particular inheritances, unequal and unearned as they might be. Slave children could expect nothing. In a social and civic sense, they simply did not exist.

Amalgamation

To secure their essential rights and interests, independent nations must maintain inviolate boundaries. Jefferson believed that Virginians who transgressed the racial boundary subverted the republic from within, blurring the line that supposedly distinguished the two nations, captive and free. Paradoxically, the despotic power of white masters over the bodies of black female slaves made Virginia most vulnerable. Merely by exercising their individual property rights, slave owners could destroy the commonwealth.

Jefferson condemned race mixing, or "amalgamation," throughout his career. The mixing of white and black, he told his young neighbor Edward Coles in 1814, "produces a degradation to which no lover of his country, no lover of excellence in the human character can innocently consent."[13] Given his strong statements against the practice, it is hard to avoid the now familiar conclusion that he was hopelessly hypocritical. But I would offer another interpretation, emphasizing the imperatives of "theory" for Jefferson and discounting his personal responses to particular slaves, including Sally Hemings. Jefferson's extravagantly stereotypical characterization of brutish blacks proceeded from the philosophical statesman's determination to draw a boundary between the two races. Only with such a boundary clearly in view would Virginians recognize that it was possible to extricate the two nations. Knowing at the same time how often the boundary was transgressed, they would also recognize the urgency of acting in a timely fashion. Colonization, the radical separation of the two races while it was still possible to distinguish them, implicitly recognized the impossibility of preventing miscegenation.

If Americans intended to do justice to the captive nation of enslaved Africans, it was first necessary to define that nation's boundaries. Where two peoples inhabited one country, the boundary was sexual not territorial. As these two peoples began to blend into one, their separation would require the increasingly arbitrary and violent destruction of evermore complex ties in mixed race families. Ultimately, "scruples of humanity" would overshadow and obscure the greater good that colonization promised: the equality and independence of the unjustly enslaved and exploited African people. Could justice ever be done in a mixed race society where slave owners continued to exercise sexual prerogatives over female property?

Jefferson's task in Query 14 of his *Notes* was to make colonization conceivable to a slaveholding class not accustomed to thinking of their slaves as fellow human beings with "rights" of any kind. The scenario of race war signaled the danger that black men presented to the survival of white Virginia. Every passing generation would produce additional legions of enemy soldiers. Returning to this theme in 1824, Jefferson left Sparks "with this admonition, to rise and be doing." The present slave population, by Jefferson's estimate, "a million and a half," might still be manageable, "but six millions, (which a majority of those now living will see them attain,) and one million of these fighting men, will say, 'we will not go.'"[14] Within the space of one of Jefferson's generations (approximately twenty years), the enslaved population would have put down permanent roots that its "fighting men" would be able to vindicate. In this portentous declaration—"we will not go"—Jefferson imaginatively identifies with these black men, having them articulate an attachment to their "country" that echoes his earlier acknowledgment that slave women were attached to their children. Of course, as long as he remained in bondage, a slave could have no true "amor patriae," for if he "can have a country in this world, it must be any other in preference to that in which he is born to live and labour for another."[15] America would become the former slaves' country, because they would take it from their masters. In this reversal of fortunes, self-emancipated black men would seize white women, whose "superior beauty" would goad them on to conquest. According to Jefferson's sexualized chain of being, the preference of black men for white women was as "natural" as "the preference of the Oranootan for the black women over those of his own species."[16] Was Jefferson therefore genuinely fearful of black male sexuality? Or was he simply acknowledging that the master class, whether white or black, exercised sexual dominion over unprotected women of the other race?

That white men exploited black women in Jefferson's Virginia was the ugly reality. In doing so whites were not responding to the natural impulse that animated black men, to mate up the sexual chain and produce superior offspring. White men not only defied the natural racial order (the one that "lovers of natural history" were supposed to cherish) but they failed to heed "nature's" sexual cues. By Jefferson's account, white women should have been much more attractive than black women. The only plausible explanation for slaveholders' unnatural and demoralizing behavior was the institution of slavery itself. Jefferson believed that the fundamental flaw of Indian societies was that native men tyrannized their women, forcing the weaker sex to perform hard labor while they lived idly as frontier aristocrats. He contrasted the degraded condition of Indian women with the "natural equality" that white women enjoyed in republican society, where "civilized" white men had learned to restrain their passions and to protect, not exploit, weak and dependent family members.[17] But the comparison did not work to the advantage of whites where black women were concerned, for Indian women, however much abused, were still acknowledged as members of their families. White slave owners exploited their "property" in slave women with impunity, heedless of the demographic consequences. By mixing the races, they finally would make the stain of blackness ineradicable.

The problem was the unrestrained sexual predation of white male slaveholders, "lovers" of black women and therefore no lovers of their own country. Yet Jefferson characteristically avoided harsh judgments on his fellow slaveholders—or on himself. His letter to Coles suggests that he recoiled more from the children of mixed race unions, the "degradation" that must be eradicated, than from the sexual practices of slaveholders. Miscegenation simply happened, as if by some perversely unnatural but irresistible process. After all, nothing could be done to control white men as long as they had absolute power over their slave property. But *post-nati* colonization would eliminate the results of these unions and, by deporting the next generation of young female slaves before they reached breeding age, make miscegenation impossible in the future.

The most troubling implication of Jefferson's colonization scheme was that white Virginians were incapable of governing themselves. Sons would sink to the same degraded level as their fathers, for slavery was nothing less than a school for petty despots. As Jefferson wrote in his *Notes*:

The whole commerce between master and slave is a perpetual exercise of the most boisterous passions, the most unremitting despotism on the one part, and degrading submissions on the other. Our children see this, and learn to imitate it; for man is an imitative animal. This quality is the germ of all education in him. From his cradle to his grave he is learning to do what he sees others do. If a parent could find no motive either in his philanthropy or his self-love, for restraining the intemperance of passion towards his slave, it should always be a sufficient one that his child is present. But generally it is not sufficient.[18]

Nothing could curb these "boisterous passions," not "philanthropy" or "self-love," not even the solicitude of a father for his child's character. Young masters, emulating their elders, would take slave concubines and the dark, degrading stain of miscegenation would spread across the country.

To redeem the republic from the pathologies of slavery, Jefferson looked beyond the plantation to the world of politics. Here, before the gaze of his fellow planters, the despotic master discovered his better nature. The imperious patriarch learned to think of himself as a citizen of the republic, as a member of a self-governing, "living generation," whose highest responsibility was to provide for the moral and civic well-being of the rising generation and of generations to follow. Jefferson did not ordinarily think of politics, the domain of vain self-assertion, cold calculation, and "every thing which can be disgusting," as an ennobling pursuit.[19] It was a measure of the demoralizing effect of slavery on the character of Virginians that Jefferson's customary valuation of the relationship between home and world, family and society, should be turned on its head. In this case, the virtues of family life did not constitute the republic's moral foundation. On the contrary, the republic—slaveholding men self-consciously acting as citizens—had to act decisively to protect their families from the moral contagion of slavery. To secure "the blessings of domestic society," citizens must renounce their patriarchal prerogatives as slaveholders. Since no restraint could operate effectively within the domestic sphere, the only solution was radical surgery on the body politic. As enlightened citizens, slave-owning men would see the need for such heroic measures, even though—or rather, precisely because—they were incapable in their private lives of respecting the sexual boundary between the two nations.

The Costs of Colonization

When Jefferson first articulated his colonization proposal, he focused on the steps Virginians must take to redeem their republic from the cancer of slavery. By 1824, when he wrote to Sparks, the politics of colonization had become hopelessly snarled in the sectional divisions that increasingly threatened the union. Suspicious of the motives of many of those who rallied to the colonization cause, Jefferson (unlike James Madison) declined membership in the American Colonization Society. Appealing to reason—and obsessively concerned with the question of costs—his letter to Sparks reveals his contempt for the ACS and its temporizing measures and his powerful sense of sectional grievance, unappeased by the recent Missouri compromises. Speaking to fellow Virginians in his *Notes,* Jefferson had offered a devastating critique of the demoralizing effects of slavery; now, as he demanded a national commitment to compensated emancipation and colonization, Jefferson defended the slave states against any hint of moral responsibility. Most remarkably, this great proponent of limited government called for a massive exercise of federal governmental power to underwrite and implement his colonization plan. The practical effect of his proposal might have been to raise the bar so high as to guarantee failure. But Jefferson was less concerned with such practicalities than with respect for his own and his region's honor. Framing the slavery problem in these convoluted terms, Jefferson could insist that his transgressions of the racial order were nobody's business but his own. Responsibility for the continuing evil of slavery ultimately lay with those who failed to recognize and promote the sort of national solution Jefferson proposed to Sparks.

Jefferson's hostility to the ACS was barely disguised by his own reiterated commitment to colonization, his great panacea. The ACS approached colonization in piecemeal fashion, inspired by their humane feelings, deluded in thinking that real "benefits" would begin "when the first colonist left the country, and . . . increase as others go after them."[20] Cost was not a major concern. "The Society has sent out emigrants at fifty dollars a piece," Sparks wrote, "and it might have done much lower, if the business were prosecuted on a large scale." As operations expanded, more and more free blacks with property might be induced to pay for their own removal; vessels of the U.S. Navy could be deployed for the purpose "at an expense, very little exceeding that, which is now required to keep them in service"; and, finally, if necessary, "a portion of the national revenue [might] be appropriated."[21] But Jefferson thought the ACS's approach was woefully inadequate. By introducing Africans to "the arts of cultivated life, and the blessings of civilization and science," a new colony would make "some retribution for the long course of injuries we have been committing on their population." The point of colonization, however, should be to redeem the American republic from a great evil threatening its imminent destruction, not to spread the light of civilization to benighted Africans. "Without repeating the other arguments which have been urged by others," Jefferson would "appeal to figures only, which admit no controversy": any site on the coast of Africa was "entirely impossible."[22]

Jefferson insisted that colonization could only succeed if Americans were committed to a comprehensive national solution based on a rational accounting of true costs. The initiatives of private individuals or benevolent associations would produce no useful result until the federal government acted on behalf of the whole people. There must be a national commitment to compensate slave owners for the full value of their property, for colonization would succeed only when all black people, slave or free, were finally expatriated.

Sparks and his fellow colonizationists expected that state emancipation schemes, such as those already in effect in the North and periodically discussed in Virginia and other slave states, would produce a growing stream of prospective colonists. Federal sponsorship of the new African colony would galvanize state and private action. Virginia could then "pursue her long meditated plan of providing for the colonization of her free blacks," and "other states would follow the example."[23] But for Jefferson and many other wary southerners, the Missouri controversy radically transformed the political and constitutional context of colonization. The clear message southerners took from efforts to bar slavery from the new state of Missouri was that "restrictionists" saw slavery as a sectional problem that slave states must address on their own. By refusing to allow the "diffusion" of the slave population in new states formed out of the national domain, restrictionists—whatever their intentions—would increase the danger of servile insurrection and therefore *strengthen* the institution of slavery. When Jefferson appealed to "figures . . . which admit no controversy," he implicitly warned northerners that this next great national discussion on the future of slavery must proceed from different premises. Only by talking about what the nation must do for slave owners, not for slaves, would it be possible to devise a colonization scheme that would not insult the honor or jeopardize the vital interests of southern states.[24]

Sparks began his optimistic review of the Society's proceedings with the cost of transporting a *single* colonist to the coast of Africa: $50. In response, Jefferson estimated the total cost of compensated emancipation at fair market value for the *entire* slave population, including children born before the process of removal was complete.

> There are in the United States a million and a half of people of color in slavery. To send off the whole of these at once, nobody conceives to be practica-

ble for us, or expedient for them. Let us take twenty-five years for its accomplishment, within which time they will be doubled. Their estimated value as property, in the first place, (for actual property has been lawfully vested in that form, and who can lawfully take it from the possessors?) at an average of two hundred dollars each, young and old, would amount to six hundred millions of dollars, which must be paid or lost by somebody. To this, add the cost of their transportation by land and sea to Mesurado [Liberia], a year's provision of food and clothing, implements of husbandry and of their trades, which will amount to three hundred millions more, making thirty-six millions of dollars a year for twenty-five years, with insurance of peace all that time, and it is impossible to look at the question a second time.[25]

The resulting figure, $900,000,000, was clearly prohibitive. But it was important for Jefferson to establish the principle that slave owners were entitled to full compensation for their loss of slave property. With the nation as a whole assuming responsibility for this national problem, the slave states would avoid the moral stigmatization and economic dislocation that the Missouri debates promised. For republicanism to survive, it was crucial that slave owners not be diminished or degraded below the level of their fellow American citizens.

Jefferson wanted Sparks to accept the premise that Americans were collectively responsible for the slavery problem, not to conclude "that the getting rid of them is forever impossible." As nonslaveholding northerners recognized their own stake in colonization, they would eschew moralistic condemnation of southern slaveholders; treated with the respect due fellow citizens, slaveholders would happily collaborate in a collective effort to cleanse the nation of the foul "blot" of slavery.[26] In their private lives, despotic masters were undoubtedly guilty of countless crimes against human nature, including the sexual exploitation of their female chattels. But in their civic capacity, slaveholders could rise above class interest—and individual guilt—to act in the republic's best interests.

Having conjured up the $900,000,000 price tag to make this fundamental point about the nation's collective responsibility, Jefferson proceeded to suggest that much of this cost could be saved through implementation of his *post-nati* scheme. Returning to the proposal he had "sketched in the Notes on Virginia" some forty years earlier, Jefferson would emancipate "the after-born, leaving them, on due compensation, with their mothers, until their services are worth their maintenance, and then putting them to industrious occupations, until a proper age for deportation."[27] The only difference between the two proposals, significantly, had to do with costs. The earlier proposal would have "emancipate[d] all slaves born after passing the act"; these children would be "brought up, at the public expence, to tillage, arts or sciences, according to their geniusses," but no compensation was offered for masters' property rights.[28] In 1824, however, property rights came first in Jefferson's accounting.

Under Jefferson's *post-nati* scheme, the cost of compensation would be dramatically reduced, almost—but not quite—to a low enough level to ignore altogether. "The estimated value of the new-born infant is so low, (say twelve dollars and fifty cents,) that it would probably be yielded by the owner gratis," he predicted, "and would thus reduce the six hundred millions of dollars, the first head of expense, to thirty-seven millions and a half; leaving only the expense of nourishment while with the mother, and of transportation."[29] On behalf of his fellow slaveholders, Jefferson came close to offering a voluntary, uncompensated emancipation, only to retreat in the following phrase, leaving the "thirty-seven millions and a half" in place as a principled assertion that slave owners had a right to their slave property. If the right were recognized, then it would be "yielded." As Jefferson told former congressman John Holmes during the Missouri crisis, "the cession of that kind of property, for so it is misnamed, is a bagatelle which would not cost me a second thought." The property right might well be defective— on what just grounds could one people hold another in bondage?—and Jefferson would gladly cede this "bagatelle" if Virginia could thus be rid of slavery, "the wolf" that threatened its "self-preservation."[30] But precisely be- cause such vital interests were at stake, northerners must act *as if* the prop- erty rights of slaveholders were legitimate: only then, and in the context of a shared national commitment to end slavery, would slave owners freely yield their claims over their slaves.

Jefferson's elaborate calculations about the costs of colonization probably baffled Jared Sparks. The "appeal to figures" ostensibly provided a common ground for reasonable citizens to chart a prudent course, and so transcend the inflamed passions that threatened to destroy the union. But what the fig- ures really "said" was that all Americans, particularly antislavery northern- ers, must recognize their shared responsibility for putting an end to slavery: the object, "although more important to the slave States, is highly so to the others also, if they were serious in their arguments on the Missouri ques- tion." They must dedicate national resources to the cause of colonization. In ceding its vast western domain to Congress, Virginia had been the nation's benefactor, considering only "the general good of the whole." It would only be fitting if revenues from public land sales were now "appropriated" to the great "object" of colonization, thus prompting the "slave States . . . to contribute more by their gratuitous liberation, thus taking on themselves alone the first and heaviest item of expense."[31] Jefferson thus asked the Yankee-dominated Congress to take the critical first steps to address the slavery problem, carefully avoiding any challenge to the rights of the slave states or to their peculiar institution. Genuine opponents of slavery would recognize that even the slightest imputation of slaveholder guilt would rip the union apart and fasten the shackles of bondage still more tightly on the captive nation. It was therefore imperative that slave owners not be blamed for slavery.

Jefferson knew that masters *were* guilty. Yet it was only by imagining a distinction between the virtuous citizen and the vicious slaveholder that he could see an escape from the great moral and political dilemma of slavery. In Virginia fellow slaveholding citizens must appeal to each other's better natures, making the commitment to end the institution on behalf of future generations. In Congress nonslaveholders must deal with slaveholders as fellow citizens equally committed to promoting the public good, not as a dangerous and immoral class with a particular responsibility for the evil institution entailed on them. All good citizens must avert their gaze from the brutality—and sexual transgressions—of despotic masters.

Jefferson's letter to Sparks did not offer useful advice or inspiration to the colonization movement. In his solicitude for the honor of slave owners and slave states, Jefferson underscored and exaggerated the sectional animosities that colonizationists sought to overcome. Proponents of colonization shared many of Jefferson's concerns, "recoil[ing] with horror" as he did "from the idea of an intimate union with free blacks," but they were more likely to focus on the horrors inflicted on a degraded servile population.[32] For their cause to succeed, Sparks and his colleagues had to appeal to benevolent impulses—and to the guilty consciences of slaveholders who would free their slaves. But Jefferson thought that misguided philanthropy would only postpone "the hour of emancipation."[33]

Jefferson's Children

By 1824 Jefferson had little good advice to offer colonizationists. But his letter to Sparks provides a commentary on the circumstances of his mixed race children as they embarked on their own internal colonization. Of Sally Hemings's four surviving children by Jefferson (two daughters died in infancy), Beverley (b. 1798) and Harriet (b. 1801) had already found their way to freedom; their still underage younger brothers, Madison (b. 1805) and Eston (b. 1808), would be freed under the terms of Jefferson's will in 1826.[34] According to their father's understanding of Virginia law, they were all white: "our canon considers two crosses with the pure white, and a third with any degree of mixture, however small, as clearing the issue of the negro blood." Because a child's status depended on his or her mother's, he or she would remain enslaved, however "white," until freed by his or her owner and likely father. But once emancipated, Jefferson concluded, "he becomes a free *white* man, and a citizen of the United States to all intents and purposes."[35] When Jefferson's children passed into the white world, all connections with their father—and their previous servile condition—would be erased. Like the young colonists Jefferson would send to the coast of Africa, this rising generation could gain its freedom only by severing family ties, by denying that they were Jeffersons.

How did Jefferson think about the fate of his mixed race children? Of course, given the absence of evidence, it is impossible to know. But when Jefferson talked about fulfilling the promise of freedom for an entire generation of enslaved Virginians through colonization, he was also talking about his personal situation.

The letter to Sparks is most remarkable for its tone of cold calculation. Colonizationist appeals to benevolent impulses were counterproductive, for if "scruples of humanity" about separating "mothers" from "infants" are given too much weight, a *post-nati* scheme could never be implemented. Jefferson's explicit recognition of the mother-child bond also deflected attention from all the other family ties that colonization would obliterate, thus avoiding any discussion of the "amalgamation" of the races. The reference to black mothers and their infant children thus reduced the question of family to a single relationship, the very one that under Virginia law perpetuated slavery, while denying all other connections—including paternity. For colonization to succeed, masters must act as if they were not fathers; in giving the infant child of one of their slave "breeders" to the state as a kind of tax or by "voluntary surrender," they would deliver "an object which they have never yet known or counted as part of their property." The worthless slave child, the mere "object" with no real value as property—in whom the master (father?) had yet to make any other emotional investment—would be made free.[36]

Could Jefferson really think this way, linking claims to freedom with worthlessness? If slavery is a form of "social death," was Jefferson saying that, from the master-father's position, liberation from slavery, the negation of family ties, was yet another form of death?[37] Jefferson would not go into "all the details of the burdens and benefits of this operation" in his letter to Sparks.[38] Perhaps they would not bear contemplating. But "who could estimate [the] blessed effects" of colonization (or of the freedom that Jefferson's unacknowledged children would one day enjoy)? Certainly the great good Jefferson had in view was of his own beloved Virginia purged of a dangerously hostile slave population. But the next generation would also enjoy the glorious moment when the enslaved nation would gain its independence. And when the two nations were finally separated, Jefferson's children would be "free *white* . . . citizen[s] of the United States." Was this the "beatitude forbidden to my age?"[39]

Of course, proper Virginia gentlemen did not talk about the shadow families they produced with their slave concubines. Jefferson's silence on the subject of miscegenation in the Sparks letter represented the same kind of conventional accommodation to a ubiquitous practice that historian Joshua Rothman analyzes at the neighborhood level.[40] If everyone knew that there were many such unions—the human evidence was everywhere apparent—it was important not to talk about it. By knowing but not knowing, neighbors paid due respect to the sensibilities (and property rights) of recognized white families. Jefferson himself was punctilious in this regard; as Jan Lewis suggests, over generations, the conventional silence of neighbors and family was transmuted into a compelling lie that only now has been fully exposed.[41]

But Jefferson surely understood that Virginians' customary silence about miscegenation exacerbated the underlying problem that colonization was supposed to address. Indeed, Jefferson's colonization plan itself expressed his despair about maintaining the sexual boundary. Once it was finally implemented, his *post-nati* scheme would secure the next generation from sexual temptation by deporting slave girls before they began to reproduce. As the races continued to mix and the slave population became perceptibly whiter, the need for colonization would become more and more compelling. It was too late for Jefferson himself to act, for "I have overlived the generation with which mutual labors & perils begat mutual confidence and influence." "This enterprise is for the young," Jefferson told Edward Coles, the ardent young opponent of slavery. This was why it was so urgent that Coles should stay in Virginia. Colonization, the only alternative to "the bloody process of St Domingo," could only be "brought on by the generous energy of our own minds," in a revolution of "public sentiment." Jefferson implored Coles to "reconcile yourself to your country and its unfortunate condition; that you will not lessen its stock of sound disposition by withdrawing your portion from the mass. That, on the contrary you will come forward in the public councils, become the missionary of this doctrine truly christian; insinuate & inculcate it softly but steadily, through the medium of writing and conversation; associate others in your labors, and when the phalanx is formed, bring on and press the proposition perseveringly until its accomplishment."[42]

The logic of Jefferson's appeal to Coles is not immediately apparent. Coles had simply asked that the revered elder statesman throw his moral support behind the antislavery cause. Jefferson acknowledged that the greatest obstacle to colonization, the only practicable solution to the slavery problem, was the unwillingness of Virginians to talk about it, "an apathy unfavorable to every hope." "Your solitary but welcome voice," Jefferson told Coles, was "the first" to break the "general silence which prevails on this subject." Yet Jefferson's own silence seems willfully perverse. Why, when he had been so intimately involved in deliberations about colonization in the wake of Gabriel's Rebellion in 1800–1802, should Jefferson tell Coles that "till my return from Europe in 1789, and I may say till I returned to reside at home in 1809, I had little opportunity of knowing the progress of public sentiment here on this subject"?[43] Jefferson and his colleagues had certainly not forgotten this desperate flurry of activity. As Charles Fenton Mercer later wrote, they had instead chosen to treat it as a "state secret" that only inadvertently came to the attention of the next generation of colonizationists.[44]

Perhaps Jefferson's silence, his reluctance to respond publicly to Coles, constituted an admission that on this important issue Jefferson's own position was hopelessly compromised. Silence was the refuge both for individuals who had transgressed the sexual boundary between white and black and for a whole generation that had failed to do justice to the captive nation. If Coles "abandon[ed] this property"—that is, if he freed his own slaves—"and your country with it," he would be rendering an awful judgment on Jefferson and his generation. Coles's departure would testify to his belief that Virginia was beyond redemption, that those enlightened young whites who most cherished freedom—like the black slaves they held in bondage—could only find it in another country. By freeing his own slaves immediately, Coles also would make it clear that he considered Jefferson's colonization scheme a dangerous delusion, an excuse for inaction rather than an enlightened program for fulfilling the Revolution's promise of liberation. Coles thus called into question the fundamental premises of Jefferson's republican faith. His honor and the honor of his generation challenged, Jefferson turned Coles's judgment back on Coles. Just as Jefferson would later accuse Missouri restrictionists of committing "treason against the hopes of the world," he now warned Coles that he would be a traitor if he emancipated his slaves and left his country.[45]

Jefferson hoped that Coles's generation, with "the generous temperament of youth, analogous to the motion of their blood, and above the suggestions of avarice, would have sympathized with oppression wherever found, and proved their love of liberty beyond their own share of it."[46] Moved by a passion for liberty, the sons would redeem Virginia from the "boisterous passions" of their fathers so that their common estate would descend to subsequent generations without the dangerous, demoralizing encumbrance of slavery. In this matter, perhaps more than any other, the younger generation must be an "independant nation," recognizing that their elders' "avarice"—and lust—was at the root of the problem. Yet, by addressing the problem obliquely, by deporting slave children, the sons could avoid both the conflagration of race war and a violent rupture with their fathers, an equally devastating war between the generations. The sons would honor the fathers by banishing all evidence of the gross injustices they had committed. This was the silence, the oblivion on his own and his generation's transgressions, the absolution that "shall have all my prayers."[47]

Colonization faced enormous obstacles. The most formidable were not the costs of compensation and deportation, though Jefferson warned that these would increase proportionally as the slave population continued to multiply. The great challenge to Coles's "living" generation was instead to liberate itself from the inertia and resistance of its predecessors. The fact that Jefferson had "overlived" his time, that his own generation had already passed from the stage, thus should have been encouraging to Coles. On this great question, the interests and attachments of Jefferson's generation—including Jefferson himself, for all his prayers—had to be considered hostile to those of the commonwealth. Whether because of "avarice," or the perverse joys of dominion over their human chattel, or because of affectionate ties with slave concubines and their offspring, the generation of the fathers would never take decisive steps against slavery. But they were prepared to submit to the unacknowledged costs of colonization, including the radical separation from their own black families, if the sons would respect their property rights in their slaves by offering appropriate compensation. Under Jefferson's *post-nati* scheme, the slave owners' mixed race children would be deported. But the breakup of families would affect all Virginians, whether or not they were guilty of sexual transgressions, for all were implicated in the complex and proliferating web of family connections that made the boundary between black and white increasingly difficult to define.

Jefferson never explicitly discussed the pain white fathers might feel by being separated from their unacknowledged slave children. All he would admit was that the "separation of infants from their mothers . . . would produce some scruples of humanity": the silence about fathers (surely some would suffer?) is poignant, given what we now know. Could his insistence that masters would "yield" slave children to the state "gratis," provided that their right to compensation was recognized, be an implicit acknowledgment that fathers would be trafficking with the lives of their own children? Would masters forgo payment for their slave property (a mere "bagatelle," after all), because of "scruples" they could not openly acknowledge about selling their sons and daughters?

Jefferson sold many slaves, but not his own mixed race children. The price of their freedom was instead the denial of their family connections. Jefferson thus fulfilled his promise to their mother, Sally Hemings, but in a way that did not threaten the sensibilities—and property interests—of his recognized white family. Madison Hemings remembered that his father "was not in the habit of showing partiality or fatherly affection to us children."[48] Through this casual, day-to-day denial of his fatherhood, Jefferson prepared for the day when his children would leave him. If Virginians collectively were ever to embrace colonization, they too would have to deny their complex family ties with the emancipated and expatriated generation whose independence they would declare.[49] Jefferson's silence preserved the myth of his white family's perfect happiness.[50] Colonization would do the same thing for Virginia. The costs of this massive deportation would not be charged against the estates of particular, "guilty," families but rather to the state or even the union as a whole. By removing the living evidence of their sexual transgressions and freeing the next generation from the temptations to which they had succumbed, the fathers of Virginia would redeem their republic. The perfect republican families that constituted the commonwealth would no longer be contaminated and corrupted by slavery and the passions it unleashed.

Notes

This essay was originally published in *William & Mary Quarterly* 57 (2000): 155–72.

1. Thomas Jefferson (hereafter TJ) to Jared Sparks, Feb. 4, 1824, in Andrew A. Lipscomb and Albert Ellery Bergh, eds., *The Writings of Thomas Jefferson*, 20 vols. (Washington, DC, 1903–4), 16:8–14.

2. Bill 51, A Bill concerning Servants, The Revisal of the Laws, 1776–1786, in Julian P. Boyd et al., eds., *The Papers of Thomas Jefferson*, 32 vols. to date (Princeton, NJ, 1950–), 2:470–73; TJ, *Autobiography* (Jan. 6–July 29, 1821), in Merrill D. Peterson, ed., *Thomas Jefferson Writings* (New York, 1984), 3–101, quotations on 44.

3. The most authoritative edition now in print is William Peden, ed., *Notes on the State of Virginia* (Chapel Hill, NC, 1954); TJ to James Heaton, May 20, 1826, in Peterson, ed., *Jefferson Writings*, 1516.

4. TJ to James Heaton, May 20, 1826, in Peterson, ed., *Jefferson Writings*, 1516.

5. Beverley and Harriet "ran away" in 1822 (see Annette Gordon-Reed, *Thomas Jefferson and Sally Hemings: An American Controversy* [Charlottesville, VA, 1997], 25–27); TJ's will provided for the freedom of Madison and Eston Hemings, but stipulated that they would serve as apprentices of their uncle John Hemings until reaching their majority (ibid., 39–43). Gordon-Reed writes: "Jefferson may well have been attempting to undercut . . . the inevitable speculation about why he freed Sally Hemings's last two sons" (42).

6. TJ to Jared Sparks, Feb. 4, 1824, in Lipscomb and Bergh, eds., *Writings of Jefferson*, 16:8–14, quotation on 13. He did not say here, as he had four decades earlier in his *Notes on the State of Virginia*, that the "griefs" of slaves "are transient" (TJ, Query 14 ["Laws"], in Peden, ed., *Notes*, 139). For my understanding of the colonization movement, I am indebted to Marie Tyler-McGraw, "Thomas Jefferson and the American Colonization Society," paper presented at the International Center of Jefferson Studies, Monticello, Sept. 1998. See also P. J. Staudenraus, *The African Colonization Movement, 1816–1865* (New York, 1961).

7. TJ to James Madison, Sept. 6, 1789, in Boyd et al., eds., *Jefferson Papers*, 15:392–98, quotations on 395, emphasis in original. The best study of this letter and theme is in Herbert Sloan, "'The Earth Belongs in Usufruct to the Living,'" in Peter Onuf, ed., *Jeffersonian Legacies* (Charlottesville, VA, 1993), 281–315. See also Sloan, *Principle and Interest: Thomas Jefferson and the Problem of Debt* (New York, 1995).

8. Peter S. Onuf, *Jefferson's Empire: The Language of American Nationhood* (Charlottesville, VA, 2000), chap. 5.

9. TJ, Query 14 ("Laws"), in Peden, ed., *Notes*, 138.

10. James Madison was skeptical about the very possibility of distinguishing

one generation from the next (Madison to TJ, Feb. 4, 1790, in Boyd et al., eds., *Jefferson Papers,* 16:146–50; this correspondence is discussed and reprinted in Lance Banning, *Jefferson and Madison: Three Conversations from the Founding* [Madison, WI, 1995], 27–55, docs. on 159–92).

11. TJ, Query 14 ("Laws"), in Peden, ed., *Notes,* 143, 138.

12. TJ, Query 18 ("Manners"), ibid., 163; TJ, Query 14 ("Laws"), ibid., 138, 143.

13. TJ to Edward Coles, Aug. 25, 1814, in Peterson, ed., *Jefferson Writings,* 1343–46, quotation on 1345.

14. TJ to Jared Sparks, Feb. 4, 1824, in Lipscomb and Bergh, eds., *Writings of Jefferson,* 16:8–14, quotations on 13.

15. TJ, Query 18 ("Manners"), in Peden, ed., *Notes,* 162.

16. TJ, Query 14 ("Laws"), ibid., 138. See the discussion in Winthrop Jordan, *White over Black: American Attitudes toward the Negro, 1550–1812* (Chapel Hill, NC, 1968), 488–90, passim.

17. TJ, Query 6 ("Productions Mineral, Vegetable, and Animal"), in Peden, ed., *Notes,* 60. See the discussion in Onuf, *Jefferson's Empire,* chap. 1.

18. TJ, Query 18 ("Manners"), in Peden, ed., *Notes,* 162.

19. TJ to Martha J. Randolph, May 31, 1798, in Sarah N. Randolph, *The Domestic Life of Thomas Jefferson* (1871; Charlottesville, VA, 1978), 250. I am indebted to Jan Lewis for my understanding of the relationship between family and politics in TJ's thought (see Lewis, "'The Blessings of Domestic Society': Thomas Jefferson's Family and the Transformation of American Politics," in Onuf, ed., *Jeffersonian Legacies,* 109–46).

20. [Jared Sparks], review of "The Sixth Annual Report of the American Society for Colonizing the Free People of Color of the United States," *North American Review* 42 (Jan. 1824): 40–90, quotation on 63.

21. Ibid., 83–84.

22. TJ to Jared Sparks, Feb. 4, 1824, in Lipscomb and Bergh, eds., *Writings of Jefferson,* 16:8–14, quotations on 8–9.

23. [Sparks], "Sixth Annual Report," 88.

24. Onuf, *Jefferson's Empire,* chap. 4.

25. TJ to Jared Sparks, Feb. 4, 1824, in Lipscomb and Bergh, eds., *Writings of Jefferson,* 16:8–14, quotation on 9–10.

26. Ibid., 16:10. For the "blot" reference, see TJ to James Monroe, Nov. 24, 1801, in Peterson, ed., *Jefferson Writings,* 1097.

27. TJ to Jared Sparks, Feb. 4, 1824, in Lipscomb and Bergh, eds., *Writings of Jefferson,* 16:10.

28. TJ, Query 14 ("Laws"), in Peden, ed., *Notes,* 137.

29. TJ to Jared Sparks, Feb. 4, 1824, in Lipscomb and Bergh, eds., *Writings of Jefferson*, 16:8–14, quotation on 11.

30. TJ to John Holmes, April 22, 1820, ibid., 15:248–50, quotations on 249.

31. TJ to Jared Sparks, Feb. 4, 1824, ibid., 16:8–14, quotations on 11–12.

32. [Sparks], "Sixth Annual Report," 59, quoting Robert Goodloe Harper.

33. TJ to Edward Coles, Aug. 25, 1814, in Peterson, ed., *Jefferson Writings*, 1345.

34. Gordon-Reed, *Jefferson and Hemings*.

35. TJ to Francis C. Gray, March 4, 1815, in Lipscomb and Bergh, eds., *Writings of Jefferson*, 14:267–71, quotations on 270, emphasis in original.

36. TJ to Jared Sparks, Feb. 4, 1824, ibid., 16:13.

37. I borrow the term from Orlando Patterson, *Slavery and Social Death: A Comparative Study* (Cambridge, MA, 1982), see esp. 38–45.

38. TJ to Jared Sparks, Feb. 4, 1824, in Lipscomb and Bergh, eds., *Writings of Jefferson*, 16:8–14, quotation on 13.

39. TJ to Francis C. Gray, March 4, 1815, ibid., 14:270, emphasis in original; TJ to Jared Sparks, Feb. 4, 1824, ibid., 16:13.

40. Joshua Rothman, "James Callender and Social Knowledge of Interracial Sex in Antebellum Virginia," in Jan Lewis and Peter Onuf, eds., *Sally Hemings and Thomas Jefferson: History, Memory, and Civic Culture* (Charlottesville, VA, 1999), 87–113.

41. Jan Lewis, "The White Jeffersons," in Lewis and Onuf, eds., *Hemings and Jefferson*, 127–60.

42. TJ to Edward Coles, Aug. 25, 1814, in Peterson, ed., *Jefferson Writings*, 1345, 1344, 1346.

43. Ibid., 1345, 1344.

44. Charles Fenton Mercer to Jared Sparks, Jan. 5, 1824, in Herbert Baxter Adams, *The Life and Writings of Jared Sparks: Comprising Selections from His Journals and Correspondence*, 2 vols. (Boston, 1893), 1:246–52.

45. TJ to Edward Coles, Aug. 25, 1814, in Peterson, ed., *Jefferson Writings*, 1346; TJ to John Holmes, April 22, 1820, in Lipscomb and Bergh, eds., *Writings of Jefferson*, 15:250.

46. TJ to Edward Coles, Aug. 25, 1814, in Peterson, ed., *Jefferson Writings*, 1344–45.

47. Ibid., 1346.

48. "The Memoirs of Madison Hemings," in Gordon-Reed, *Jefferson and Hemings*, 247. My discussion of Jefferson's white family is indebted to Lewis, "The White Jeffersons," in Lewis and Onuf, eds., *Hemings and Jefferson*, 127–60.

49. This does not mean that Jefferson's descendants would not keep the memory of their connections with him; see the moving essay by Lucia Stanton and Dianne Swann-Wright, "Bonds of Memory: Identity and the Hemings Family," in Lewis and Onuf, eds., *Hemings and Jefferson,* 161–83.

50. Lewis, "The White Jeffersons," ibid., 127–60.

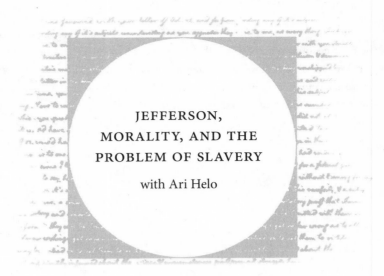

JEFFERSON, MORALITY, AND THE PROBLEM OF SLAVERY

with Ari Helo

How could Thomas Jefferson, advocate of equal rights to life, liberty, and the pursuit of happiness, have justified his ownership of human beings in moral terms? How, in his draft of the Declaration of Independence, could he have accused King George III and the British nation of imposing slavery on the American colonies?

Jefferson never thought that slavery was morally justifiable. In order to grasp his understanding of the issue of personal guilt, we need to historicize Jefferson's moral thought. Much of modern moral understanding begins with the autonomous individual and his "inalienable rights." We consider all people first and foremost as individuals, fellow claimants of dignity and respect whose inherent and irreducible rights constitute the foundations of modern morality. Our language, borrowed directly from the Declaration, is Jeffersonian. Yet, while the "individual" is certainly important in his moral thought, Jefferson constantly made judgments about individuals on the basis of his exalted standard of virtuous behavior, recognizing that their capacity to act morally differed widely. In Jefferson's view, men were to be judged according to the manifestation of their moral dispositions. Slaves were beyond—or beneath—such judgments. As long as they were slaves, they were by definition unable to exercise free will or to enforce claims to rights, "inalienable" or otherwise, and therefore could not be held morally accountable for their actions.

But if slaves were beyond the pale of moral judgment, the institution of slavery nonetheless raised profound moral problems for the new republic. "Nothing is more certainly written in the book of fate than that these people are to be free," Jefferson wrote in his *Autobiography*, "nor is it less certain that the two races, equally free, cannot live in the same government."[1] Jefferson's solution to the slavery problem was to institute a program of gradual emancipation, separating slave children from their parents in order to prepare them for freedom, sending them to their own country—perhaps on the west coast of Africa—and "declaring them a free and independant people."[2]

Jefferson's deep awareness of both the progressive and destructive elements in contemporary developments of Western civilization—both so well exemplified in the history of the French Revolution—fundamentally shaped his understanding of humanity. His optimism about the *continuity* of certain positive trends in recent history did not lead him to embrace any utopian notions of the ultimate moral end of the still ongoing historical process. It is remarkable how little interest Jefferson ever showed in metaphysical speculations about man's essence or in any other kinds of extrahistorical truths about human nature. Within this fundamentally historical intellectual framework Jefferson can be accurately identified as a progressive republican in the Lockean mode, albeit with serious reservations about the dangers of civic corruption under any human, and thus historical, government.[3] Jefferson was acutely conscious of the need for general civic education in order to guarantee that citizens fulfill the promise of their own history. As Jefferson lectured the Marquis de Lafayette, gaining minimal control over this historical process required "the administration of reasonable laws favoring the progress of knowledge in the general mass of the people." Otherwise, there could never be an end to the repetitious cycle of falling into a tyranny of "the many, the few, or the one."[4]

Yet, whatever the limits of Jefferson's faith in the future, his own failure to take any effective steps against the institution of slavery—by his own account, a major obstacle to the fulfillment of the republican promise in Virginia—remains conspicuous and demands explanation. To uncover the logic of Jefferson's position on slavery, even within the historicist-republican intellectual context delineated above, three fundamental points must be emphasized.

First, throughout his political career, both as a legislator in Virginia and as the President of the United States, Jefferson never aimed to weaken the legal, institutional basis of slavery itself.[5] Breaking with the historical legacy of slavery—an institution as ancient as Western civilization itself—would constitute yet another revolution, as momentous as any in human history. But such a revolution, however desirable, could not violate the fundamental premise of the republican revolution against British tyranny, that the "people" were the source of legitimate authority and should not be subjected to the rule of the few—even if the few were enlightened enough to discern the direction of historical development.[6] A democratic, majority decision was absolutely necessary before the existing legal order and the property rights in slaves that it secured were overturned.

Second, Jefferson never acknowledged that his proposed schemes for emancipating slaves violated natural human affections by separating children from their parents and then expatriating them.[7] He apparently considered this program morally defensible because these children would be given some basic education before gaining freedom in their new homes.

Third, Jefferson's "suspicions" about the natural inferiority of enslaved Africans did not constitute his justification for expelling them. His distaste for any permanent mixture of the races derived from his conviction that it would inevitably lead to genocidal violence. He also believed that the formation of a large, racially distinct class of semifree Americans—emancipated but not expatriated—would jeopardize a process of gradual emancipation and compulsory expatriation that could take as long as a half century. Emancipation was only possible if the community of free men came to recognize the moral and political necessity of destroying an institution that they still believed was fully legitimate. Jefferson was therefore convinced that the determination to emancipate the slaves had to emerge from within the community of free men, as a new, practical standard of virtuous behavior. Any premature effort to interfere with the institution would violate the fundamental rights of free citizens and jeopardize the progress of the community as a whole toward a more enlightened understanding of its true collective interests.

Moral development could only take place in a specific civic context, and not as the result of the heroic struggles of a few crusaders against the customary complacency, narrow self-interest, and moral obtuseness of established social orders. It is a nice irony that Jefferson himself looms so large in American national mythology as just such an heroic individual, inspired by his implacable sense of the corruption of the old regime. But Jefferson did not portray himself as a member of a morally enlightened revolutionary vanguard, far out in front of the American people. In 1825 he offered an extraordinarily modest assessment of his role in drafting the Declaration, his most famous contribution to the Revolutionary cause. "All American whigs thought alike on these subjects," he recalled: "Neither aiming at originality of principle or sentiment, nor yet copied from any particular and previous writing, [the Declaration] was intended to be an expression of the American mind."[8] Jefferson's self-effacement helps explain the self-righteous moral tone so characteristic of his political writing: progressive moral standards were generated within—and inconceivable without—enlightened civic communities. It was Jefferson's fundamental belief in the righteousness of the Revolution, the most compelling demonstration of the possibility of political and moral progress in history, that shaped his thinking about all other moral issues, including slavery.

Jefferson's conception of moral development in history is reflected in his indictment of George III in his draft of the Declaration. By enslaving innocent Africans, "a distant people who never offended him, captivating & carrying them into slavery in another hemisphere, or to incur miserable death in their transportation thither," the British king "has waged cruel war against human nature itself, violating it's most sacred rights of life and liberty." The slave trade was a "piratical" form of "warfare" that was now universally condemned, even by "*infidel* powers." Participating in this universal moral development, the legislatures of Virginia and Maryland had sought "to prohibit or to restrain this execrable commerce," but George III rebuffed their initiatives, "prostitut[ing] his negative" in order "to keep open a market where *men* should be bought & sold."[9] Diverging attitudes toward the slave trade thus reflected profound moral differences that now made it impossible to sustain the idea that Britons and Americans could sustain their identity as a single people. Indeed, Jefferson suggested that it was their shared sense of moral outrage at these crimes against humanity that enabled Americans both to see themselves as a distinct, independent people and to identify with enlightened people everywhere in their revulsion against a barbarous, retrograde institution.

Modern commentators are united in their contempt for Jefferson's moralizing about George III's culpability for "imposing" an institution on the Americans that was in fact the basis of their material prosperity and even, in the case of the staple-producing plantation colonies, of their very existence. Jefferson's congressional editors thus get high marks for expunging this embarrassing passage. Certainly they saw what seems so clear to us:

that American slaveholders were much better advised to deflect attention away from the institution, and their implication in it. But it would be a mistake to conclude that Jefferson's charge was merely opportunistic. Instead, we suggest, Jefferson's indictment of George III was grounded in a coherent and deeply held moral perspective: if he merely had wanted to score rhetorical points, he surely would have been more circumspect.[10]

Let us be clear about what Jefferson is saying in this controversial passage. First, he is not displacing responsibility for slavery from American slaveholders to British slave traders. When the institution was established in the American colonies, it was not yet clear to either merchants or planters that the traffic in human flesh violated the norms of civilized society. Nor did the question merely concern the slave trade. Jefferson recalled this condition of universal moral obtuseness in his famous letter to Edward Coles in 1814: "Nursed and educated in the *daily habit* of seeing the degraded condition, both bodily and mental, of those unfortunate beings," colonial Virginians had few doubts that their slaves "were as legitimate subjects of property as their horses and cattle . . . not reflecting that that degradation was very much the work of *themselves & their fathers*."[11] Yet if the establishment of this monstrous institution was very much the "work" of Jefferson's Virginian forbears, it did not follow that they were morally responsible for it. They could not then know, given the primitive state of moral development, that they were entailing this legacy of degradation on their descendants. It is important to emphasize that it is the fathers, not the sons, who are getting the clean bill of health here: because slavery has become a moral problem, it is incumbent on the younger generation to do something about it. And this is the same criterion for judging George III—and not his ancestors, who also knew no better.

In their admittedly modest efforts to regulate slave imports, Virginia and Maryland had nonetheless demonstrated their responsiveness to the broadening moral horizons of an enlightened age. These were tentative steps, to be sure, and Jefferson would doubtless acknowledge that prudential and economic considerations influenced legislators concerned about the continuing growth of an apparently redundant and potentially dangerous servile population: after all, such considerations had always been a spur to moral progress. Virginians began to recognize their moral dilemma as they came to understand that the buyer or driver of slaves was equally responsible with the slave trader for the increasingly conspicuous injustice of the institution. This knowledge came to them from the outside world, from their exposure to evolving moral standards, and from their vulnerability to the despotism of a corrupt, retrograde regime that perpetuated the slave trade—making war on "a distant people who never offended him"—and now compounded the crime by "exciting those very people to rise in arms among us, and to purchase that liberty of which *he* has deprived them, by murdering the people upon whom *he* also obtruded them; thus paying off former crimes committed against the *liberties* of one people, with crimes which he urges them to commit against the *lives* of another."[12] In this critical passage, Jefferson simultaneously identified with the innocent victims of George III's "war against human nature" and cast those victims in the role of the Revolutionaries' most bitter enemies. This was the crux of the American dilemma. The patriots constituted a moral community, and if their quest for independence had any world historical significance, it was because they resisted their former sovereign on the moral grounds that were so fully—and, for us, tediously—elaborated in the body of the Declaration. But they were also locked in an ongoing war with their own slaves, for that is precisely what slavery was: an institutionalized state of war. It was therefore morally incumbent on Virginians and on Americans generally to work toward a just peace that would vindicate their own claims to nationhood.

Contemporary moral and political philosophy enabled Jefferson to formulate the problem of slavery, and the excised passages from the Declaration reveal the direction of his thinking. Jefferson cribbed shamelessly from John Locke in his eloquent invocation of social contract theory and the right to revolution in the Declaration's opening paragraphs. But Locke's teaching on war and slavery was much less useful to Jefferson, for Locke failed to anticipate the subsequent progress of enlightened thought on this crucial question. Jefferson's indictment of George III is also, implicitly, an indictment of Locke. Jefferson's dissent from Locke on slavery was prophetic, for the liberal apotheosis of property rights would be the slaveholders' most powerful bulwark.[13]

John Locke asserted that slavery was the legitimate outcome of a just war. By turning the state of peace into a state of war without justification and thus wantonly violating the natural rights of other men, the instigator of violence became a criminal who deserved the death penalty. This is Locke's description of "the perfect condition of Slavery," which "is nothing else but the State of War continued, between a lawful Conqueror, and a Captive":

> This Freedom from Absolute, Arbitrary Power, is so necessary to, and closely joyned with a Man's Preservation, that he cannot part with it, but by what forfeits his Preservation and Life together. For a Man, not having the Power of his own Life, cannot, by Compact, or his own Consent, enslave himself to any one, nor put himself under the Absolute, Arbitrary Power of another, to take away his Life, when he pleases. No body can give more Power than he has himself; and he that cannot take away his own Life, cannot give another power over it. Indeed having, by his fault, forfeited his own Life, by some Act that deserves Death; he, to whom he has forfeited it, may (when he has him in his Power) delay to take it, and make use of him to his own Service, and he does him no injury by it. For whenever he finds the hardship of his Slavery out-weigh the value of his Life, 'tis in his Power, by resisting the Will of his Master, to draw on himself the Death he desires.[14]

The victor in a just war had the moral authority to postpone the death sentence by enslaving any individual who had violated his rights. Because he had divorced himself from the law of nature, the slave ought to desire his own death: in terms of Locke's normative view of morality, the slave did not deserve to live. But Locke did not make it the duty of the lawful conqueror to punish his enemies by either death or slavery. Instead, the conqueror "may" demand such retribution for the injustice he had suffered. And even if the conqueror "should" enslave his captives, his right did not extend to the captive's estate or family connections.[15]

Whether or not Locke's implicit justification for British involvement in slavery and the slave trade is consistent with his philosophy, his position is ambiguous in only one respect.[16] His acceptance of African slavery in the American plantations as an inheritable condition must either be attributed to sheer racism or to some unarticulated line of reasoning: that, for instance, when an enslaved individual is deprived of his land—or his country—nothing in natural law prohibited his children from inheriting his new, degraded status.

Locke insisted that a slave could not make a compact regarding his servitude because he had alienated his natural right to life "by his fault"—that is, by "some Act that deserves Death." The slave did not possess the moral power to consent to any kind of compact. Even a servant was presumed to possess such a power when negotiating a compact that rendered him utterly dependent on his master—and therefore incapable of entering into other compacts—during a fixed term of service.[17] In Locke's view, any man worthy

[242]

of his natural rights would only sell his freedom and consent to drudgery under the authority of another man on a temporary basis, as an indentured servant: an individual's permanent enslavement presupposed the violation of his free will.[18] Locke's definition of the "slave" thus excluded the notion of the morally competent and accountable individual, the central figure of modern moral philosophy.

Jefferson was not persuaded by any such logic. As possessors of certain morally inalienable rights, individuals were free agents; as such, they could not coherently forfeit their freedom. Following the lead of more recent writers on the law of nations, such as Baron de Montesquieu and Jean-Jacques Burlamaqui, Jefferson did not believe that even a "just" war could justify enslaving captured enemy combatants. Further, and most crucially, reprisals and retribution were matters of public international law, according to which any war, by definition, was a conflict between nations, not between individual soldiers. By contrast, Locke's interest in punishing individuals indicates that he considered the question of slavery only in terms of his purely theoretical notion of political society, an ahistorical category that functioned as the judicial criterion for assessing different historical governments in moral terms.[19] The black slaves of the "Old Dominion" were not justly held in bondage according to the tenets of natural law, Jefferson thought, but rather because of an unfortunate human error in moral reasoning—exemplified by Locke's teachings—that had justified the establishment and consolidation of the institution of slavery during the formative decades of colonial development. Jefferson's conception of the origins of slavery in a British error of natural jurisprudence was fundamental to his indictment of George III in the Declaration and would continue to shape his understanding of slavery as a moral problem in future decades.

Lord Kames provided Jefferson with the profoundly historicized view of the issue of morality that led him to challenge Locke—and indict King George.[20] "The sense of common good is too complex, and too remote an object to be a solid foundation for any positive law, if it has no other foundation in our nature," Kames wrote in his *Essays on the Principles of Morality and Natural Religion.*

> What is just now observed will lead us to a more rational account of these laws. They are no other but gradual refinements of the original law of nature, accommodating itself to the improved state of mankind. The law of nature,

which is the law of our nature, cannot be stationary. It must vary with the nature of man, and consequently refine gradually as human nature refines. Putting an enemy to death in cold blood, is now looked upon with distaste and horror, and therefore is immoral; tho' it was not always so in the same degree.[21]

This was the passage that inspired the young Jefferson to challenge Locke on the slavery issue in an extraordinary marginal note. The more humane treatment of prisoners, wrote Jefferson, constituted

a remarkeable instance of improvement in the moral sense. the putting to death captives in war was a general practice among savage nations. when men became more humanized the captive was indulged with life on condition of holding it in perpetual slavery; a condition exacted on this supposition, that the victor had right to take his life, and consequently to commute it for his services. at this stage of refinement were the Greeks about the time of the Trojan war. at this day it is perceived we have no right to take the life of an enemy unless where our own preservation renders it necessary. but the ceding his life in commutation for service admits there was no necessity to take it, because you have not done it. and if there was neither necessity nor right to take his life then is there no right to his service in commutation for it. this doctrine is acknowledged by later writers, Montesquieu, Burlamaqui & c. who yet suppose it just to require a ransom from the captive. one advance further in refinement will relinquish this also. if we have no right to the life of a captive, we have no right to his labor; if none to his labor we have none to his absent property which is but the fruit of that labor. in fact, ransom is but commutation in another form.[22]

The natural lawyers' first law of nature, self-preservation, simply did not provide a sufficient basis for enslaving human beings, however they may have violated the natural rights of their combatants. In this respect, even Locke's theoretical considerations had been hopelessly equivocal. According to Jefferson's marginal note, the Lockean state of war could not be prolonged by the act of enslavement once the state of peace had resumed.[23] This principle had now been incorporated in the law of nature and nations, superseding the contrary views of earlier authorities. As Jefferson noted, this was a remarkable example of the Kamesian notion of the improved state of mankind, resulting from the progressive refinement of sentiment in an enlightened age and manifest in the development of academic jurisprudence. It had overcome John Locke's historically determined and restricted view.

Kames, whom Jefferson called "one of the ablest" of the moral sense philosophers, attempted to resolve the controversy between Francis Hutcheson and David Hume about the human sense of justice as either a natural or an artificial virtue.[24] Kames criticized Hutcheson for a too idealistic conception of the moral sense as distinguishable from all considerations of self-interest. In Kames's view, Hutcheson's position would compel us to handle the notion of human justice as something less than a morally motivated phenomenon, and thus he leaves his whole system an easy prey for Hume's criticism. Kames's main target, however, is Hume, for whom justice is more or less sociologically derivable "artificial virtue." Because a peaceful, just social order requires nothing more than proper understanding of our self-interests as social beings, Hume suggests, our sense of justice is, morally speaking, artificial: it precedes all strictly unselfish motives of truly virtuous action.[25]

Kames's response to this problem is based on the notion that in fact every mode of social behavior has a moral dimension. On the whole, Kames holds that in order to conceive of any human action in moral terms, we must consider all human behavior as already regulated by some more or less internalized natural principles of action. Even savage people act according to the minimum standards of justice. Their cruel customs represent "brutish principles of action." It is only through the process of "great refinement in the art of living" that the Kamesian natural principles of action—self-preservation, self-love, fidelity, gratitude, and benevolence—can develop into complex, practical ideas of proper behavior.[26] Contrary to the general scholarly understanding, therefore, the so-called new social virtues in Kames's theory cannot be distinguished from moral virtues. Rather than making distinctions between virtues, Kames distinguishes between our social and properly moral affections, the latter being those that we "indulge" or "restrain," according to our inborn moral sense.[27]

Proceeding from his premise that man is an active being, Kames first challenges the Lockean view of our motives as derivable either from our selfish inclination to avoid pain and seek pleasure or from our natural, but equally self-centered desire for happiness.[28] Kames insists, presumably against Locke, that once we distinguish our instinctive appetites and affections from their objects, we can see that sympathetic, social affections are fully natural to man. The miseries of others prompt sympathy without causing any feeling of aversion. To an extent, therefore, human feelings of

sympathy do not devolve from sheer self-love, even while they are compatible with our interests as social animals. Such natural affections, in fact,
comprise "the cement of society," claims Kames, thus inverting Blackstone's
notion of our natural weakness as such "cement."[29] But most important, the
Kamesian view of man as an emotionally social being is distinguishable
from his image of man as a moral agent.[30] Kames's long second essay most
fully elaborates his view of man as capable of moral development in terms
of his moral affections. The foundation of natural law, he asserts, cannot be
anything other than human nature itself. Thus, an effective system of laws
should accord with the historical development of human nature in a particular community. Kames aims at constructing a practical system of law
that fully complies with "humanity" itself, neither requiring an unrealistic
commitment to benevolence in our everyday life nor precluding progressive
changes in our common standards of behavior.[31]

In elaborating the theoretical basis for his principles of action, Kames
offers a fully teleological account of our "internal constitution" as a species.
Like all other species, men must have been created with certain functional
characteristics that are reflected in their behavior. The internal constitution
of each species "manifests itself in a certain uniformity of conduct": "two
things cannot be more intimately connected than a being and its actions."[32]
It is not clear whether Kames believes that the notion of creation was needed
to make his teleological argument comprehensible, but it is crucially important to his theory that the manifestation of the human constitution can be
viewed as epistemologically equivalent to our actual behavior.

The inescapable implication of the empirical observation that moral
codes varied among different nations at different times was that human action—unlike the merely instinctive modes of behavior of other species—
was susceptible to progressive development. The ancient practice of killing
war criminals "is now looked upon with distaste and horror, and therefore
is immoral; tho' it was not always so in the same degree." Building on the
premise, generally accepted by the natural law writers, that the substance of
natural law was not yet known in its details, Kames derived the principles
of his morality from his understanding of the evolution of human behavior.
All principles of action, moral as they must be, must be compatible with the
ideal of "universal, equal benevolence" and function as guides to real action in
developing human systems of laws. The figure of man in Kames's theory arises
from this capacity to see the world of human action in moral terms.[33]

Kames's moral theory is based on the idea that our given internal constitution as actively social, natural beings can be viewed as "a system of benevolence" encoded in every individual. As he states the issue: "to say all in one word, this system of benevolence, which is really founded in human nature . . . is infinitely better contrived to advance the good and happiness of mankind, than any *Utopian* system that has ever been produced, by the warmest imagination."[34] The view of man as endowed with a system of benevolence, therefore, provides the theoretical basis for understanding the logic of our morals, and indeed for any systematic effort to construct a workable system for promoting our moral development.[35]

For Kames, our moral sense is an innate, pre-reflective perceptual capacity for gathering data about human actions "proceeding from deliberate intention." Such actions are the "object" of the "power or faculty" that "passes under the name of the moral sense." Moreover, the moral sense never ceases to affect even our reflective capacities, for, as Kames notes, "the moral sense, both in the direct feeling, and in the act of reflection, plainly supposes and implies liberty of action."[36] According to Kames, the fundamental error of utopian moralists such as Shaftesbury and Hutcheson is their claim that "partial benevolence" would not count as benevolence at all. Even when originating in emotions rather than in rationality, Kamesian morality remains a matter of learning morality by its constant practice. History, in this view, appears not only as the narrative of man but as the process by which morality is actualized.[37]

Kames believes that civilization is a moral blessing to mankind as a whole. But because human action always takes place in particular circumstances, people must resort to such terms as "our country" and "our government." These terms are useful not only due to their communicative value in a single society, but also because "they serve for a much nobler purpose, to excite us to generous and benevolent actions . . . not confined to particulars, but grasping . . . all mankind."[38] The methods for achieving such nobler purposes are strictly related to the progress of civilization. It is, therefore, only "by education and practice that we acquire a facility in forming complex ideas, and abstract propositions. The ideas of common interest, of a country, of a people, of a society under government, of public good, are complex, and not soon acquired even by the thinking part of mankind. They are scarce ever to be acquired by the rude and illiterate; and consequently do not readily become the object of any of their affections."[39] Kames thus rejects all notions of the inevitable progress of human development: "nations" may well "advance to industry, commerce, and perhaps to conquest and empire,"

[247]

but "this state is never permanent," for "luxury has been the ruin of every state where it prevailed."[40] Acquiring and maintaining a refined sensibility to genuinely moral aspects of our social development necessitate a constant and conscious practice of the virtues. As Kames warns us, even our desirable passions "decay by want of exercise."[41]

It is logical for Kames to assert that "the moral sense, tho' rooted in the nature of man, admits of great refinements by culture and education."[42] Kames distinguishes our natural affections, which comprise the "cement of society," from the ongoing development of moral feelings that arise from the dialectical relation between our instinctive moral reactions and abstract moral thinking. Thus, he writes, "refinement in taste and manners, operating by communication upon the moral sense, occasions a stronger feeling in every vicious action, that would arise before such refinement."[43] According to Kames, our "moral sense becomes daily more acute . . . in a civilized society" and our duties "multiply by variety of connections" so that "benevolence becomes a matter of conscience in a thousand instances which formerly were altogether disregarded."[44] In terms of our growing moral sensitivity, human nature itself may change in the course of history.

Kames taught that moral progress can only take place within particular civic communities, in a "society under government." Of course, the critical challenge for Jefferson and his fellow Revolutionaries was to prove to the world—and to themselves—that they constituted such a community. After all, they had been free people with their own colonial governments even before the Revolution, unwilling to be "reduced to a state of nature" by Parliament's effort to dissolve those governments.[45] By detailing the progressive alienation of the English king's American subjects, the Declaration gave a new people an instant historical pedigree. Made conscious of themselves as a community through their accumulated grievances, American patriots were now called upon to act upon the stage of world history. Kames's historical conception of morality thus fit their situation perfectly. On one hand, his writings encouraged Jefferson to measure morality by making cross-cultural comparisons: the English failure to foster the progress of political civilization stood in stark opposition to the Americans' heroic efforts to vindicate their rights. At the same time, however, Kames's morally charged notion of human history mitigated the impact of universal, ahistorical natural rights principles on revolutionary thought and practice. This is why Jefferson was not interested in the ahistorical individual, abstracted from the civic and cultural context that made him a responsible moral agent. Slaves were no part of the revolutionary civic community, but rather a captive nation, only kept from unleashing vengeance on its oppressors by the institution of slavery. Jefferson's famous commentary on racial difference in the *Notes on the State of Virginia* was yet another cross-cultural comparison that illuminated the challenges to the Revolutionary Virginians' capacity for continuing moral development, and underscored the danger of an unjustly enslaved and hostile servile population to the Commonwealth's existence.[46]

All civil legislation was based on the notion of reciprocity of rights. But there could be no such reciprocity under slavery, for the slave by definition could claim no rights at all.[47] This made it difficult for Jefferson to define rebellious slaves as either criminals or as enemies in a "civilized" war. The insurgents in Gabriel's Revolt in 1800 had justice on their side—again, by definition. However, the original breach of natural law could not be imputed to the "living generation" of slave owners, but rather to their forefathers who had been unconscious of the injustice. Here, not coincidentally, was another flattering cross-cultural, or rather transhistorical, comparison that enabled Jefferson to situate Revolutionary Virginia in the grand sweep of moral progress. The problem of defining the status of African Americans did not reflect a phobic obsession with proving the racial inferiority of the slaves.[48] Jefferson instead approached the problem from the perspective of historical jurisprudence. Free Americans were dealing with an enslaved people who had been carried to America against their will. As a result, Jefferson lamented, slaves and their masters alike were victims of the institution of slavery, locked in a perpetual war that threatened to destroy both peoples.[49] For Jefferson, national identity itself was thoroughly associated with the historical, institutionalized forms of freedom that had developed in the Anglo-American colonies. The inalienable rights of free men constituted the normative, extra-historical basis of all free institutions. Such institutional arrangements, however, naturally varied among nations because they reflected only the contemporary level of "morals" among the people in question. In this respect, Jefferson's profound cultural concerns encompassed not only African Americans but also Native Americans and ignorant European urban masses. Similarly, it can be seen in Jefferson's never-fading concern about the dangers of civic corruption in his home state. As he made clear in the case of the newly freed Colombian people in 1816, "the ignorance and bigotry of the mass" made them temporarily unable "to understand and to support a free government." Thus, he advised P. S. Dupont de Nemours to assume the role of a Solon, giving "your Columbians, not the best possible government, but the best they can bear."⁵⁰

Enslaved Africans had been deprived of their rights when they were brought to the New World, against their will, and therefore could not enjoy the benefits of this institutional development. Instead, as slavery itself became institutionalized, free whites claimed and exercised rights over their slave "property." Jefferson would never have assented to the proposition that he violated the natural rights of man simply by virtue of being born into a slaveholding family. If he had believed this, the emancipation of his own slaves would have discharged him of any further moral responsibility. The challenge instead was to find a practical solution to the slavery problem that would enable Virginians collectively to extricate themselves from the institution, reversing the process of historical development that had deprived Africans of their freedom, but doing so in a way that would not jeopardize the free institutions that were themselves the products of history. Everything would be lost, Jefferson feared, if he moved too precipitately. He could not risk jeopardizing civic community, and therefore the very possibility of moral action, by alienating fellow citizens who were equally endowed with inalienable rights.

Jefferson's historical conception of morality explains both his legendary caution on the slavery issue—a caution amounting to inactivity—and his apparent obtuseness to the damage done to the human victims of the institution. His primary goal was not to free black people but to free white people from the moral evil of being slaveholders. By definition, slaves could not suffer any violation of "rights" in the jurisprudential meaning of the term. Only by uniting under some government and determining their own destiny as a people, could any group of individuals claim rights and become proper historical subjects. In the case of Virginia's slaves, this was not going be the government that white Virginians had constituted for themselves. As Jefferson wrote in one of his famous letters on "ward republics," even if Virginia "were . . . a pure democracy, in which all its inhabitants should meet together to transact all their business, there would yet be excluded from their deliberations, 1, infants, until arrived at years of discretion. 2. Women, who, to prevent depravation of morals and ambiguity of issue, could not mix promiscuously in the public meetings of men. 3. Slaves, from whom the unfortunate state of things with us takes away the right of will and of property."⁵¹ The civic community should be expanded, the radical democratic reformer urged, but never beyond its natural limits. In the case of slaves, the community's progress toward achieving universal and equal benevolence was fundamentally circumscribed by deeply rooted racist suspicions of white society. These were suspicions Jefferson confessedly shared, although they were at least partially qualified by his skepticism about the present state of natural sciences. Even as "a lover of natural history," he was a man of prudence who preferred the precautionary principle that seemed to offer him an "excuse" to keep the human races "as distinct as nature has formed them."[52]

Jefferson elaborated his historical-legal conception of the "nation of Virginia" and its moral agency in another well-known letter, in this case explaining his opposition to federal common law jurisdiction to Edmund Randolph in 1799. Virginians had developed institutions of government and made laws for themselves, and so had emerged as a distinct people with a civic and moral identity, long before the American Revolution. "The common law . . . was not in force when we landed here," Jefferson asserted, nor was it "till we had formed ourselves into a nation, and had manifested by the organs we constituted that the common law was to be our law." The American "nation," by contrast, only came into being with independence, and then "only for special purposes, to wit, for the management of their concerns with one another & with foreign nations, and the states composing the association chose to give it powers for those purposes & no others."[53] The "axiom of eternal truth in politics" dictates that political "independence can be trusted nowhere but with the people in mass," Jefferson later told Judge Spencer Roane, hurrying to add that the people "are inherently independent of all but moral law."[54] Jefferson's understanding of the law of nature and nations proceeded from the notion of a moral agent, whether it be an individual or a nation, progressively reinterpreting the meaning of this moral law under constantly changing historical circumstances. The very concept of nation denoted a free agency within the historical domain of natural law. As John Taylor of Caroline, the leading Old Republican ideologist, maintained, it was clear that "a nation is both a natural and a moral being. Its natural powers we call physical, its moral, metaphysical or political." It was equally "obvious that a nation, like an individual, could never become a tyrant over itself."[55]

How could this "moral being," Virginia, be persuaded to engage with the slavery problem? The enlightened Jefferson might well believe, as he wrote in his *Autobiography*, that "nothing is more certainly written in the book of fate than that these people are to be free."[56] But Jefferson could not compel other free men to share his vision or obey his will. As long as they submitted to a legal regime that expressed the moral sense of their fellow citizens, Virginians could not be deprived of their property in human beings. Jefferson's constant advocacy of both public education and the widening of the Virginia electorate to non-freeholders reflects his hopes that the legislature would one day better express the sentiments of a more refined majority of the free citizenry. Only when the community as a whole progressed toward a new understanding of its moral responsibilities could any effective steps be taken against the institution. In the meantime, Virginia's slaves remained a "nation in chains."

Masters and slaves belonged to distinct, hostile nations. Only when emancipated slaves became a "free and independant people" in a country of their own could they consider their former oppressors as they would "the rest of mankind, enemies in war, in peace friends."[57] "If a slave can have a country in this world," Jefferson wrote in his *Notes on Virginia,* "it must be any other in preference to that in which he is born to live and labour for another: in which he must lock up the faculties of his nature, contribute as far as depends on his individual endeavours to the evanishment of the human race, or entail his own miserable condition on the endless generations proceeding from him."[58] Eventually, Jefferson persuaded himself, his fellow Virginians would recognize that emancipation and expatriation were morally imperative. The slave himself would surely welcome the opportunity to develop his own moral potential, to unlock "the faculties of his nature." It was unimaginable to Jefferson that any man would prefer remaining a slave to gaining freedom, wherever he could find it.

But neither slaves nor free blacks could claim equal rights until white Virginians were prepared to act—and Jefferson could always say that that day had not yet come. From the standard, obligation-centered moral perspective of our own day, Jefferson's diffidence to community sentiment in a society of slaveholders epitomizes the failure of moral reasoning. The lesson that he drew from Kames, however, was that moral problems always arise within particular historical frameworks and that effective solutions depend on taking historical reality into account. Man was always bound to find himself practicing morality in some historically circumscribed role.[59] When Jefferson approached the problem of American independence, Kamesian logic made him a "radical" who believed that he spoke for a suddenly enlightened community determined to vindicate its rights. And as he made the kind of historical and intercultural comparisons favored by the Scottish school, Jefferson became absolutely convinced that a great moral gulf separated righteous Revolutionaries from their oppressors. But the same logic counseled caution in the case of slavery: a "revolution" in Virginia's racial order would not advance the progress of civilization. The only solution was to eliminate the institution of slavery and expatriate the former slaves to some distant location so that white Virginians could fulfill their moral potential as a civilized community.

Jefferson drew a crucial distinction between habitual human behavior and the beneficent actions that a man may practice in his own society without compromising his personal honesty. Karl Lehmann's classic study of Jeffersonian humanism demonstrates that Jefferson's attachment to the notion of the moral sense—as an instinctive capacity that develops or deteriorates with the communal standards of time and place—can be inferred without so much as a single reference to Francis Hutcheson. All the essential elements of this historically charged moral view are present in a quotation from Cicero in *Jefferson's Literary Commonplace Book*: "The seeds of virtue are inborn in our dispositions and, if they are allowed to ripen, nature's own hand would lead us on to happiness of life"; unfortunately, "as soon as we come into the light of day, we at once find ourselves in a world of iniquity amid a medley of wrong beliefs" and are easily led astray.[60] Human morality was about constant and conscious practice of man's capacity for proper action, his natural virtue. And failing to provide a favorable social environment for each man's development in his moral and intellectual capacities meant that only a general corruption would follow. This was the premise of Jefferson's lifelong concern with public education as the only means for making the mass of the people capable of self-government.

All this fits well with the general Kamesian, historicist position described above, as well as with Hutcheson's general view of the subject in his *Short Introduction to Moral Philosophy*. There, Hutcheson affirms the correctness of the Ciceronian doctrine of virtue as "the sole good" and then states that, as moral philosophy also deals with natural goods, it may well be viewed as "the art of regulating our whole life."[61] Dugald Stewart—the best metaphysician alive, according to Jefferson—could offer just as much intellectual support as Hutcheson or Kames. Stewart explains the commonsense thinkers' "active and moral principles" by invoking Hutcheson's and Adam Smith's speculations about human sentiments. The argument, in brief, is that any principle of action may lose its link to its original end and thus to its "utility." Avarice, for example, is a perverted natural desire for the mere means of acquiring our daily necessities, money. According to Stewart's formulation, when human desires descend into the class of "secondary affections," as they frequently do, a natural human pattern of action is simply turning into a vice. Thus, the corruption of human desires is explained as both a social and amoral phenomenon.

Utility, in this account, has little to do with the later utilitarian moral argument, for it refers simply to the given teleological connection between an act and its end as either natural or moral. Stewart's moderate skepticism about human dignity, which he attributes to the teachings of Mandeville and Hobbes, flows from the view that all our "principles" are "acquired." Not at all surprisingly, Stewart also holds, against Kames, that no theory is yet possible for discerning such principles as "laws" of nature by any scientific criterion. Even so, moral principles can only be understood in terms of the practical, teleological notion of an end and the act in question. Whenever the notion of "private happiness" is inconceivable as the ultimate end of our approbations and affections, proclaims Stewart, we are dealing with something "properly called habits."[62]

When Jefferson insisted that "habit alone confounds what is civil practice with natural right," he simply held that habits often reflect corrupt morals, because they are no longer associated with our ideas of the law of nature. This was not to claim that civil practice, even while always seeking to take natural jurisprudence into account, could ever fully reflect divine natural law.[63]

Jefferson's understanding of moral duties was compatible with the Ciceronian notion of "offices." Cicero first invoked the conception of honesty, *honestum,* as the sum of all virtue that governs the agent's response to every particular situation he confronts so as to preserve his moral rectitude; second, however, the honest man's rational consideration of which course of action to choose was affiliated with its utility, *utilitatem.* What the Scottish Enlightenment taught Jefferson was that there had to be some instinctive foundation for honesty, while he appears to have thought it inconsequential whether such a moral perspective was acquired—or, more accurately, rationalized—by naturalistic, deistic, or ontological reasoning.[64]

When Jefferson affirmed his belief in the existence of the moral sense in his famous letter to Thomas Law in 1814, he invoked the language of virtue ethics. "Nature has constituted utility to man the standard and test of virtue," Jefferson insisted, adding that "men living in different countries, under different circumstances, different habits and regimens, may have different utilities."[65] Real virtue had to derive from the notion of justice inherent in every man and to comply with human sociability in its various forms. The distinction between virtue and its mere appearance depended on whether or not the individual practicing virtue had successfully cultivated a virtuous disposition, or—we would say—internalized authoritative norms. Utility was not a moral maxim by itself, but a practical maxim for an individual already committed to the notion of justice.[66]

The principle of utility offered guidance to the moral agent dealing with a practical ethical dilemma in a particular historical situation.[67] As a practical principle, utility referred to the rational consideration not of ends but of the means of achieving ends already known to be fully moral. Jefferson thus endorsed the practicality of a virtuous moral agent who never set his own self-interest above the community's, but who prospered and flourished with his community. When it came to the question of whether the community should wage a just war in the name of "national morality," Jefferson proclaimed, "the most honest men often form different conclusions."[68] None of this called into question the purely theoretical, or psychological, view that the human sense of justice devolves from natural human affections (or feelings) rather than from some fully rationalized dispositions. And Jefferson often chose some particular course of action with "a bleeding heart."[69]

In the much discussed Adam and Eve letter, Jefferson warned his close friend William Short not to be overcome by sentimental scruples when assessing the French Revolution. "The liberty of the whole earth was depending on the issue of the contest," Jefferson averred, and went on to note that his "own affections have been deeply wounded by some of the martyrs to this cause, but rather than it should have failed, I would have seen half the earth desolated. Were there but an Adam and an Eve left in every country, and left free, it would be better than as it now is."[70]

When President Jefferson refused his public support for Thomas Brannagan's antislavery pamphlet in 1805, he, again, explained that "it is highly painful to me to hesitate on a compliance which appears so small" regarding the cause "so holy." But, he went on, "that is not it's true character," for his compliance would be injurious to Brannagan's purposes. "Should an occasion ever occur," however, "in which I can interpose with decisive effect, I shall certainly know & do my duty with promptitude & zeal."[71] Satisfying his personal moral sentiments was not the same thing for Jefferson as executing what he knew to be his duty as a statesman.

When Jefferson wrote that "what is practicable [for the statesman] must often controul what is pure theory," he had a criterion for determining the practicable, namely, that "the habits of the governed determine in a great degree what is practicable."[72] Such a maxim did not sanctify the habits derived from "ignorance and bigotry" of the Colombians or justify the "wrong beliefs" inherited from the ancient Romans, but instead underscored the importance of considering human behavior as the proper subject of continuing education. It was thus in perfect accord with Kames's teaching that a people's actual behavior constitute the basis for judging their level of moral development—and that theorizing about an all-embracing, transhistorical ideal of universal benevolence was a waste of time.[73]

How, then, could moral progress take place in relation to the problem of slavery, the unhappy institutional legacy of bad reasoning by less enlightened generations about the requirements of natural law? The only way to gain fuller understanding of natural law was through the progressive refinement of manners. It was precisely for this reason that Jefferson worried so much about the degradation of manners and the lack of moral reflection among slaveholding white Virginians. The ability to grasp and resolve moral problems, Jefferson lectured his nephew Peter Carr, was not a function of social class or education: "state a moral case to a ploughman & a professor. The former will decide it as well, & often better than the latter, because he has not been led astray by artificial rules." One crucial condition had to be taken into account, however: neither should be "biassed by habits." In the real world, the most intractable moral predicaments—most notably, that of slavery in Jefferson's Virginia—were inextricably tied to the habits and customs that governed community life.[74] This was the case with Virginia slaveholders whose moral instincts suddenly ceased to function when their property in slaves was in question: "What a stupendous, *what an incomprehensible* machine is man!" lamented Jefferson, when noting how an individual could "inflict on his fellow men a bondage, one hour of which is fraught with more misery than ages of that which he rose in rebellion to oppose."[75]

If slaves were victims of a historic injustice, it did not follow that they occupied a higher moral plane in Jefferson's scheme of things. To the contrary, their "bias" against their oppressors was so absolute—and so perfectly mirrored the slaveholders' bias—that Jefferson considered a genocidal race war the inevitable consequence of emancipation without expatriation. The institution of slavery might restrain their vengeful impulses, but while they remained in bondage, slaves necessarily remained uncivilized, outside of history and without morality. Jefferson was convinced that black people in general acted on the basis of their sensations and appetites, without forethought and deliberation, because they were not educated to exercise and improve their faculties. The slave's as well as the freedman's "disposition to theft" was symptomatic of this moral underdevelopment.[76]

Jefferson's concern with the development of human faculties and the general refinement of manners makes his thoroughly practical view of ethics comprehensible. "Habits" constituted the practical, reflexive moral sense of a community at a particular moment in history and therefore the empirical fabric by which the behavior of any group of men could be judged. Freedom meant the free use of human faculties. As Jefferson lectured Jean Nicolas Démeunier in 1795, the United States had become an asylum for many Europeans, offering them only "an entire freedom to use their own means & faculties as they please."[77] He made the same point in his first inaugural address: Americans were in possession of a "chosen country," where they could entertain "a due sense of our equal right to the use of our own faculties, to the acquisition of our own industry, to honor and confidence from our fellow-citizens, resulting not from our birth, but from our actions and their sense of them."[78] Even as great a genius as Isaac Newton did not have the right to exercise his faculties in a way that would interfere with the free exercise and development of anyone else's faculties.[79]

The idea that Jefferson's "observations" about his slaves could warrant the "suspicion" that their faculties were naturally inferior was clearly racist or, to use his own term, hopelessly "biassed." It could not be reconciled with his own conception of moral development through history. But what Jefferson did not doubt for a single moment—and this, he would insist, was much more than a mere suspicion—was that the actual behavior of these people, as he had observed it, was far inferior to the progressively improving standards of the civilized world. Jefferson's comparative judgment on the moral condition of masters and slaves in Virginia is, of course, profoundly offensive to modern sensibilities, and even contemporary readers questioned his methodology. He asserted, astonishingly, that "it would be unfair to follow them to Africa for this investigation. We will consider them here, on the same stage with the whites."[80] His comparison was made on the basis of how these faculties had been used by African Americans in the context of Western civilization. Yet this is exactly what his thoroughly historical and cultural notion of morality required. The standard was not, as we might be tempted to conclude, merely a self-interested deduction from the sorry state of affairs in a fundamentally immoral society, but was instead a conception of the progressive tendencies for moral improvement throughout the "civilized" world that the provincial Jefferson shared with enlightened Europeans.

This interpretation of Jefferson's historical conception of moral development dissents from Garry Wills's influential account of Jefferson as a sentimentalist. Wills focuses on Jefferson's comment in the *Notes on Virginia* that, although "nature has been less bountiful" to slaves "in the endowments of the head, I believe that in those of the heart she will be found to have done them justice." Wills's conclusion that Jefferson thus acknowledged the enslaved African American as his moral equal only makes sense if we assume that the moral sense was equivalent to good sentiments.[81] The error here proceeds from the unwarranted assumption that Jefferson's conception of the moral sense made people morally equal regardless of their actual behavior. But even Francis Hutcheson, the leading Scottish sentimentalist—and Wills's favorite authority—believed that bad conduct did not follow from "any irregularity" in our moral sense, but from wrong judgments.[82] When Jefferson discussed the bad behavior of slaves, emphasizing their disposition to theft, he was chronicling the corruption in morals in a population that had yet to cross the threshold of national identity and moral responsibility.

It did not follow that masters could wield despotic authority over their slaves without violating moral norms. To the contrary, Jefferson insisted, the slaves' equal endowments of heart meant that they must be treated with respect as fellow human beings. This was equally true of all dependents: in this respect, the black man was equal to any white child. The praiseworthy human qualities of children—or of slaves—did not, however, make them equal to their parents—or masters. Parental authority over children devolved from a more mature understanding and from the moral responsibility resulting from that understanding. Slavery was perpetual childhood: the benevolent instincts that slaves shared with all children would never be nurtured and developed as the moral faculties that ultimately justified claims to equality. In moral terms, uncultivated human faculties were useless.[83] Whether or not their mental endowments were "inferior," Virginia's slaves could never develop their individual faculties as long as they remained in bondage—and in Virginia.

For Jefferson, all virtues were specific human excellences. The exercise of the moral faculty was thus necessary to moral development, just as the cul-

tivation of other faculties was necessary for the development of other human virtues. As he wrote to Richard Price, a prominent spokesman of moral
rationalism, "we may well admit morality to be the child of understanding
rather than of the senses, when we observe that it becomes dearer to us as
the latter weaken, & as the former grows stronger by time & experience."[84]
Being "cultivated" in manners simply meant being a cultural being. Moral
conduct was thus to a large extent a product of culture, for the cultivation of
an individual's faculties depended on the general capability of any group of
people to absorb more refined understandings of what constituted morally
desirable conduct. Human cultures had to be assessed according to their
demonstrated capacity for development as civilized Western man understood the term. The central tenet of modern moral thinking, that there is an
intrinsic, irreducible value in each individual, was inconceivable to Jefferson.
The end of man was to develop his moral conduct in a social setting. Any
other form of "individualism" was of no interest to Jefferson. A thoroughly
cultural conception of man thus lurks in the background of Jefferson's image
of man and is fully compatible with Kames's maxim that we are how we act.
The Jeffersonian "morals of the people" consisted of both the Kamesian taste
and manners. Regarding an individual citizen, "the manners of his own nation" are "familiarized to him by habit," wrote Jefferson. Were the manners
of the nation not too corrupted, they would enable any free Virginian to reflect critically the immorality of contemporary legalism among proslavery
Virginians. Such thinking was only intelligible within the context of some
specified culture, namely that of the civilized West. Even this culture, however, was inconceivable as a fixed ideal in itself, for it ultimately existed for
its own refinement. In this view, even natural law appeared self-corrective
and self-regenerating according to the growth in human understanding.[85]

When Jefferson spoke of corruption of manners in Virginia, he could
refer either to the Indians or the African Americans: On one occasion,
Virginia seemed to be "sinking into barbarism of our Indian aborigines," on
another, it was "fast becoming the Barbary of the Union and in danger of
falling into the ranks of our own negroes."[86] Freedom distinguished Indians
from slaves, although it was not clear that Indians would seize the historic
opportunity of moral uplift through assimilation with white Americans.
Neither group, in its present degraded condition, could be compared with
the enlightened societies of the civilized West.[87] But Jefferson's understanding of human dignity, as expressed in the idea of the inalienable rights of a
free agent, had nothing to do with his assessments of the culturally circum-

scribed conduct of slaves, or of free blacks, or of Africans, or of the white "mobs of the cities," or of the white "drunkards and idlers" of Virginia.[88] The only culture he was interested in was the culture of human refinement as epitomized in the Enlightenment view of a progressive history.

The ultimate obstacle to the integration of emancipated slaves into republican society was their retarded moral development after generations of unjust captivity and brutal exploitation. In moral terms, they were still children, yet to be raised to even a rudimentary understanding of the requirements of a free society. Either as slaves or as freedmen, they would be dangerous to the success—and perhaps even the survival—of the American experiment and therefore to the general progress of mankind. Jefferson's standard for making comparisons between ethnic groups was the improvement of man. According to that standard, he concluded, the moral and political development of the black population would take generations. In the meantime, American republican society would be riven by deep inequalities that would belie and subvert the progressive and enlightened principles on which it was founded. The failure to emancipate and expatriate Virginia's slaves and then "to declare them a free and independant people" would unleash a horrific race war that would reduce both "nations" to the barbaric conditions of an anarchic state of nature in which any sort of moral life— much less its progressive refinement—would be impossible.[89]

Notes

This essay was originally published, with Ari Helo, in *William & Mary Quarterly* 60 (2003): 583–614.

1. Thomas Jefferson (hereafter TJ), *Autobiography* (Jan. 6–July 29, 1821), in Merrill D. Peterson, ed., *Thomas Jefferson Writings* (New York, 1984), 3–101, quotations on 44.

2. The quotation is from TJ, *Notes on the State of Virginia,* ed. William Peden (Chapel Hill, 1954), 138. TJ elaborated his emancipation scheme most fully in a letter to Jared Sparks, Feb. 4, 1824, in Peterson, ed., *Jefferson Writings,* 1486–87. For further discussion, see Peter S. Onuf, *Jefferson's Empire: The Language of American Nationhood* (Charlottesville, VA, 2000), 147–88.

3. Recognition of the historicist dimension of early American political thought reveals striking historiographical differences *within* both the "republican" and Lockean "liberal" paradigms, complicating the conventional juxtaposition of the two

schools. J. G. A. Pocock's analysis of Machiavellian republicanism as an early, nascent form of modern, historicist thinking remains suggestive. Successive "moments" in Pocock's conceptual history—classical, Machiavellian, and Rousseauean—can be seen as part of the complex historical pedigree of what he calls a modern "Western awareness of human historicity" (J. G. A. Pocock, *The Machiavellian Moment: Florentine Political Thought and the Atlantic Republican Tradition* [Princeton, NJ, 1975], 551).

4. TJ to Lafayette, Feb. 14, 1815, in Peterson, ed., *Jefferson Writings*, 1361.

5. See Paul Finkelman's strong criticism of TJ in this respect, in "Jefferson and Slavery: 'Treason against the Hopes of the World,'" in Peter Onuf, ed., *Jeffersonian Legacies* (Charlottesville, VA, 1993), 181–221.

6. For the accusation that TJ simply chose "political usefulness" over "active opposition to slavery," see John Chester Miller, *The Wolf by the Ears: Jefferson and Slavery* (1977; Charlottesville, VA, 1991), 279.

7. I qualify this assertion in "Every Generation Is an 'Independant Nation': Colonization, Miscegenation, and the Fate of Jefferson's Children," in this volume.

8. TJ to Henry Lee, May 8, 1825, in Peterson, ed., *Jefferson Writings*, 1501. On TJ's authorship, see the brilliant discussion in Jay Fliegelman, *Declaring Independence: Jefferson, Natural Language, and the Culture of Performance* (Stanford, CA, 1993).

9. TJ, "original Rough draft" and Declaration of Independence as Adopted by Congress, July 4, 1776, in Julian P. Boyd et al., eds., *The Papers of Thomas Jefferson*, 32 vols. to date (Princeton, NJ, 1950–), 1:423–28, quotation on 426, emphasis added.

10. The most persuasive critique along these lines can be found in Pauline Maier, *American Scripture: Making the Declaration of Independence* (New York, 1997).

11. TJ to Edward Coles, Aug. 25, 1814, in Peterson, ed., *Jefferson Writings*, 1344, emphasis added.

12. TJ, "original Rough draft" and Declaration of Independence as Adopted by Congress, July 4, 1776, in Boyd et al., eds., *Jefferson Papers*, 1:426, emphasis added.

13. We are indebted here to Jan Ellen Lewis, "The Problem of Slavery in Southern Discourse," in David Thomas Konig, ed., *Devising Liberty: Preserving and Creating Freedom in the New American Republic* (Stanford, CA, 1995), 265–97.

14. John Locke, *Second Treatise*, in Peter Laslett, ed., *Two Treatises of Government* (1698 edition) (Cambridge, UK, 1994), § 24:1–3, p. 284; § 23, p. 284. On the concept of the state of war in Locke, see ibid., § 7:3, p. 271; § 19:8–10; § 212:3–4, p. 407.

15. Ibid., § 183:4, p. 390; § 189:7, p. 393.

16. Ibid., § 24, pp. 284–85. Peter Laslett remarks that, in light of "The Instructions to Governor Nicholson of Virginia" (1698), Locke indeed "seems satisfied that the

forays of the Royal Africa Company were just wars of this sort, and that the negroes captured had committed such acts" (§ 24, pp. 284–85n).

17. TJ's "A Bill concerning Servants" thus provided that no further compact between master and servant was to be regarded as valid, because the servant had consented to such an exceptional compact (Boyd et al., eds., *Jefferson Papers*, 2: 473–75).

18. Locke, *Second Treatise*, in Laslett, ed., *Two Treatises of Government*, § 24:9–12, p. 285. Locke explained here that selling oneself could mean only selling oneself "to Drudgery, not to Slavery."

19. For Peter Laslett's widely accepted view that the Lockean notion of political power is fundamentally judicial, see ibid., p. 97. On Locke's account of the origins of property as linked to his views on the origins of political society, see, for example, James Tully, *A Discourse on Property: John Locke and His Adversaries* (Cambridge, UK, 1980). On Locke's anti-Hobbesian conception of the so-called historical origins of government, consider, for example, his formulation that "whether a Family by degrees grew up into a Common-wealth . . . or whether several Families . . . at first put the rule into the hands of a single person, certain it is that no body was intrusted with it but for the public Good and Safety." It was only because of the general human inclination to ambition and luxury that "Men found it necessary to examine more carefully the Original and the Rights of Government" (*Second Treatise*, in Laslett, ed., *Two Treatises of Government*, § 110–11, pp. 341–43). Francis Hutcheson made the case against the apparently realist "origins" of civil government in even more simple terms. While "a potent head of a family . . . might have conquered and thus compelled his neighbours around to submit to him as their prince," wrote Hutcheson, "we are not inquiring into the possible injurious methods of usurpation, but into the just causes of just power" (Hutcheson, *A Short Introduction to Moral Philosophy* [Glasgow, 1747], 282).

20. Important works on Kames include William C. Lehmann, *Henry Home, Lord Kames, and the Scottish Enlightenment: A Study in National Character and in the History of Ideas* (The Hague, 1971); Arthur E. McGuinness, *Henry Home, Lord Kames* (New York, 1970); and Ian Simpson Ross, *Lord Kames and the Scotland of His Day* (Oxford, 1972). On Kames's legal thinking, see David Lieberman, *The Province of Legislation Determined: Legal Theory in Eighteenth-Century Britain* (Cambridge, UK, 1989). One of the central themes of the Scottish common-sense school was, of course, to block routes to moral skepticism that Berkeley's and Hume's treatment of the general Lockean epistemology seemed to offer. For a good introduction to the problematic issue of how to see Locke's moral thought as the link between the older school of natural law theorists and the Scottish Enlightenment, see also Knud

Haakonssen's illuminating account of contemporary natural jurisprudence and its religious premises, in Haakonssen, ed., *Thomas Reid, Practical Ethics: Being Lectures and Papers on Natural Religion, Self-Government, Natural Jurisprudence, and the Law of Nations* (Princeton, NJ, 1990).

21. Lord Kames (Henry Home), *Essays on the Principles of Morality and Natural Religion* (Edinburgh, 1751), 147.

22. E. Millicent Sowerby, comp., *Catalogue of the Library of Thomas Jefferson,* 5 vols. (Charlottesville, VA, 1983), 2:11–12.

23. Garry Wills's contention (in *Inventing America: Jefferson's Declaration of Independence* [Garden City, NY, 1978], 293–94) that this extract separates TJ's position from Locke's understanding of the state of war being continued between the master and his slave is misleading. Wills's adherence to the notion of all-embracing benevolence as equivalent to the emotionally determined moral sense of man leads him to the erroneous conclusion that TJ rejected the Lockean understanding of the state of war. The argument merely affirmed the validity of the Lockean notion of the state of war between the oppressor and the oppressed without any suggestion that human affections could alter the situation in moral terms. In fact, TJ denied the Lockean right to retribution by the victor only insofar as it concerns individuals and not nations.

24. See TJ to Thomas Law, June 13, 1814, in Dickinson W. Adams, ed., *Jefferson's Extracts from the Gospels: "The Philosophy of Jesus" and "The Life and Morals of Jesus"* (Princeton, NJ, 1983), 358. TJ's moral statements convey a moderate skepticism about all moral theories rather than any definite position among such moral sense theorists as Hutcheson, Kames, Reid, and Shaftesbury. Modern philosophers still differ on how to interpret Hutcheson's moral sense doctrine. See, for example, P. J. E. Kail, "Hutcheson's Moral Sense: Skepticism, Realism, and Secondary Qualities," *History of Philosophy Quarterly* 18 (2001): 57–77, where Hutcheson's approach is analyzed as a kind of "non-realism" and contrasted with the old interpretations of Hutcheson's sentimentalism as well as with his alleged moral realism.

25. David Hume, *A Treatise of Human Nature* (London, 1739), bk. 3, pt. 2, § 1:24; Kames, *Essays,* passim. Hutcheson, according to Kames, says "there is naturally an obligation upon all men to benevolence," a view that "falls far short of the whole idea of obligation." For Kames, the term "obligation" covers, first and foremost, the necessary duties of justice without which no human society can survive. It is something we, indeed, occasionally neglect, but only against our instinctive orientation toward the moral good, so that conscious reflection is always involved when "a wrong" is done (see Kames, *Essays,* 57, 70).

26. Kames, *Essays,* 136, 111, 88–90.

27. Ibid., 76–77.

28. On criticism of Locke, see ibid., 15. For the distinction between social and moral affections, see ibid., 23–25, 38, 119, 132.

29. Ibid., 24. "The most sociable" people are the most interested in reading histories, novels, and plays that excite sympathy for the suffering of their protagonists (see ibid., 1–30, quotation on 18). On Blackstone, see Knud Haakonssen, "From Natural Law to the Rights of Man: A European Perspective on American Debates," in Michael J. Lacey and Knud Haakonssen, eds., *A Culture of Rights: The Bill of Rights in Philosophy, Politics, and Law—1791 and 1991* (New York, 1991), 19–61, esp. 41.

30. Kames is not Hume, who erroneously (according to Kames) "endeavours to resolve the moral sense into pure sympathy" (Kames, *Essays*, 57).

31. Ibid., 34. Here, Kames criticizes both utopian and skeptic philosophical positions as unsuitable for any system building: moralists tend either to require "angelic nature" from us, or simply to reduce us to a level "more suitable to brutes than to rational beings."

32. Ibid., 37–38.

33. Ibid., 84, 147. For an almost identical formulation, see Kames's *Principles of Equity* (Edinburgh, 1760), v. In accordance with four-stage theories of history, Kames took all non-Western societies to be mere relics of the previous stages of human refinement, reflecting the common past of all mankind. It is not coincidental that Kames was inclined to find moral unity in time (in the continuity of history) rather than in place (in utopia rather than in eutopia), since that was precisely what the burgeoning notion of history as a singular concept, concerning the whole of mankind throughout time, amounted to.

34. Kames, *Essays*, 86, emphasis in original.

35. Ibid., 82. What the moral sense qualifies is not a mere natural affection, but a natural *principle* of action. To clarify this crucial point, Kames proclaims that "our nature, so far as concerns action" is made up of two things: first, there are the natural principles of action consisting of our various appetites, passions, and affections; and second, there is the moral sense that provides us with the simple ideas of approbation or disapprobation of any act initially motivated by these principles. This is why he claims that, since the moral sense remains "our guide only, not our mover," the "principle of benevolence" can be founded only on the cooperation between our natural principles of action and the moral sense (76–78). What needs to be grasped here is that, for example, the *principle* of "self-love" cannot be a merely instinctive impulse for action, because it necessarily involves the agent's rational capacity for considering some means as contributing to the proposed end, in this case, the agent's own well-being (11). Thus, whenever thought of as principles, even

our natural affections involve the classical notion of practical reasoning concerned with the ends-and-means relation. Kames further distinguishes these principles as natural, moral, and legal principles of action (89–90, 125–26, 129–30). Even so, all of them begin with the natural, human inclination to self-preservation and end with a more or less extensive notion of benevolence.

36. Ibid., 50, 70. This brings Kames's moral argumentation close to that of ancient virtue ethics, albeit with a stern historical conviction that the domain of morality should be conceived of as a process leading man toward a more refined mode of behavior. Hutcheson's tenet that we are "obliged" to the notion of equal and universal benevolence is, in Kames's opinion, simply utopian and uninformative. On the other hand, he aims to explain or, at least, crucially diminish the Humean tension between "ought" and "is" by situating it in time. This move, consequently, demands viewing refinement as a moral rather than simply a social phenomenon. While Kames holds that refinement requires social intercourse, he also notes that by giving up "those principles of action which operate by reflection, and whose *objects are complex* and general ideas," we would end up endorsing some more primitive principles (141, emphasis added).

37. For Kames's remarks on the utopian notion of "benevolence" that erroneously "excludes justice," see ibid., 55, 121. Knud Haakonssen, in *Natural Law and Moral Philosophy: From Grotius to the Scottish Enlightenment* (Cambridge, UK, 1996), characterizes Dugald Stewart—another TJ favorite among the Scottish philosophers—as one of the optimists about the progress of civilization for whom it appeared evident that the thus far merely "natural history" of man "would soon be changed into a no less natural, but now properly moral, history" (239).

38. Kames, *Essays*, 85–86.

39. Ibid., 139–40.

40. On the recurrent theme of corruption as related to both the Kamesian notion of civilization as well as to his esthetic theory, see McGuinness, *Henry Home, Lord Kames,* 120–39, quotation from Kames on 125.

41. Kames, *Essays*, 28.

42. Kames ascribes both the lack of the moral sense and its abundance to "peculiar circumstances." This is why developing society is so central in his scheme (see ibid., 138–43).

43. Ibid., 146.

44. Kames, *Principles of Equity*, 8.

45. TJ, *The Rights of British America,* in Peterson, ed., *Jefferson Writings,* 111.

46. These themes are elaborated in Onuf, *Jefferson's Empire,* 147–88.

47. Because TJ thought that no "just war" could justify the institution, it fol-

lowed that the only method to reestablish reciprocity was to abolish the institution. Its liberalization would have made no difference in this respect. James Oakes points out that it was well after the Civil War that the real disfranchisement of the African American took place: "Defining slavery not as a labor system, which had clearly been destroyed, but as one of 'race control,' which was now being restored, leading Southerners argued that the social order of their own age was largely continuous with its antebellum counterpart" (*Slavery and Freedom: An Interpretation of the Old South* [New York, 1990], 204).

48. See TJ to James Monroe, Nov. 24, 1801, in Peterson, ed., *Jefferson Writings*, 1098, for his confusing, ambiguous formulations about the relation between the colonization of Virginia slaves and slave rebellions, with such remarks as, that "acts deemed criminal by us" might be deemed "meritorious, perhaps" by the Haitian revolutionaries.

49. The concept of perpetual war was constantly present in TJ's remarks about the nature of the institution of slavery. In his *Notes on the State of Virginia*, TJ invoked the specter of genocide: "Deep rooted prejudices . . . will divide us into parties, and produce convulsions which will probably never end but in the extermination of the one or the other race. . . . [T]he slave rising from the dust, his condition mollifying, the way I hope preparing, under the auspices of heaven, for a total emancipation, and that this is disposed, in the order of events, to be with the consent of the masters, rather than by their extirpation" (TJ, Query 14 ["Laws"]; and Query 18 ["Manners"], both in Peden, ed., *Notes*, 138, 163).

50. TJ to P. S. Dupont de Nemours, April 24, 1816, in Peterson, ed., *Jefferson Writings*, 1388. TJ's caution about the prospects for political progress also made him favor only moderate reforms in Revolutionary France in 1789. He later confessed to having been too skeptical about the capacity of the French to acquire a republican form of government under "the constitution of 1791." In 1815 it was, once again, evident to Jefferson that the political education of a whole new French generation would be necessary before that nation could ever secure itself from falling into tyranny again (see TJ to Lafayette, Feb. 14, 1815, ibid., 1361).

51. TJ to Samuel Kercheval, Sept. 5, 1816, in Andrew A. Lipscomb and Albert Ellery Bergh, eds., *The Writings of Thomas Jefferson*, 20 vols. (Washington, DC, 1903–4), 15:71–72. Writing about political developments in France, TJ asserted that the "government she can bear, depends not on the state of science, however exalted, in a select band of enlightened men, but on the condition of the general mind" (TJ to Lafayette, May 14, 1817, in Peterson, ed., *Jefferson Writings*, 1407).

52. "Will not a lover of natural history," viewing "the gradations in all the races of animals . . . excuse" his preference for keeping "those in the department of man

as distinct as nature has formed them" (TJ, Query 14 ["Laws"], in Peden, ed., *Notes*, 143). With regard to women's political rights, the principle appears to have been the same; TJ stated that the "appointment of a woman to office is an innovation for which the public is not prepared, nor am I" (TJ to Albert Gallatin, Jan. 13, 1807, in Paul Leicester Ford, ed., *The Works of Thomas Jefferson*, 12 vols. [New York, 1904–5], 10:339).

53. TJ to Edmund Randolph, Aug. 18, 1799, in Peterson, ed., *Jefferson Writings*, 1068.

54. TJ to Judge Spencer Roane, Sept. 6, 1819, ibid., 1426.

55. John Taylor, *An Inquiry into the Principles and Policy of the Government of the United States* (Fredericksburg, VA, 1814), 394, 390. For TJ's favorable commentary on this part of Taylor's work, see TJ to John Taylor, May 28, 1816, in Peterson, ed., *Jefferson Writings*, 1391–95.

56. TJ, *Autobiography* [1821], in Peterson, ed., *Jefferson Writings*, 44.

57. Declaration of Independence, ibid., 23.

58. TJ, Query 18 ("Manners"), in Peden, ed., *Notes*, 163.

59. It is important to bear in mind that for most eighteenth-century moral philosophers "duty" denoted the virtues of man in his various roles as a family member, a statesman, or an individual under the moral law of nature. Alasdair MacIntyre, in *After Virtue: A Study in Moral Theory*, 2d ed. (London, 1985), illustrates the meaning of the functional notion of man in moral theory by noting that "it is only when man is thought of as an individual prior to and apart from all roles that 'man' ceases to be a functional concept" (58–59). The various theories about the most extensive catalogue of Ciceronian "daily" duties must be kept separate from the highly complex question of the extent to which the obligatory notion of morality was elaborated in the various pre-Kantian moral doctrines with which TJ was familiar.

60. See the discussion in Karl Lehmann, *Thomas Jefferson, American Humanist* (1947; Charlottesville, VA, 1985), 122. The quotation is in Douglas L. Wilson, ed., *Jefferson's Literary Commonplace Book* (Princeton, NJ, 1989), 60n.

61. Hutcheson, *A Short Introduction to Moral Philosophy*, iii, 1. Even if TJ, as Michael P. Zuckert asserts, "never spoke of Hutcheson at all," "never once recommended Hutcheson's book to those who sought guidance on reading in politics and law," and "never owned Hutcheson's major work" (Zuckert, *Natural Rights and the New Republicanism* [Princeton, NJ, 1994], 19), this book was recommended by TJ to John Minor for studies in no lesser a field than that of ethics and natural religion (TJ to John Minor, Aug. 30, 1814, in Ford, ed., *Works of Jefferson*, 11:422n).

62. Dugald Stewart, *The Elements of the Philosophy of the Human Mind* (1792), vol. 1 of *The Works of Dugald Stewart* (Cambridge, UK, 1829), 284–89, quotation on 237.

63. TJ to Thomas Earle, Sept. 24, 1823, in Lipscomb and Bergh, eds., *Writings of Jefferson*, 15:471.

64. In TJ's famous "Head and Heart" letter, it is Heart that explains how the foundation of morals is laid "in sentiment, not in science." TJ's commitment to virtues as human excellences characterizes the whole dialogue. Even Head speaks of persons "of the greatest merit, possessing good sense, good humour, honest hearts," while Heart claims to be capable of such judgments on its own: "I receive no one into my esteem till I know they are worthy of it." This commonplace distinction between moral and contemplative powers of man can be found in TJ's other letters as well. To Peter Carr he speaks of the "honest heart" as the "first blessing" and of the "knowing head" as the "second" (see TJ to Maria Cosway, Oct. 12, 1786, in Boyd et al., eds., *Jefferson Papers*, 10:450, 446, 451; and TJ to Peter Carr, Aug. 19, 1785, ibid., 8:406).

65. TJ to Thomas Law, June 13, 1814, in Adams, ed., *Jefferson's Extracts from the Gospels*, 357.

66. According to Jefferson's much discussed summary of his own Epicurean faith, in a letter to William Short in 1819, "happiness" was "the aim of life" and the four cardinal virtues—prudence, temperance, fortitude, and justice—were the necessary "means to attain" it. The puzzle to be solved in this account of human virtue concerns the status of prudence as apparently a moral rather than an Aristotelian, intellectual virtue. That some inherently intellectual human capacity, however, was critical to TJ's moral outlook is clearly discernible in this as well as in other formulations. In his summary of Epicureanism, "prudence" not only represented the opposite force of "folly," but was the first, key virtue among the (Stoic) virtues, just as it had been in Pierre Gassendi's summary presentation of Epicurean doctrines and in Cicero's *De Officiis,* where it is handled as a kind of practical maxim for the common man in lack of absolute wisdom. Moreover, there was also involved "the test of virtue," which was "utility" in TJ's syllabus on Epicurianism. No wonder, then, that reason was one of TJ's three standards for sound morality, along with justice and philanthropy, "sound" being the type of morality Jesus of Nazareth had taught. Or, as TJ later clarified the issue: the human qualities of wisdom, justice, and benevolence—all of them best embodied by the historical figure of Jesus—were necessary to attain the "social utilities which constitute the essence of virtue" (see TJ to William Short, Oct. 31, 1819, in Peterson, ed., *Jefferson Writings*, 1433; and TJ to Joseph Priestley, April 9, 1803, ibid., 1121; on "social utilities," see TJ to William Short, Aug. 4, 1820, ibid., 1437).

67. Jean M. Yarbrough's suggestion that TJ somehow misunderstood his own ethics arises partly from her failure to distinguish fully the notion of moral obligation from the widely accepted practical notion of duties as Ciceronian "offices." By

equating some more or less given notion of moral obligation with the common-place, Pufendorf-inspired, catalogues of "duties we owe to others" and "to God" (and these, in turn, with the Jeffersonian moral virtues), Yarbrough ends up pro-claiming that, "for Jefferson, all our *obligations* are meshed together into a seamless web of *social* utility" (*American Virtues: Thomas Jefferson on the Character of a Free People* [Lawrence, KS, 1998], 153, 194–95, emphasis added). No virtuous action, according to TJ, could be obligatory beyond the minimum contemporary standard of justice, whereas any virtuous act beyond this minimum could be genuinely be-neficent to some people if not harmful to any others.

68. TJ to Robert R. Livingston, Sept. 9, 1801, in Peterson, ed., *Jefferson Writings,* 1091–95.

69. TJ to James Monroe, July 14, 1793, in Boyd et al., eds., *Jefferson Papers,* 26:503.

70. TJ to William Short, Jan. 3, 1793, ibid., 25:14.

71. TJ to George Logan, May 11, 1805, in Ford, ed., *Works of Jefferson,* 10:141.

72. TJ to P. S. Dupont de Nemours, Jan. 18, 1802, in Peterson, ed., *Jefferson Writings,* 1101.

73. In any case, TJ thought the greatest moral teacher, the historical Jesus of Nazareth, had said all that needed to be said on the issue. What Jesus had failed to do was to translate the principle of universal benevolence into a fully developed "system" of morality that would offer guidance in practical decision making (see TJ to Benjamin Rush, "Syllabus of an Estimate of the merit of the doctrines of Jesus," April 21, 1803, in Adams, ed., *Jefferson's Extracts from the Gospels,* 333).

74. TJ to Peter Carr, Aug. 10, 1787, in Boyd et al., eds., *Jefferson Papers,* 12:15. On either a "savage" or a civilized man being "unbiassed by habits," see TJ, Report on Negotiation with Spain, March 18, 1792, in Ford, ed., *Works of Jefferson,* 6:425.

75. TJ to Jean Nicolas Démeunier, June 26, 1786 (Jefferson's answers to Démeuni-er's queries), in Boyd et al., eds., *Jefferson Papers,* 10:63, emphasis added.

76. TJ, Query 14 ("Laws"), in Peden, ed., *Notes,* 142. On freedmen's customary thefts, see TJ to Edward Bancroft, Jan. 26, 1789, in Boyd et al., eds., *Jefferson Papers,* 14:492.

77. TJ to Jean Nicolas Démeunier, April 29, 1795, in Peterson, ed., *Jefferson Writings,* 1028.

78. TJ, First Inaugural Address, March 4, 1801, ibid., 494.

79. TJ to Henri Gregoire, Feb. 25, 1809, ibid., 1202.

80. We will forgo extensive quotation from this oft-quoted discussion. TJ, Query 14 ("Laws"), in Peden, ed., *Notes,* 143, quotation on 139.

81. TJ, Query 14 ("Laws"), in Peden, ed., *Notes,* 142; Wills, *Inventing America,* 224–26.

82. Francis Hutcheson, *An Inquiry Concerning Moral Good and Evil* (1725–26; 1964), § 4, 3:122, in *An Inquiry into the Original of Our Ideas of Beauty and Virtue* (London, 1726).

83. This was the thrust of TJ's scheme for public education in Virginia: "By that part of our plan which prescribes the selection of the youths of genius from among the classes of the poor, we hope to avail the state of those talents which nature has sown as liberally among the poor as the rich, but which perish without use, if not sought for and cultivated" (TJ, Query 14 ["Laws"], in Peden, ed., *Notes,* 148). When emphasizing that individuals are genuinely different in their talents, TJ also held that it is possible that the "want or imperfection of the moral sense in some men" is just like the want of "the senses of sight and hearing in others" (TJ to Thomas Law, June 13, 1814, in Adams, ed., *Jefferson's Extracts from the Gospels,* 357).

84. TJ to Richard Price, July 11, 1788, in Sowerby, comp., *Catalogue of the Library of Thomas Jefferson,* 2:9.

85. TJ, Query 18 ("Manners"), in Peden, ed., *Notes,* 162.

86. TJ to Joseph C. Cabell, Jan. 22, 1820, in Ford, ed., *Works of Jefferson,* 12:155; TJ, quoted on the threat of descending to the level of the black man, in Miller, *Wolf by the Ears,* 257.

87. It was appropriate to let the Indians know only "their present age" of history, while it was equally clear that the Latin American republics were probably incapable of maintaining free government. On the Indians, see TJ to William Henry Harrison, Feb. 27, 1803, in Peterson, ed., *Jefferson Writings,* 1120; on the Latin American peoples, see TJ to Alexander von Humboldt, Dec. 6, 1813, ibid., 1311. For further discussion of Indians and the problem of civilization, see Bernard W. Sheehan, *Seeds of Extinction: Jeffersonian Philanthropy and the American Indian* (Chapel Hill, NC, 1973); and Onuf, *Jefferson's Empire,* 18–52.

88. TJ, Query 19 ("Manufactures"), in Peden, ed., *Notes,* 165; TJ to Joseph C. Cabell, Feb. 2, 1816, in Peterson, ed., *Jefferson Writings,* 1381.

89. TJ, Query 14 ("Laws"), in Peden, ed., *Notes,* 138.

Index